SDG&E

Reflections

1
3

San Diego Calª April 18. 1881

A meeting was held in the Parlor of the Consolidated Bank for the purpose of organizing a Gas Light Company for the City of San Diego.

There were present, O.S. Witherby, Bryant Howard, R.M. Powers, J.S. Gordon and E.W. Morse.

On motion O.S. Witherby was elected Chairman and E.W. Morse Secretary.

On motion it was voted that the name of the Corporation shall be the "San Diego Gas Company"

Articles of Incorporation were adopted and signed.

The following persons were elected as Directors for the first year O.S. Witherby, Bryant Howard, R.M. Powers J.S. Gordon and E.W. Morse.

The following officers were then elected,

O.S. Witherby President
Bryant Howard Treasurer
E.W. Morse Secretary

On motion Mess. Morse and Howard were appointed a committee to draft a set of By-laws.

On motion it was voted that the price of Gas be fixed at five dollars ($5.00) per thousand

The meeting then adjourned to Friday April 22nd at 10 O'clk a.m.

E.W. Morse
Secretary

Minutes from the first Company board of directors meeting on April 18, 1881, signed by Ephraim Morse, first secretary.

REFLECTIONS

A History of the San Diego Gas & Electric Company 1881–1991

IRIS ENGSTRAND

KATHLEEN CRAWFORD

Published by
The San Diego Historical Society
and San Diego Gas & Electric Company
1991

EXECUTIVE EDITOR
Richard L. Manning

PROJECT MANAGER:
Betty L. Timko

HISTORICAL PHOTOGRAPHY EDITOR:
Fred Vaughn

MANUSCRIPT EDITOR:
Pauline McKnight

DESIGNERS:
John Odam and Tom Gould

DESIGN COORDINATOR:
Stephanie Swiggett Gould

COPY EDITOR:
Shaun Doole

COVER PHOTOGRAPHY:
Stephen Simpson

PRINTER:
BookCrafters

Electric crews in the early 1900s used horse-drawn vehicles to install and maintain power lines.

Library of Congress Catalog Number

ISBN 0-918740-13-4

CONTENTS

A squadron of Navy biplanes passes over Station B on its way to North Island about 1930. The trolley car is on Kettner Boulevard between Broadway and E Street.

To the employees, shareholders and customers of San Diego Gas & Electric Company

Every era should reflect upon its history to understand the lessons of the past, the fleeting reality of the present and the infinite directions of the future. To know only one's own generation is to remain a child. Reflections about an institution's past can give us perspective in historic time and bring to light recurring themes. San Diego Gas & Electric Company has been a pioneer in service to the community—a service that has provided light, heat and power to a people and to a region without interruption for 110 years.

As we reflected upon the history of SDG&E, we saw the Company's transformation from a primitive "gas works" operating in a fledgling city with no natural fuel supplies into a multimillion-dollar utility that stresses its diverse energy sources—oil, natural gas, nuclear and purchased power. The story became a remarkable tale of people developing new techniques of production and meeting constant challenges imposed by the environment. The successes of SDG&E reflected the strength and ingenuity of its employees and the faith of its shareholders; its failures mirrored the times when forces—economic and environmental—created problems with no easy solutions.

San Diego is an "energy desert." From the very first moment, coal and oil had to be imported to manufacture gas. A few years later imported fuel provided the power to generate electricity. Within a short time, even water for the growing community had to be brought in from the distant mountains. Nevertheless, through a combination of optimism, engineering skills, careful planning, hard work and enthusiasm, San Diego's early pioneers improved their systems and expanded their gas and electric service. That the city and the county attained their present size and productivity is a genuine triumph over natural limitations. And integral to that growth, critical to that triumph, has been a steady, dependable, essential supply of energy from SDG&E, providing a lifestyle that most people take for granted.

The Electric Building, as it stands against the San Diego skyline, is a symbol of a Company that works with people. As we move toward the 21st century, SDG&E will remain in the vanguard of service, reflecting a proud history and lighting the way into the future.

Iris Engstrand and Kathleen Crawford
University of San Diego
October 27, 1991

HIGH
VOLTAGE

Lineman on "diving board" (at right) works to pull in a conductor (wire) with a hand winch. The wire will be connected to an insulator before being energized.

Chapter 1

1881-1890
A Decade of Firsts

When five prominent San Diegans met in the parlor of the Consolidated Bank on April 18, 1881, to incorporate the San Diego Gas Company, they formed a successful enterprise that would serve a fledgling city whose population—divided between Old Town and New Town—had just passed 3,000. They quickly asked that the city trustees authorize the purchase of 25 street lamp posts, the first ones to be maintained for public use. Could they possibly have imagined that just 110 years later, San Diego's 99,159 street lights would serve the sixth largest city in the country? Could they have believed that their company's gas customers would grow from an original 89 to 670,000 and their electric customers from none to 1.1 million? The founders were optimistic, especially during this period of unprecedented city growth, but most likely were not projecting 100 years into the future. In fact, they would have some trying times just surviving the 1880s!

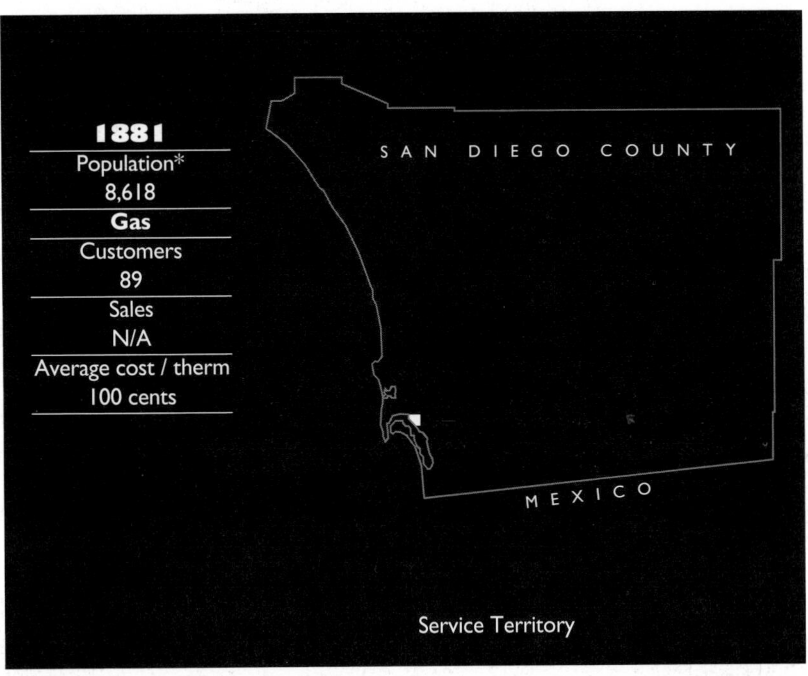

Map showing area first served by gas in 1881. Electricity service started in 1884.
*County population based on census 10-year estimates

The city of San Diego had started as a small village at the foot of Presidio Hill during the 1820s when Mexico had achieved its independence from Spain. The founding families of Estudillo, Bandini, Carrillo, Machado, Lopez and Pico had built their homes around the little plaza in the center of what is now Old Town and ran the affairs of the pueblo. After 1848, with the ending of the Mexican-American War, numerous soldiers and sailors from the eastern and midwestern United States joined the local residents and soon decided to make San Diego their permanent home. Some married the daughters of local Hispanic "dons" and moved to outlying ranches in the county, while others started businesses on the plaza. Newcomers,

Old Town, from Presidio Hill. Believed to be the first photograph of San Diego, about 1867, taken by J. Henfield. This is probably what Alonzo Horton saw when he arrived in San Diego the same year. (Photo courtesy of San Diego Historical Society–Ticor Collection)

< Ole Gylling (above) and James McCarty pause from their work at the Springer water gas set, the Company's first water gas generator. Before this unit was installed in October 1887, demand from a growing San Diego had exceeded the capacity of the Company's earlier gas generators. The coal piled in the left foreground was the raw material for the gas generators.

EPHRAIM W. MORSE

Ephraim W. Morse, first secretary of the Company, has been characterized as San Diego's "ideal citizen." Born in Amesbury, Massachusetts, in 1823, Morse had an excellent common-school education and worked on his parents' farm until he was 25 years old.

Excited by the reports of California gold, he sailed from Boston on February 4, 1849, and entered San Francisco Bay on July 5. Having caught malaria during his sea voyage, Morse decided that San Diego's climate would be more healthful. Within a month, the southern climate cured his ills. He traveled to Massachusetts to claim a bride in 1851 and returned to San Diego in 1852.

Aside from keeping a store, Morse had the agency for Wells Fargo Express, served as associate justice of the court of sessions, secretary of the board of trade, county treasurer and city trustee. Morse had been admitted to law practice in 1856 and was knowledgeable in banking, public lands, transportation, and water matters. He spoke Spanish fluently.

Morse, who was married first to Lydia Gray until her premature death, and then to Mary Chase Walker, died in January 1906.

such as Ephraim W. Morse from Massachusetts and New Yorker Thomas Whaley, liked the town's location and opened stores, but others, like merchant William Heath Davis, thought the town lay too far from the bay.

Davis promoted what he called "New San Diego" by the present harbor and built a wharf to encourage development. His plan was premature, and he failed to attract settlers away from their comfortable Old Town. In April 1867, the steamer *Pacific* brought Alonzo Horton and several passengers to the foot of present-day Market Street. Since nothing but a few pilings remained of Davis' wharf, the group was rowed ashore and helped to dry land. While Horton was awaiting a buckboard to take him to the plaza, he looked around at the harbor and thought it "must be a Heaven on Earth . . . the best spot for building a city I ever saw." He met Ephraim Morse, by then a city trustee, who showed him what land was available for purchase. Sheriff James McCoy held an auction on May 10, 1867, at which Horton purchased 960 acres for $265 or 27½ cents an acre. The city trustees gave Horton a deed to the land on May 11, and he registered as a voter in San Diego. Within a short time, Horton's Addition became a reality.

By 1870, Horton had sold a number of lots, joined in the creation of a Chamber of Commerce, built a hall, and succeeded in having the county order all of its records removed from the Whaley House in Old Town and placed in the Express Building in New San Diego. The Bank of San Diego was organized in June with Alonzo Horton as president and Bryant Howard as treasurer. Later that month *The San Diego Union* moved its offices to Fourth and D (now Broadway), and the Horton House Hotel opened its doors on October 10.

Although Alonzo Horton was not directly connected with the formation of the San Diego Gas Company, he was definitely an indirect force. His lavish hotel, located on Broadway across from today's Horton Plaza, had 100 rooms richly carpeted, lighted with gas and supplied with fresh water. Gas was piped into the hotel from a pneumatic gas works at the rear of the building, and water came from a 55-foot well under the building. A 7,000-gallon tank stored water that could be piped both hot and cold into each room. George Marston, the young desk clerk, saw to it that guests had all the comforts of home. The opening of the hotel served as a catalyst for the young city and, together with San Diego's excellent climate, attracted guests from throughout the country.

Prospects for the city were bright during the 1870s. Congress passed a bill approving construction of the Texas & Pacific Railroad to San Diego in 1871, and the new courthouse at D and Front streets was completed in 1872. The economy experienced a setback, however, during the panic of 1873, causing the collapse of railroad plans but leaving the city with a substantial nucleus for a quick recovery. The San Diego Water Company, organized in 1872, drilled wells and built a reservoir at Fifth and Hawthorn streets. Efforts were continued to attract a railroad to the state's southwestern corner, and by October 1880, the California Southern Railroad was incorporated. Its route would begin at National City, pass through Temecula and Colton, and join the Atlantic & Pacific at Waterman Junction (Barstow).

Several efforts had been made during the 1870s to launch a gas company and, even though machinery had been brought in by steamer, none of the ventures had succeeded. Nevertheless, the city had expanded sufficiently to be ready for gas illumination. Seven well-connected San Diegans met with M.G. Elmore of the San Francisco Petroleum Gas Company early in 1881 to plan the founding of the San Diego Gas Company. They were men of substance, experience and vision. All were born in the East but had come to San Diego because of pleasant living conditions and business opportunities. They were involved in the Chamber of Commerce, the founding of several banks, trusteeship of the public library, promotion of the railroad, beautification of the park, and the bringing of water to the city.

Ephraim Morse, lawyer and city trustee, had written a pamphlet on the "Climate, Resources, and Future Prospects of San Diego" for the Chamber of Commerce; Bryant Howard from New York had become treasurer of the Bank of San Diego; Oliver S. Witherby from Ohio had been elected first judge of the Southern District in 1850 and became the Company's first president from 1881 to 1886; George Cowles, a rancher and banker from Connecticut, was former president of the New York Cotton Goods Exchange; James S. Gordon and George W. Hazzard, from Indiana, were both former presidents of the Chamber and owned a store for general merchandise; and Dr. Robert M. Powers, also from Ohio, had just arrived in 1880 to improve his health. He decided not to practice medicine but to enter the business community.

By the time these astute San Diegans joined with Elmore on April 18, 1881, to file Articles of Incorporation, construction of the "gas works" had already begun with machinery shipped in on the steamer *Orizaba*. Organ-

LIGHTING REFLECTS ITS PAST

It now appears as if the electric light will ultimately supersede all other kinds of illumination. There is as yet no recorded failure, so far as we have been able to learn. One of these days not far in the future, we shall probably see lofty towers erected in this city from whose tops will flash brilliant lights, revealing long rows of imposing buildings, a fleet of ships nestling cozily in the harbor, and cars rumbling along crowded thoroughfares—all evidencing the life and energy of a stirring metropolis.
The San Diego Union, July 30, 1881

Dr. Robert M. Powers, one of the original founders, served as the Company's top officer between January 1889 and June 1905, a period covering the land depression of the 1890s and the coming of the Byllesby Company in 1905.

Original engraving of the Company's light works, from *The Golden Era* magazine of 1889. This location is still used by SDG&E as a substation and auto repair shop.

Map of early San Diego, circa 1873.

The *Ancon* and her sister steamship, *Orizaba,* carried oil in 1882 from Ventura down the coast to San Diego for the Company's oil gas manufacturing plant. Oil, however, proved impractical for the plant and was replaced with coal, imported from Australia.

izing the Company with a capital stock of $100,000, they had authorized a plant costing $30,000 to be constructed at Tenth and M (Imperial) streets. Plans were made for connections to the main buildings in town, such as the county courthouse, the banks, the Horton House Hotel and commercial buildings. The new gas company advertised that its gas would be of the same quality as that used in the Palace and Grand hotels of San Francisco—a city that had organized a gas company in 1852—and would be in place by June 1. The technology was available, since Baltimore had produced gas since 1816 and Boston and New York since 1822 and 1823, but Midwestern towns like Chicago did not generate gas light until 1850, and San Francisco was the first on the West Coast to do so.

On June 5, 1881, *The San Diego Union* reported that "Fifth Street was thronged last evening by our citizens, old and young, who had turned out to witness the novelty of the inauguration of the new gas works, and the stores and business places presented a brilliant appearance." Just the day before, the Company's board of directors had authorized the secretary "to sign the lease of Samuel Stephens to San Diego Gas Co. for lots 'A' & 'B' of block 157 and all buildings thereon for one year from June 1, 1881 at $12.50 per month." George Merritt, who later became a Company director, would occupy the residence for $10 per month, and the gas company could use "the work shop and premises for business purposes." This was part of the present complex of Station A, and the Company's first bill for tools amounted to $8.10.

The original gas plant and nearly three miles of gas mains had been completed on June 2 to serve the 89 charter subscribers. Gas capacity reached about 25,000 cubic feet per day—sufficient for a town of 20,000 inhabitants. On Tuesday, June 14, 1881, the board of directors voted that a phone be placed at "the works," which occupied the block bounded by Ninth, Tenth, M and N streets. This was the first office phone and joined those of Gordon & Hazzard, the local banks, and about 20 other telephones in use in the city; more instruments were en route from San Francisco. San Diego served as a metropolitan center for the mining companies of Julian and the agricultural interests in East and North County.

With these innovations, San Diego's past seemed to be slipping away. The advance of civilization caused a group of Indians living on a rancheria at 12th and M to move to the Chollas area. The once-open fields were becoming dotted with houses as Horton's Addition began to fill up. The gas company directors were optimistic about future growth since the California Southern Railroad had completed track between National City and San Diego, and more was under construction to the north. It would reach Colton by August 1882 and from there could hook up to the East with Santa Fe's Atlantic & Pacific Railroad.

San Diego Telephone Exchange,

CENTRAL OFFICE, COR. SIXTH AND G STREETS.

(With the Western Union Telegraph, Wells, Fargo & Co's Express, and General Stage Offices.)

LIST OF SUBSCRIBERS.

NAMES.	No.	LOCATION.	NAMES.	No.	LOCATION.
Allison Brothers.	14_2	Market.	Kimball, F. A.	4_5	National City
" "	14_6	Slaugh. House.	Leach & Parker	18	Office.
California Southern R. R.	4_2	General Office.	Luce, M. A.	20	Office.
" " "	4_3	National City.	Pacific Coast S. S. Co.	8_2	Office.
Campo	25		" " " "	8_3	End of Wharf.
Chase, Chas. A.	9	Drug Store.	Reed, D. C.	14_4	Residence.
Clark & Russell	22	Stable.	Remondino, Dr. P. C.	12_1	Residence.
Consolidated Bank	17		Russ & Company	5	Lumber Yard.
Court House	11		" "	4_4	National City.
Fairchild, J. A.	3_2	Office.	San Diego Flour Mills	7_3	
" "	3_3	Residence.	Steiner, Klauber & Co.	7_2	
Francisco, Silliman & Co.	15		Stockton, Dr. T. C.	12_3	Residence.
Gas Works	16		" " " "	12_5	Office.
Hamilton & Co.	24		Stewart, W. W.	21	Warehouse.
Hinton & Gordon	10_2	Livery Stable.	Sun Office	6	
Hinton, J. B.	10_3	Residence.	Thompson, J. W.	13	Residence.
Horton, A. E.	14_3	Residence.	Union Office	2	
Horton House	19		Wentscher, A.	1_2	Office.
Infirmary	12_4		" "	1_3	Warehouse.
			" "	23	Residence.

NOTICE.

To facilitate rapid switching, each subscriber's wire will be designated by a number placed opposite his name on the right hand. Subscribers having more than one telephone station on the same wire, are designated by a small figure at the right of their telephone number, which figure is also the number of bells for that station. Call the Central Office, and give the number of the wire instead of the name of the person you wish to converse with. When switch is made ring again for the number wanted. Do not place the mouth too near the transmitter when talking. Report all interruptions to the Central Office.

Always hang the Telephone on the hook when not in use.

J. W. THOMPSON, Manager.

In 1882, the Company bought oil for making gas first from Peru and then from Ventura, California; it was shipped down the coast by the paddle-wheel steamer *Ancon* and her sister ship *Orizaba.* This crude petroleum, used to manufacture gas in cast-iron retorts, proved unsatisfactory, and the Company changed to the production of coal gas in April 1883. Coal was brought in from Australia and from England at a cost as high as $20 per ton. As the volume increased, the price dropped to between $6.50 and $9.50 per ton.

Discussions at the board of directors meetings in 1882 ranged from buying a screen door (July 5) to digging a well (September 5) in case the city water supply failed and it was needed "for washing gas or such other purposes." The directors began to advertise in *The San Diego Union* to promote the use of gas stoves, promising that they would "Save Labor, Save Expenses, Save Worry" with "no smoke, no ashes, no dirt." Their stoves, which could be bought or rented—with a deduction in the price of gas—were "always reliable, ready and safe" and would "roast, broil, bake, boil or stew in less time and better manner than any other method." Gas mains

This is believed to be the original oil gas generator, installed in 1881. Vapors from heated oil were collected and piped to homes and businesses.

The gas plant as it looked from 1883 through 1886. The brick building at left and the adjoining wooden building comprised the original gas plant built in 1881 on a 50- by 100-foot lot, the brick building fronting west on Ninth between M and N (Imperial Avenue and Commercial Street today). In 1883, the plant was altered for coal gas manufacturing.

were run to the Florence Hotel on Fir Street between Third and Fourth avenues, and pipes ran up Second Avenue to the Catholic Church. By mid-1884, Dr. Powers asked the city trustees to place gas lamps along Fifth Avenue, and later that year the Company installed a gas heater in the Episcopal Church on Fourth Avenue that "looked cheerful" and warmed the church sufficiently.

The first transcontinental railroad had reached San Diego in early 1884, but a flood had cut off service after just a short time. The tracks were washed out in Temecula during a 20-inch downpour, and the track was not replaced until November 1885. This event linked San Diego with the Santa Fe at Waterman Junction near San Bernardino and introduced a period of boom prosperity to the city. The gas company also looked to improving its transportation capabilities, and in May 1885 the board thought it wise to purchase "a horse and wagon suitable for the business of the Company." Negotiations continued through the summer, and it was finally decided to have a wagon built. When it was completed, the horse was purchased, and a short entry in the minutes of October 15, 1885, "Horse and wagon—$100," marked the beginning of the Company's vehicle department. The gas company continued to expand and also began making plans for the introduction of electricity.

Regular monthly meetings of the San Diego Gas Company were held at the Company's office in the Masonic Building at Sixth and H with Judge Oliver Witherby presiding. The board frequently discussed electric lighting, and it was the subject of a resolution on November 25, 1884, when the group decided to contact different manufacturers of electric street lighting apparatus to "ascertain which may be the best and cheapest" for providing the city with that service. It came up again when the city trustees appointed a committee to prepare a contract for electric lighting in March 1885.

Horse-drawn streetcar in front of the old Florence Hotel, looking south from Fir Street. The Florence was owned by W.W. Bowers when this photo was taken in 1888. Gas mains had been run to the hotel to provide lighting and heating.

The challenge of understanding and using electricity has fascinated men since ancient times. In 600 B.C., the Greek philosopher Thales first observed static electricity when he stroked a piece of iridescent amber and found that it could attract and repel light objects such as lint or feathers. William Gilbert, physician to Queen Elizabeth I, repeated Thales' experiment. In his book, *De Magnete,* he named the mysterious force "elektron," the Greek word for amber. In 1752, Benjamin Franklin, with his famous kite, identified lightning as electricity, and in 1800, Alessandro Volta produced a continuous current. Sir Humphrey Davy used Volta's discovery to produce the arc light, and his pupil Michael Faraday developed the dynamo as a source of electric power. The Gramme dynamo, invented in Europe in the 1850s, produced a sustained electric current. This event made the use of arc lights for outdoor illumination practical for such things as lighting the streets of Paris and, in 1878, made possible the first evening football game for 30,000 people in England.

In the United States, Charles F. Brush, an engineer employed by the Cleveland Telegraph Supply Company, patented his first dynamo in 1877 and improved the design of both the generator and the arc lamp. On October 21, 1878, Thomas Alva Edison perfected the first practical incandescent lamp, consisting of a loop of carbonized cotton thread mounted in a vacuum to prevent oxidation. It burned for more than 40 hours. In San Francisco in 1879, George Roe, an early pioneer in lighting, began his California Electric Light Company. He used arc lighting because Edison's lower-illumination incandescent lamps, always in the process of being improved, were not readily available on the West Coast until the early 1890s. A representative of the Brush manufacturing interests proposed to illuminate Los Angeles streets by means of arc lights placed upon 150-foot-high masts early in 1882. The Los Angeles Electric Company, organized later that year, became the city's pioneer electric utility.

The first electric plant in San Diego had been installed by the Jenney Electric Company of Indianapolis at Second and J at a cost of $30,000. The plant, which began operating in March 1886, had two 100-horsepower boilers supplying two 75-horsepower engines that operated four 30-light direct-current arc light generators furnishing current to six electric-carbon arc lamps mounted on 110-foot-tall towers. The Jenney Company's first contract with San Diego provided for 24 lamps at $288 each per year,

OLIVER S. WITHERBY

Judge Oliver S. Witherby, the Company's first president, was born in Cincinnati, Ohio, in 1815 and was graduated from Miami University in 1836. He studied law at Hamilton, was admitted to the bar in 1840, and was elected prosecuting attorney for Butler County.

Witherby arrived in San Diego with the Mexican–American Boundary Commission in 1849 and, with a successful business and legal career behind him, was elected San Diego County's representative at the first state assembly in Monterey in 1850. He was then elected judge of the newly created Southern District Court, where he served until his appointment as collector of customs for the Port of San Diego from 1853 to 1857.

Judge Witherby purchased the Escondido Rancho in 1858, farmed for 10 years, then sold the ranch and reentered the business field. He amassed quite a fortune but lost much of it in the panic of 1893. He died in December 1896.

This rare photo from inside the Company's gas facility, looking northwest toward the corner of Ninth Avenue and M, shows the Company's first horse and wagon amid scattered oil drums and coal waste. The first water gas generator (see frontispiece photo) is at left.

One of San Diego's 125-foot electric-arc street light towers. This one was located at Fifth and F streets. The view in this picture, taken in 1886, looks southwest from the tower, with G Street running diagonally from left to right. Beyond G is Market (then known as H Street), at the foot of which is the tree-encircled U.S. Army Barracks. Point Loma and Coronado's North Island are in the background.

A closeup of an original 110-foot arc light tower. (Photo courtesy of San Diego Historical Society–Ticor Collection)

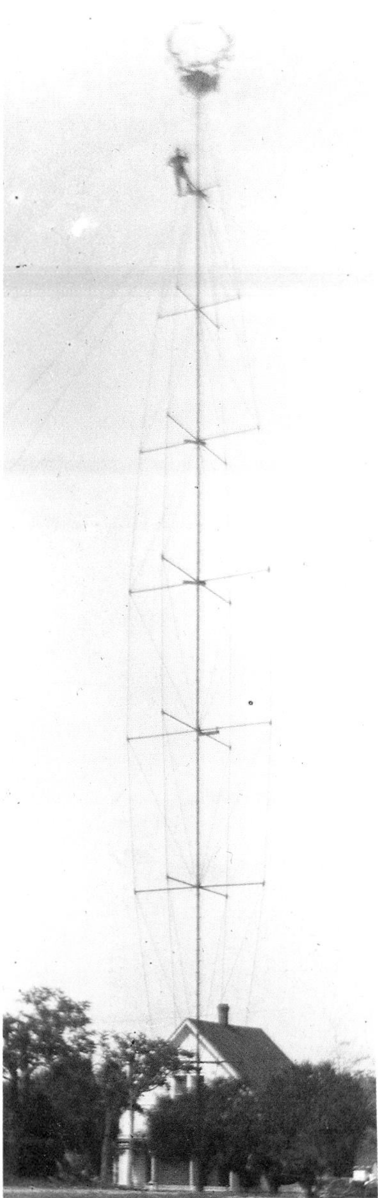

This early view inside the original Jenney Electric Company arc light works was taken probably about 1886, the first year arc lighting was offered San Diego residents. One of the two 75-horsepower engines seen here could drive two generators using wide leather belts. Each generator could produce enough electric "juice" to light 30 lamps.

burning only until midnight. A workman had to ascend the towers daily to install new carbons.

The venture failed, however, and the Jenney plant and properties were purchased in September 1886 by Elisha S. Babcock and H.L. Story, developers of Coronado, who were also planning to install water gas manufacturing equipment to supply electricity and gas to their proposed hotel. The new company, the Coronado Gas & Electric Company, was short lived. Babcock and L.M. Vance approached the San Diego Gas Company with plans for consolidation, and the new San Diego Gas, Fuel and Electric Light Company was formed on April 15, 1887, with O.S. Hubbell as president, just as construction began on the Hotel del Coronado. The structure would include electric bells throughout, 2,500 Mather incandescent light bulbs, and several arc lights; it also had gas jets for backup lighting, with gas supplied by the hotel's coke gas oven.

The San Diego company bought the Coronado machinery, and Dr. R.M. Powers continued on the board of the new organization. The San Diego Gas and Electric Light Company was incorporated on May 12, 1887, by Simon Levi, D.C. Reed, S.C. Bigelow, Joseph A. Flint, and William Iglehart, each holding 500 shares valued at $50,000. Pending completion of a new electric-light plant, Coronado's arc machinery was placed in the old Jenney plant; the new water gas equipment was installed by October 1. With it in operation, the Company could make about 150,000 cubic feet of gas per day.

On May 20, 1887, with a deposit of $10, *The San Diego Union* became the Company's 44th gas customer with one 5-light meter and one 3-light meter. George White Marston, former desk clerk at Horton's hotel and owner of a dry-goods store, was one of the Company's first electric-light customers, putting up an $18 deposit on May 23, 1887. While the Hotel del Coronado was under construction in 1887 and 1888, one of the first underwater power

W.J. Hunsaker, a native Californian, was president of the Company from April 15, 1886, to April 14, 1887. Hunsaker, a prominent San Diego lawyer, served as mayor in 1888.

lines crossed beneath San Diego Bay to supply electricity to the building site, especially for night work. After the hotel was formally opened on February 1, 1888, the underwater line was abandoned.

According to an article in *The Golden Era* magazine of September 1889, the demands for gas and electric light during most of 1887 were much greater than could be supplied by the old works.

People would beg for "just one or two gas jets," urging that such a small amount would not be felt, but since the gas holder was emptied of its contents every night, sometimes as early as 9, it would be unsafe to grant the requests. It was a trying time for the officers of the Company, but they pushed the work rapidly, and by the first of October 1887, the water gas plant was in operation and there was gas enough to spare. Work on the coal gas works continued, and by the following March they were in full operation. The Company had the satisfaction of knowing that it was even ahead of the boom, and could furnish gas for a city of 100,000 people without any further additions to its plant.

The struggle between the Southern Pacific and the Santa Fe railroads to control the passenger trade to Southern California had resulted in a rate war. The usual $150 fare from Chicago and St. Louis kept falling until on March 6, 1887, the fares opened at $12, dropped to $6 and then, by noon, stood at $1. Fares then rose again to about $25 for the remainder of the year. Because of these low fares and widely distributed promotional literature, approximately 4,750 people settled in San Diego in June. The number averaged 5,000 per month during the summer. Business lots soared to $2,500 a front foot, and property valuation rose from $4,582,213 to $13,182,171 during 1887.

During this era of progress, the San Diego Street Car Company, known for its horse-drawn trolleys, built a carbarn 150 feet long by 36 feet wide with

BRYANT HOWARD & JAMES GORDON

Bryant Howard and James S. Gordon, both elected directors at the Company's first meeting, were successful San Diego businessmen and active in various civic projects.

Howard, who arrived in San Diego in 1870, joined in the founding of both the Bank of San Diego and the Commercial Bank, and eventually became cashier of the Consolidated National Bank. He was one of the first library trustees, served as city treasurer in 1882, and succeeded Ephraim Morse as president of the San Diego flume project.

Gordon, a general merchant, had a store in partnership with George W. Hazzard in National City and later with John Capron in San Diego. He served as vice president of the Chamber of Commerce in 1871, president in 1873 and 1874, treasurer in 1881 and vice president in 1886. Gordon resided at the corner of Tenth and H streets.

Station A power plant, around 1889. View is south and west from the corner of 11th and M streets. The gas-making plant was at the opposite corner of the block, but the gas-storage holder built in 1887 can be seen at left. The woman and child are unidentified but possibly could be Mrs. Robert Powers and her child.

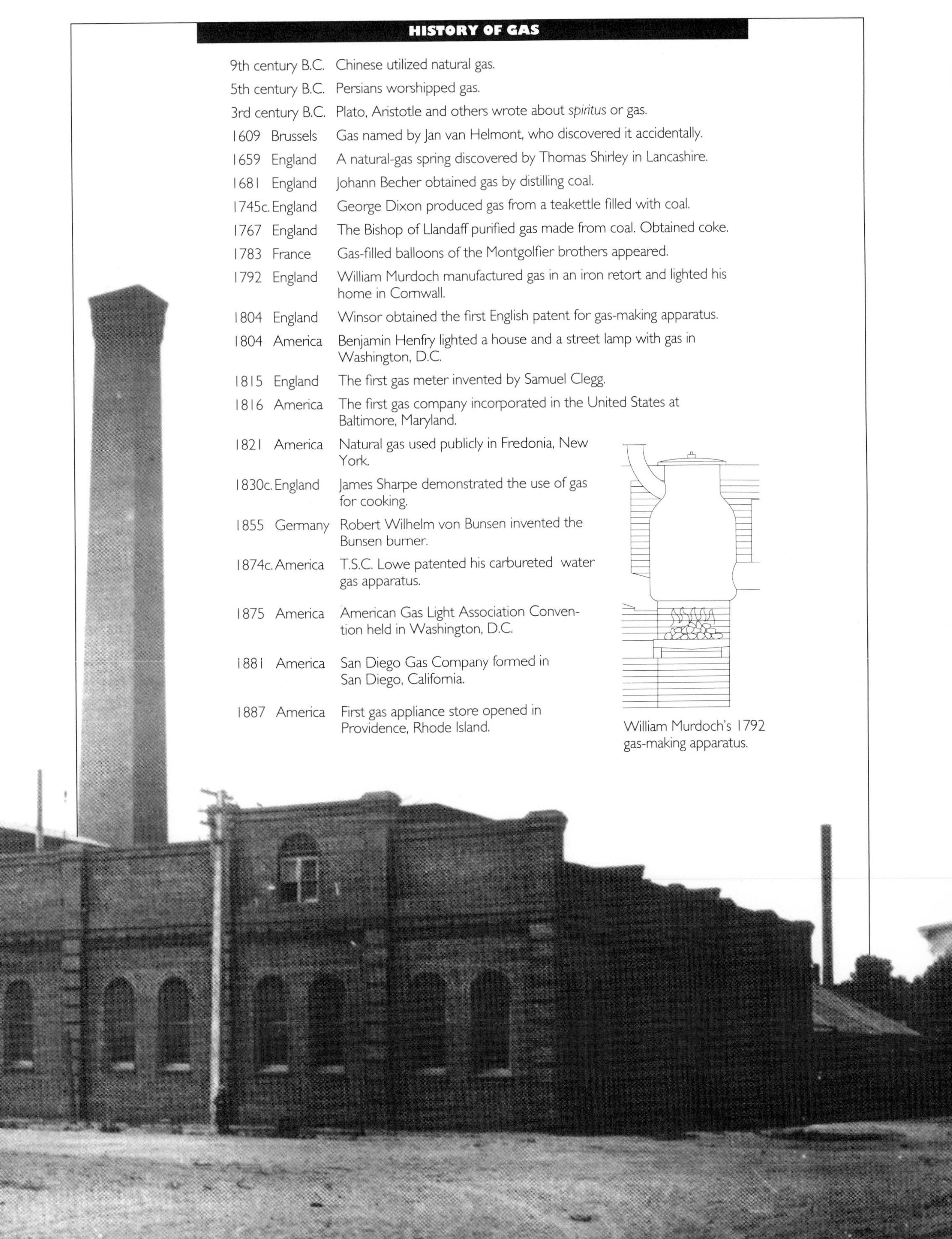

HISTORY OF GAS

9th century B.C.	Chinese utilized natural gas.
5th century B.C.	Persians worshipped gas.
3rd century B.C.	Plato, Aristotle and others wrote about *spiritus* or gas.
1609 Brussels	Gas named by Jan van Helmont, who discovered it accidentally.
1659 England	A natural-gas spring discovered by Thomas Shirley in Lancashire.
1681 England	Johann Becher obtained gas by distilling coal.
1745c. England	George Dixon produced gas from a teakettle filled with coal.
1767 England	The Bishop of Llandaff purified gas made from coal. Obtained coke.
1783 France	Gas-filled balloons of the Montgolfier brothers appeared.
1792 England	William Murdoch manufactured gas in an iron retort and lighted his home in Cornwall.
1804 England	Winsor obtained the first English patent for gas-making apparatus.
1804 America	Benjamin Henfry lighted a house and a street lamp with gas in Washington, D.C.
1815 England	The first gas meter invented by Samuel Clegg.
1816 America	The first gas company incorporated in the United States at Baltimore, Maryland.
1821 America	Natural gas used publicly in Fredonia, New York.
1830c. England	James Sharpe demonstrated the use of gas for cooking.
1855 Germany	Robert Wilhelm von Bunsen invented the Bunsen burner.
1874c. America	T.S.C. Lowe patented his carbureted water gas apparatus.
1875 America	American Gas Light Association Convention held in Washington, D.C.
1881 America	San Diego Gas Company formed in San Diego, California.
1887 America	First gas appliance store opened in Providence, Rhode Island.

William Murdoch's 1792 gas-making apparatus.

An engine and cars from the San Diego Electric Rapid Transit trolley system pause during their travels sometime around 1888 or 1889. Poor wiring caused the enterprise to fail in the early 1890s. (Photo courtesy Herbert R. Fitch Collection)

space for 20 railed horse cars and 20 horse stalls, plus an outdoor corral, on the southwest corner of Arctic and D streets, now Kettner and Broadway. In a spirit of competition, George D. Copeland started the Electric Rapid Transit Street Car Company, the second electric street railway in the United States. The young company began operating in November 1887, but did not do well; the wiring used to supply electricity had insulation difficulties and failed after a few months. Copeland changed the plant over to an incandescent commercial lighting service at India and Kalmia streets. The amount of business was slight, so Copeland arranged to move his two 750-light generators and two smaller direct-current machines to the San Diego Gas and Electric Light Company's new plant, where they were operated by steam engines. The generators were eventually purchased by the Company in 1892. The San Diego Street Car Company also went broke and coincidentally its equipment and carbarn were sold in 1892.

In order to provide water for the growing city—and to protect the investment of the San Diego Gas and Electric Light Company—two of the original gas company founders, Ephraim Morse and Bryant Howard, became interested in the San Diego Flume Company promoted by Theodore S. Van Dyke, author of *The Conquest of Arid America*. George Copeland, George Marston, Milton Santee, Moses Luce, Colonel W.G. Dickinson and other city

fathers also recognized the need for water imported from the Cuyamaca mountains. They built a reservoir with a capacity of 4 billion gallons about 50 miles east of San Diego at an elevation of 5,000 feet. Water traveled by gravity flow through a flume 35.6 miles long. D.C. Reed, former director of the gas company and later mayor of San Diego, and California Governor Robert Waterman shared the front bench in the first boat to shoot the flume. Its completion was celebrated on February 22, 1889, amid great festivities with fountains of water 125 feet high spraying out of nozzles on street corners. (No matter that the actual flume water had been held up and they had to use well water for the party; soon the "real" water arrived!) Other water projects included construction of the Sweetwater Dam and the incorporation of the Otay Water Company.

San Diego California Dec 1st 1884

At a regular meeting of the Directors of the San Diego Gas Co on the above date there were present C. S. Witherby J. S. Gordon E. W. Morse and R. M. Powers. Minutes of the last regular meeting and special meeting of Nov 20th were read and approved. Bills for various items as follows - Freight $65.90 Expenses, water, rent &c $49.44. Pipe $3.93, Shale $111.85 Lime $18.00 Coal $829.50 Labor $296.00 and Dividend a/c $688.80 aggregating $2067.92 were read and approved.

Letters from J. Macdonough & Co. relating Cannel Coal and Shale, from Adam Weber in relation to Clay retorts, and from Page Bros on Shale from Australia were read and placed on file.

On motion of E. W. Morse seconded by J. S. Gordon the secretary was instructed to present a written statement to the Board of City Trustees requesting them to re-advertise for proposals for lighting the City with gas or electric lights as in our opinion sufficient time was not allowed to give the City the benefit of competition in the matter of the electric lights. Motion carried. There being no further business the meeting adjourned.

R. M. Powers Secy.

Handwritten minutes of directors' meeting from December 1884.

The city of San Diego experienced phenomenal growth during this period, reaching a peak of 35,000 to 40,000 people. The San Diego Gas and Electric Light Company's newly installed generating equipment at Tenth and Imperial could supply 300 arc lamps

Looking south from Broadway, this was downtown San Diego about 1882, a year after the Company started its gas service. In the background, a steamer gets under way from the Fifth Avenue docks, while the future site of the historic Hotel del Coronado lies on the horizon beyond. (Photo courtesy of San Diego Historical Society–Ticor Collection)

used from sundown to midnight—unless some influential citizen was giving a party, then they burned until 1 a.m.! As reported in the Company's minutes, ". . . all the work has been done in a first class manner and it is the opinion of all practical and expert gas and electric light engineers who have visited us that we have the most perfect and complete plant of its size to be found anywhere." The September 1889 issue of *The Golden Era* magazine reported that the Company's ten arc light towers were "much more graceful in appearance than the wooden masts and square structures used in other cities" and because of their "excellent arrangement," visitors invariably spoke about the city's public lighting "in the highest terms."

New subdivisions were mapped at Mission Bay, Pacific Beach, Ocean Beach (formerly Mussel Beach) and La Jolla. To the south were Oneanta by the Sea (in the Tia Juana River Valley), Tia Juana City (five miles inland) and Otay, "The Magic City;" to the east were La Presa (near Sweetwater Dam), La Mesa and Lakeside. National City was incorporated in 1887 and the cities of Escondido and Oceanside in 1888. A new charter made San Diego a fourth-class city and provided for the election of a mayor. The state legislature approved the new charter on March 16, 1888, and Douglas Gunn, a former editor of *The San Diego Union,* became the first elected mayor in 37 years. For the San Diego Gas and Electric Light Company, it would mean working with 18 men—nine aldermen, elected at large, and nine delegates, elected by ward—instead of the old five-man board of trustees. The new form of government, including a paid fire department, a board of public works and a board of harbor commissioners, went into operation in May, just as city and county assessments dropped se-

Looking like the front door to Hades, the retort wall in the Company's coal gas maker required strong men to shovel in the fuel. One door is open at the end of the bottom row.

riously from $40 million in 1888 to $25 million in 1890. The Horton Bank Building at Third and D became the new city hall.

The collapse of the land boom was disastrous to land speculators and especially to New San Diego's prime mover, Alonzo Horton. He was then 75 and living in his white mansion on First Avenue. During the next few years, he lost some of his remaining properties because of delinquent taxes, but he kept his hand in San Diego's development. More than half of the peak-of-the-boom population had departed, with the 1890 census listing 16,159 as living in the city and 34,987 in the county. The Company's revenues fell off to $79,000 in 1889 and decreased to $76,000 in 1890. The 173 electric arc lights in service dropped to 120, but the gas division held its own—gaining one customer in two and one-half years (450 to 451 from January 1, 1888, to June 1, 1890).

Dr. Robert M. Powers took over as president and general manager on January 17, 1889, and would serve until June 26, 1905. Even though the Company was hard hit by the collapse of the boom, the board of directors rejected an offer of $400,000 in February 1889 to sell the gas plant. They then heard rumors that a rival gas plant financed by a New York syndicate was going to be built in San Diego. According to *The San Diego Union* of December 23, 1889, it was "an open secret that E.S. Babcock Jr. was involved." Apparently nothing came of the plans. As San Diego's population stabilized, the San Diego Gas and Electric Light Company made plans for upgrading its service.

Early electrical lighting equipment provided both arc light and incandescent illumination. Each generator was connected to a steam-powered motor with a long leather drive belt.

This view up Fifth Avenue, from the intersection with I Street, shows the booming popularity of San Diego in 1887. In fewer than six years, arc lights (on tower at back) and power lines (poles at left) laced the streets. Telephones had also become popular but required a large number of cross arms to hold each customer's wire (poles at right).

SAN DIEGO GAS & ELECTRIC LIGHT Co
ELAND.
SAN DIEGO
GAS
ELECTRIC LIGHT Co

Chapter 2

1891-1900
From Panic to Progress

1891
Population*
34,986
Electric
Customers
255
Sales
N/A
Avg. cost /month per incandescent lamp
$2
Gas
Customers
672
Sales
N/A
Average cost / therm
72 cents

SAN DIEGO COUNTY

MEXICO

Service Territory

*County population based on census 10-year estimates

As the decade of the 1890s began, San Diego was experiencing a minor recession. The Boom of the Eighties, which had resulted from land speculation involving hundreds of urban lots in the center of town and along the coast, had reached its peak two years before. Many of the subdivisions in or near San Diego contained lots useful only for permanent residences, vacation cottages or businesses—all of which depended upon an influx of people. So, when the dreamed-of thousands of newcomers turned around and went home—or failed to come at all—property from Carlsbad in the north to Tia Juana City in the south went begging. San Diego, still not on any main railroad line, had also begun to feel the pinch of rivalry with Los Angeles. Southbound train passengers were warned to carry jugs of drinking water since, they were told, there were few sources of that precious liquid in the southern city.

Even management of the Santa Fe Railroad had threatened to terminate service for lack of coal, but John D. Spreckels, who had constructed a wharf for coal bunkers at the foot of G Street in 1889, laid tracks to the Santa Fe line and saved the day. Spreckels, who owned the Coronado Beach Company and Coronado Ferry Company, purchased *The San Diego Union* in 1890 and promoted the positive aspects of the city. He began to invest seriously in San Diego and work toward a direct rail connection with the East. Nevertheless, Spreckels' major business interests were in Coronado, and he supported its movement to secede from San Diego and form a separate city—which it did in 1891.

The Company's 1890 staff consisted of (from left) R.L. Clarke, R.P. Moses, C.W. Wiggins, Sam McGovney, John Starr, James McInnes and Frank Bayless. The hayburners were Company workers also, but the two dogs are unknown.

< This two-story main office building was constructed in 1898 at 935 Sixth Avenue, site of smaller quarters acquired in 1890. Accommodating trolley drivers would stop in mid-block to wait for passengers to go in and pay their bills. The Elks occupied the building's upper story and placed their symbol of an elk's head at the peak of the roof.

U.S. Grant Jr., son of the famous Civil War Union general and U.S. President, came to San Diego at the turn of the century to make his mark. Today, the U.S. Grant Hotel is his most enduring remembrance. (Photo courtesy of San Diego Historical Society–Ticor Collection)

Despite the economic slowdown, San Diegans remained optimistic and promoted the landscaping of City (later Balboa) Park under the direction of Kate Sessions, pioneer horticulturist. Some early businesses, such as George Marston's department store, remained solvent, and a few new ones opened. Joseph Jessop began his jewelry business in 1890, and the elegant Fisher Opera House, with a capacity of 1,400, opened that year on the east side of Fourth between B and C streets. Ulysses S. Grant Jr., son of the former president, arrived in San Diego in 1892 and purchased the Horton House Hotel in 1895. San Diegans made elaborate plans to celebrate the 350th anniversary of Juan Rodriguez Cabrillo's 1542 landing on Point Loma, while the city, in a more serious vein, asked the United States Congress for appropriations to widen and deepen the harbor's channel and to undertake jetty construction to prevent shoaling.

On January 5, 1890, *The San Diego Union* described the "splendid gas and electric facilities" of the Company, whose plant was believed to be "probably one of the most complete on the coast." The coal gas works, bounded by Ninth, Tenth, M and N streets, was what was termed a 10-inch plant—all connections being 10 inches in diameter except the outlet, which was "twelve inches and consisted of five benches of retorts, Weber regenerative furnaces, exhauster, tower, scrubber and condenser, four purifiers 10 x 12 each, Slatim meter of 300,000 cubic feet capacity, automatic sheet governor and a gas holder of 150,000 cubic feet capacity" with an estimated plant capacity of 250,000 cubic feet daily. The water gas plant, in a separate building, consisted of a generator, scrubber and condenser, known as the "Springer" process, with boiler and generator to operate the same. It produced "150,000 feet daily, making a total of 400,000 [cubic] feet every twenty-four hours" supplied in "twelve miles of street mains and about 600 meter connections."

The electric light works, fronting on Tenth Street, contained one "250-horsepower Corliss engine and one Buckeye high-speed engine." These were added to the "30-light dynamos of the Indianapolis Jenny [sic] system, one 30-light dynamo of the Western Electric system, and one 65-light machine of the Brush system for arc lighting and one 100-light incandescent dynamo for inside lighting, while the Jenney system is used solely for outside lighting." The Company had 10 towers, each with six 2,000-candlepower lamps, which were served by 25 miles of poles and wires. Even Eastern visitors, accustomed to the lights of Boston or New York, commented favorably.

When Station A began operating the Jenney arc light generators in 1888, the generators (three units in foreground) were operated by a single 250-hp Hamilton-Corliss piston steam engine (large drive wheel in background). The Hamilton-Corliss was the only engine to furnish lighting until 1904.

The Hamilton-Corliss was connected by a wide, leather drive belt to a single-line shaft (foreground). Other drive belts connected this drive shaft to each of the generators. This was a typical Victorian-era "power takeoff" arrangement that was popular for industrial applications before the development of small, individual electric motors.

The drive belts were so wide that one could handily serve as a New Year's dining table for employees. These employees were given $5 gold pieces. This photo may have been taken January 1, 1900, or within a few years of that date.

DR. ROBERT M. POWERS

Dr. Robert M. Powers, elected secretary of the Company in 1882, came to San Diego from Ohio in 1879 for his health. He had been a practicing physician at the time of his arrival but quickly turned his attention generally to business and specifically to the formation of a gas company. Dr. Powers carefully kept the minutes of the new corporation until 1889, when he became president and general manager. He remained as president for a time after 1905 when the Company was acquired by the Chicago firm of H.M. Byllesby & Company.

Although listed in the city directory as a physician, Dr. Powers also helped organize the Bank of Commerce in 1893 and served as its president from 1897 to 1903. He was a member of the first library board and served on the board of trustees for the State Normal School for several years. He and his family were active in social and church circles and resided at Ninth and A streets. Dr. Powers died in January 1927. His daughters remained in San Diego and were recognized as civic and cultural leaders. Julia Powers Spining died in 1973, and Miriam Powers Barney in 1983. Robert Powers II settled in Oakland in 1940.

My dear Doctor:

How much will you pay us per month to keep out of street lighting?

E.S.Babcock.

Love note or blackmail? This note was forwarded to Dr. Robert Powers after Elisha Babcock had added the typed message at the bottom. There is no record that the Company paid Babcock, developer of the Hotel del Coronado, any money.

All the Company officers, with the exception of Dr. Powers, president and general manager, had changed by the beginning of 1890. The new persons were, according to the minutes, "S. Levi, Vice-President and Treasurer; F.W. Jackson, Secretary; W.W. Steward, Ed Wescott, E.W. Bushyhead, S. Levi and R.M. Powers, Directors." At the January 16 stockholders meeting, salaries of $175 per month for the general manager and $100 per month for the secretary were approved.

The city instructed the board of public works on April 29, 1891, to award the San Diego Gas and Electric Light Company a contract to supply 91 tower masts and low electric lights at a cost of $46.37 per night since "lighting of the streets of the city is necessary for the protection of lives and property." The Company had "put up a lot of new bracket arc lamps of 2,000 candle-power" that gave a "powerful and beautiful steady light." The generating system of George Copeland's Electric Rapid Transit Street Car Company was finally purchased outright. New customers for gas were duly recorded by the secretary in the corporate minute books, and during 1891 some of the better-known names included numbers 254, Wells Fargo; 263, Sisters of Mercy (Mercy Hospital); 270, Board of Supervisors of San Diego County; 283, R.V. Dodge; 309, Joseph W. Sefton; and 343, The San Diego Union. By January 1894, there were 862 customers, including No. 857, U.S. Grant Jr.

In November 1892, Elisha S. Babcock, formerly of the Coronado Electric Light Company, was approached by a number of citizens to consider starting an electric company that would furnish light to the business houses on Fifth Avenue in San Diego. Babcock decided to refer the matter to Dr. Powers and thoughtfully inquired early in 1893, "How much will you pay us per month to keep out of street lighting?" Babcock, who was involved in water development, decided not to compete, and there are no records of Company money having been paid to him.

In San Francisco, the powerful Edison General Electric Company of New York, which owned Edison's patent rights, incorporated on July 1, 1891, as the Edison Light and Power Company in California and purchased George Roe's California Electric Light Company by an exchange of stock. It merged with the San Francisco Gas Company in 1896. Other locally owned companies, such as the Los Angeles Electric Company, were struggling to remain independent and to meet growing demands.

The nationwide financial panic of 1893 left a number of bankruptcies in its wake. Five of the eight San Diego banks failed, leaving solvent only the First National Bank at Fifth and E, the Bank of Commerce at 841 Fifth (with Dr. R.M. Powers as president), and San Diego Savings Bank (later San Diego Trust & Savings) at Fifth and F. The Consolidated Bank, a combination of the first two banks in San Diego and founded by several gas-company board members, closed its doors permanently in 1893. Its building at Fifth and G was sold to Ralph Granger and would later become the city hall.

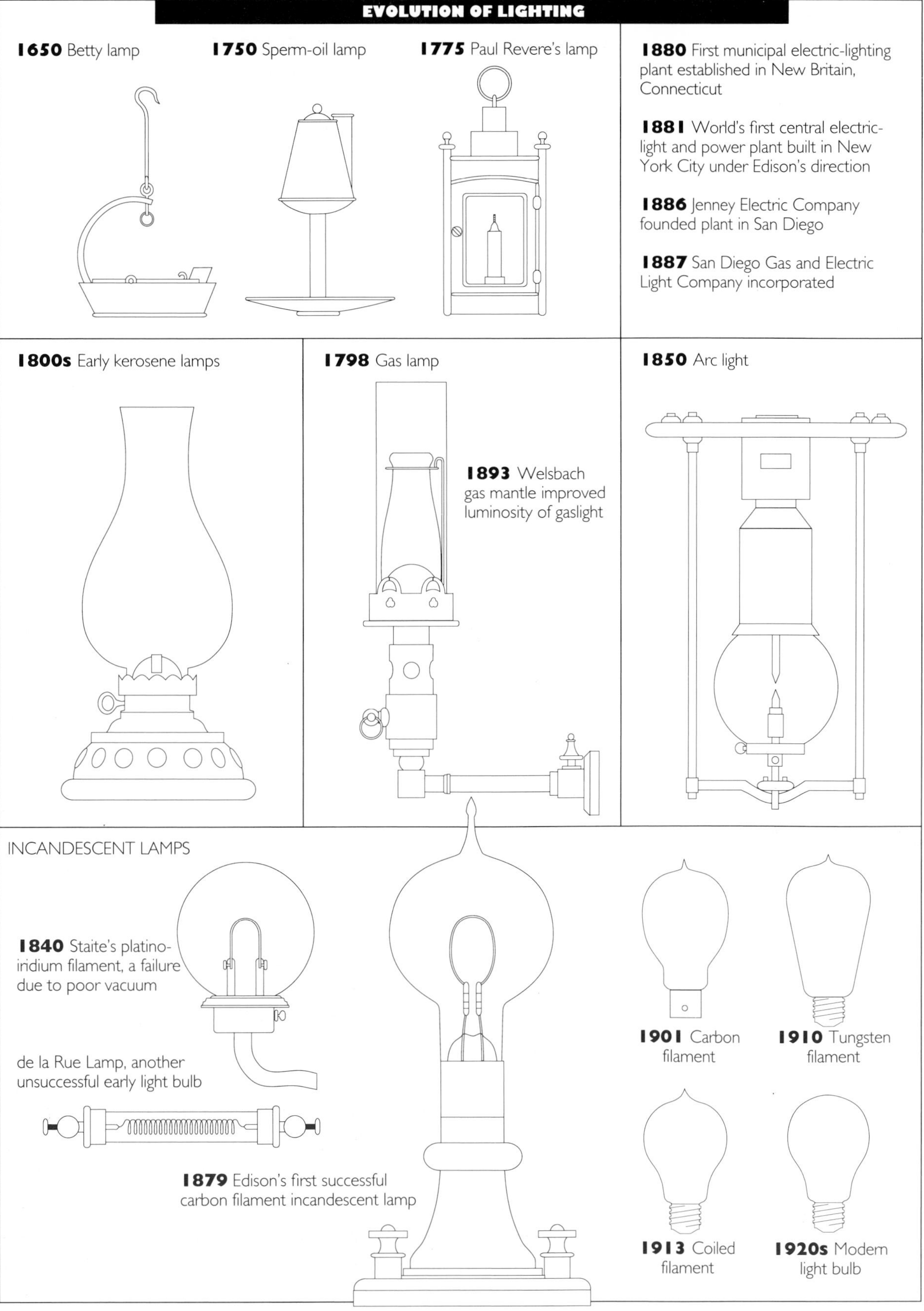
EVOLUTION OF LIGHTING
1650 Betty lamp
1750 Sperm-oil lamp
1775 Paul Revere's lamp
1880 First municipal electric-lighting plant established in New Britain, Connecticut
1881 World's first central electric-light and power plant built in New York City under Edison's direction
1886 Jenney Electric Company founded plant in San Diego
1887 San Diego Gas and Electric Light Company incorporated
1800s Early kerosene lamps
1798 Gas lamp
1893 Welsbach gas mantle improved luminosity of gaslight
1850 Arc light
INCANDESCENT LAMPS
1840 Staite's platino-iridium filament, a failure due to poor vacuum
de la Rue Lamp, another unsuccessful early light bulb
1879 Edison's first successful carbon filament incandescent lamp
1901 Carbon filament
1910 Tungsten filament
1913 Coiled filament
1920s Modern light bulb

The gas meter shop at Station A in the late 1890s. Repairing gas meters are A.P. Henning and his son, Tom (both appear in the group photos on pages 27 and 30). Although it looks like dirty work, it was cleaner than shoveling coal into the gas maker.

By 1895, Station A was operating both incandescent-light generators and arc-lighting equipment. Electric generation then was measured by the number of lights that each unit could supply. The early electric incandescent lighting was so dim, however, that gas mantel lights remained popular until about 1910.

Despite other reversals of fortune, the city of San Diego in 1894 pursued an active agenda to attract people to the area. A site on North Island was offered to the federal government for a naval training school, and efforts were made to induce steamship lines to stop in port. George Marston warned, however, that an "adequate supply of water" was "a matter fraught with weightiest and most vital public concern." The Chamber of Commerce urged that a State Normal School be placed in San Diego.

In March 1894, a controversy arose over the San Diego Gas and Electric Light Company's contract with the city to provide outdoor lighting. Mayor William H. Carlson called a special session of the city council at which he reminded the aldermen that the city would be plunged into darkness on the following night unless something was done and recommended that "some temporary arrangements for lighting the city be made." The Company was asked to continue on a temporary basis, to which Dr. Powers, general manager, replied that he had "no desire to act arbitrary [sic] in the matter" but that it cost "too much money to run 100 lamps without any prospect of compensation." Powers concluded:

"It seems to me that the citizen chosen by his constituents to represent them who . . . will allow himself to be governed by personal considerations or pique, or an unsatisfied desire to punish somebody, should select another field in which to exercise his pernicious propensities . . . I know that some business houses have arranged to have special protection of their property in case the lights are extinguished, and I have been given assurance that while the convenience and protection afforded by well lighted streets are understood and appreciated, under the circumstances our company could do nothing else than to shut down if the council does not agree upon something."

The San Diego Union of April 3, 1894, reported that the lights would continue to shine. "President Barker, the champion of municipal ownership of electric lights . . . made a vigorous denial of the charge that he was working from personal or political motives." Powers "disclaimed having made any personal attack" on the city council's president and pointed out that "Los Angeles, Santa Barbara and San Bernardino had certain advantages or differences in their contracts which made it possible to reduce the cost of lighting—as for instance, Santa Barbara was lighted only to 1 a.m. and the San Bernardino plant was run by water power." Delegate John C. Olmstead moved that the resolution accepting the Company's bid be adopted, and it passed by a vote of ten to six—with Barker voting no.

The only other newsworthy event of 1894 was the report on June 27 that "Steve Hinckley, violently insane, climbs an electric light mast." For two hours the neighborhood around 12th and H streets "was in an uproar" listening to Hinckley alternately groan and talk. A little girl finally talked the man down, "and Officers McInnes and Ellsworth and Detective James Russell immediately took charge of the fellow and . . . hurried him to the county jail, where he was placed in a padded cell in the insane ward."

Arc lights, like this one near Fifth Avenue and Beech Street in downtown San Diego, stood 125 feet high and served to illuminate large areas of streets and homes. Workers had to climb them daily to replace the burned-out arc rods. Most of the homes here probably still used oil lamps or gas jets for inside illumination.

By 1895, newspaper competition was fairly strong. There were five rival papers—E.W. Scripps' *San Diego Sun,* two smaller papers called the *Vidette* and the *Record,* and the newly founded *San Diego Tribune. The San Diego Union*, an eight-page daily, experienced its greatest growth under John D. Spreckels' ownership, installing a linotype in 1895. San Diegans demanded at this time that long-distance telephone connections be installed and that harbor defenses be improved. Soon the Chamber of Commerce would establish a branch office in Los Angeles.

The year 1896 started out well for the San Diego Gas and Electric Light Company with *The Union* reporting that the Company was one of the city's "most prominent enterprises." Its plant, located at the foot of Ninth Street, was "one of the best equipped on the Pacific coast." The Company "had made many improvements and expended large sums of money in modernizing. The gas plant is equipped with five benches of five retorts each and a Springer water gas plant with a total capacity of 400,000 [cubic] feet. The capacity of the gas holder is 150,000 feet, and the plant as a whole could supply many times more than at present required." The article continued:

Twelve masts separated by wide distances and 125 feet in height, each holding six lights of 2,000 candle power each, illuminate the city at night and there are over 100 low arc lights at prominent corners. Nearly 150 commercial lights of 2,000 candlepower each are supplied by the company as well as all the gas used for light and fuel . . . The distributing system of the company consists of twenty miles of gas mains, about forty-five miles of electric wires, the twelve towers and the many armmasts which render this one of the best lighted cities on the coast.

The Company's contract with the city dated April 1, 1896, to light the streets, avenues and parks for a term of one year, was for the sum of $1,521 per month, payable monthly. The Westinghouse Electric Light system managed by George Copeland was also running more than 700 incandescent lights in San Diego. The power for the plant was obtained from the dynamos at the San Diego Gas and Electric Light Company's plant at the foot of Ninth Street.

This view of the Company's original office at 935 Sixth Avenue was taken about 1890. Standing in the doorway are F.W. Jackson, secretary (left) and Dr. R.M. Powers, president and general manager. E.W. Hickman is seated in the Company buggy, used in contacting customers. In the window is a stove, one of the first appliances sold by the Company.

On May 23, 1896, *The Union* reported that gas rates were coming down. The prospects of a new company organized by Leon P. Lowe, son of Professor Thaddeus S. Lowe, a pioneer in gas-balloon ascensions during the Civil War, had encouraged the directors to reduce the price of gas to $1.95 per 1,000 cubic feet from $2.50 for fuel and $3 for lighting. This would undersell the promoters of the new company who had promised to give a $2 rate. Lowe, who had been invited to San Diego by U.S. Grant Jr., proposed to put in a plant and eventually sell gas at $1.75 per 1,000 cubic feet. He indicated that San Diego had great opportunities, since the little city of Pasadena, half the size of San Diego, used from 18 million to 20 million cubic feet while San Diego used only 12 million to 15 million.

This recently discovered glass-plate photograph shows the interior of the Company's office, probably the original 935 Sixth Avenue building, between 1895 and 1898. Electric-light fixtures (above the counter) and gas-light fixtures (on wall) are visible, as well as stoves on the left side.

Secretary Jackson of San Diego Gas and Electric Light Company commented that they were "not trying to shut out legitimate competition . . . but [did] not intend to have our throats cut by promoters who use the capital of unwitting citizens to work upon, and who are ready to put in a plant at excessive figures and leave the backers in the lurch." One of the local backers reported on May 24 that when U.S. Grant had first mentioned the matter, Grant was "under the impression that Mr. Lowe had some new or superior process which we ought to possess and was in favor of cheaper gas, but did not propose to put his own money into it."

On May 29, 1896, *The San Diego Union* carried two ads: "Cheapest Gas on the Coast (excepting San Francisco)—Gas at $1.95 a thousand [cubic feet] is cheaper than oil . . . gasoline or coal . . . for Light, Fuel or Power." The Company would waive all existing contracts with consumers and give them the new rate after June 1, 1896. The minutes of the board of directors of October 29, 1896, indicated that the cost of coal was $6.25 per ton for Australian coal and $6 per ton for Nanaimo (Vancouver Island, British Columbia) coal. This was the lowest price ever reached, since the average cost of coal over the life of the coal gas plant was between $8 and $9 per ton.

Gas lamps, like this ring light above the bar at the Horton House saloon in 1895, remained a popular indoor lighting system until after the turn of the century. Some builders installed both gas and electric lighting in new homes as late as 1904.

At the board meeting of January 28, 1897, San Diego Gas and Electric Light Company proposed a new contract for the city "to light the streets, avenues and parks" for another term of one year. The proposal was as follows:

Eighty-one arc lamps of 2,000 candle power each at present located upon the bidder's iron or wooden towers or masts and also thirty-six arc lamps of 2,000 candle power each, placed upon mast arms or poles as at present located and also one such mast arm arc lamp at the corner of Third and J Streets, and one at the corner of Fourteenth and K Streets, and one at the corner of Twenty-sixth and L Streets in said city. Said lamps to be

A rainy day in San Diego shortly after the Company's enlarged offices (white building, left side of street) were opened. The trolley tracks crossed at Sixth Avenue and Broadway (then known as D Street) in this view to the south. The Company used square power poles at that time, and did not want people to post notices on the poles. (Photo courtesy of the Union Title Insurance & Trust Company Historical Collection)

lighted on what is known as the "moon schedule," for the sum of $12.50 per lamp, per month, payable monthly making a total of $1500 per month for all of said lights. And when the moon is obscured by clouds or fogs, the said lights will be turned on, upon thirty minutes notice to the bidder from the proper authorities, to turn on the same, at a cost of six and one-half cents per lamp per hour.

The contract proposal was then revised and the rate lowered to $10 per lamp per month. It went into effect on April 1, 1897, and ran for one year.

The same kinds of rate conflicts were being experienced throughout the state, since all electric utilities were fledgling operations, and electric lighting was not yet perfected. There were no handbooks to guide those who installed the new equipment, and electrical engineers were in short supply. The State Constitution of 1879, which had given all cities, regardless of size, the right to grant franchises to suppliers of "gas lights or other illuminating light upon all city streets," had placed city council members in a vocal position to discuss the pros and cons of lighting costs. Cities including Los Angeles, Santa Barbara, San Jose and San Francisco were struggling to find the least expensive means to supply municipal lighting and were receiving bids from three and four competing privately owned companies. Few municipalities had the capability to enter into the industry at this time, so privately owned companies throughout the country set the trend.

Small, competitive generating plants continued to challenge the major electric companies that were striving to build their customer load, and San Diego was no exception. Early in 1897, the city received a proposition from a Mr. Sharpe "to build a new municipal electric lighting plant. . . . The specifications provided for the best of modern machinery, housed in a building of Moorish or old Spanish architecture, made of brick and cemented over on the outside. The capacity of the plant was placed at 160 2,000 candle power arc lights, with 120 lights" and 16 miles of pole line.

One council member thought offers from other companies, including San Diego Gas and Electric Light Company, should also be solicited. Dr.

These turn-of-the-century employees did not have holidays or Saturdays off. The work could be hard and dangerous, since health and safety practices had not been instituted.

AC VERSUS DC: WHAT'S THE DIFFERENCE?

Direct current (DC) was the original form of electricity discovered by the Greeks and captured by Ben Franklin's kite. Early developers of electric generating equipment, like Thomas Edison, worked with DC. Edison used direct current to power the world's first electric system in New York in 1881. DC is an electric charge moving in one direction only as it passes down a wire. DC, however, is difficult to transform into the high voltages desired for long-distance electrical power transmission.

This is where alternating current (AC) comes in. AC alters its value from positive to negative as it flows down a wire. For most home and business uses, AC power varies from a positive 120 volts to a negative 120 volts, back to a positive 120 volts, 60 times each second. These abrupt shifts in value create the characteristic "frequency," which we call "cycle." Sixty switches a second creates 60-cycle power.

AC power can be transformed easily into the high voltages needed for efficient long-distance power transmission. AC power also allowed for development of lower-cost modern appliances and business machines.

DC is still used today in a few selected locations for very long-distance (more than 400 miles) transmission of electricity. In these cases, AC is converted to DC before it is fed into the transmission line, then reconverted to AC before distribution to customers.

Powers, who was attending the council meeting, insisted that the city had to give "a hundred other electrical companies," including his own, a chance to compete. Powers warned that the present contract expired on March 31, "and if the city goes ahead and enters into this new proposition, the city will be in darkness until the new plant is in. . . . And some of the men who are now urging this thing on, and looking forward to darkness as a very nice thing, will find that the people are not with them."

The San Diego Weekly Union on May 27, 1897, reported that the city had approved the new lighting contract that would run from April 1, 1898, to March 31, 1899, and provide street lighting at "the rate of $10.50 per month per light or $1,200 per month for the entire service." By this time, the city recognized that the Company was the best qualified to meet street lighting needs, and the two entities entered into a smoother working relationship. The development of water resources began to take precedence.

San Diego's population hovered around 17,000 during this time, and the city continued to be concerned about a municipal water supply. Headway had been made in solving the problem, but an average rainfall of 10 inches per year was insufficient. Private companies had developed mountain reservoirs and were selling water to the city on a contract basis. From 1887 to 1897, these companies constructed six major dams in the county. The San Diego Flume Company was successful for a few years, but an 11-year drought between 1895 and 1905 dried up the flume's reservoir and forced it to pump brackish San Diego River water. The Southern California Mountain Water Company, organized by Elisha Babcock and taken over by John Spreckels, had built the Upper and Lower Otay and Morena dams. The city purchased the San Diego Water Company in 1901 and, as water use expanded, began negotiations with the Spreckels company.

Early in 1898, the year the Spanish-American War captured the attention of the country, San Diegans were concerned about cultural activities. Site

Riding the flume was a bit dangerous, but city residents were justly proud that abundant water was available. The lack of water and natural energy resources has always been a problem for San Diego. (Photo courtesy of San Diego Historical Society–Ticor Collection)

Interior of Station A in the 1890s. Belt-driven generators continued in operation until after 1910.

studies were made for the establishment of a Carnegie Library, and preservation of the San Diego Mission, then in ruins, was urged by George Marston. The Chamber of Commerce set a policy that no part of City (Balboa) Park would be appropriated for military purposes or, in fact, for any purpose other than that for which it was originally intended. On a smaller scale, *The San Diego Union* of February 15, 1898, reported that the directors of San Diego Gas and Electric Light Company had "decided to levy an assessment of $5 per share on the capital stock to pay floating indebtedness and place the company in a more advantageous position." The year was one of optimism, and continued growth was predicted.

At the regular monthly directors meeting of San Diego Gas and Electric Light Company on September 21, 1899, President Powers reported that he had signed an acceptance of "an offer made by the Spreckels Bros. Commercial Co. to furnish the Company with (800) eight hundred tons of Wallsend coal" at $7.62½ per 2,240 pounds. The board also adopted a schedule of discount rates for commercial incandescent lighting and set "residence and commercial installation of separate transformers and meters $1.00 minimum charge per month and 2 cents per lamphour up to $5.00 per month" with a discount given for payment by the fifth of the month. The president reported that he had entered into a contract with the city for the following year at a price of $10.50 per lamp per month. The secretary reported expenditures for March as $10,070.27; April, $2,963.85; May, $3,096.42; June, $13,158.13; July, $6,375.98; and August, $4,179.86. The directors decided to raise the rate "for arc electric lights burning from dark until midnight to be fixed at $12.50 per lamp per month" with a discounted rate of $10 per month for yearly customers who paid monthly in advance by the fifth of each month. In other business of the meeting, Superintendent Ralph Clarke asked for reimbursement of $13 for train fare to Los Angeles and Santa Barbara on Company business.

At the turn of the century, San Diego embarked upon a new era. In addition to a number of established businesses, new ones had opened.

By the late 1890s, the staff included (from left) R.L. Clarke, Ole Gylling, William Darling, George Lemon, James McCarty, A.P. Henning and his son, Tom Henning, Frank Blankenship, Bert Bangs, Fred Anderson, Oscar Carroll, Bert Sherman, Sam McGovney, Ole Lemon, L.M. Arey, Dr. R.M. Powers. Next to Powers is his son, Robert. Most of these men had been born before the invention of the electric lamp.

Automobiles and trucks began to replace horse-drawn wagons, and paved highways soon were laid over the county's dirt roads. Cash registers, adding machines, typewriters and modern packaging also were in evidence. Melville Klauber and Simon Levi, both of Bohemian descent, formed a partnership for general merchandising in 1883. Even though their store suffered a second-floor collapse and a destructive fire in the Backesto Block building, they constructed a new brick structure at the northeast corner of Fourth and H streets and became very successful. Simon Levi, a board member of the San Diego Gas and Electric Light Company, resigned from the partnership in November 1896 to become a commission merchant and shipper, dealing in honey, beeswax and produce. The Klauber Wangenheim Company, a general retail store formed in 1897 from Klauber & Levi, was in the vanguard of new developments. Klauber Wangenheim had several retail stores in the county, bought out the competing Harbison Grocery Company in 1901 and expanded into both Long Beach and Los Angeles that same year.

Out on Point Loma, some unusual newcomers belonging to the Universal Brotherhood & Theosophical Society had built their international headquarters on 130 acres of prime property under the direction of Katherine A. Tingley. Students, disciples and other followers arrived from all over the world in 1900 and occupied such exotic buildings as the Isis Conservatory of Music and Drama, the Raja Yoga Academy and the Temple of Peace. Madame Tingley attracted many wealthy people to her utopian community, including A.G. Spalding of sporting-goods fame. They built a beautiful Greek theater on a site overlooking the Pacific Ocean and took over the Fisher Opera House in downtown San Diego when it began to fail. Several of their buildings are today preserved within the campus of Point Loma Nazarene College.

In the summer of 1900, the first major accident of San Diego Gas and Electric Light Company occurred when 27-year-old E.W. McCurdy died as the result of an early-morning tragedy. McCurdy, *The Union* reported, "lost his life and the big dynamo which supplies the city with light was ruined so that there will be no street lights for three or four nights, or until a new armature for the dynamo can be shipped from San Francisco." McCurdy, an assistant engineer, apparently slipped and fell against the dynamo, "his fingers striking the positive and negative poles and permitting 7,000 volts of electricity to pass through his body." Dr. D. Gochenauer, who was called to the scene, found that every safeguard against danger was provided. "The idea of those who have investigated is that McCurdy stumbled and, in attempting to catch himself, threw his hands against the poles on the dynamo. He evidently did not grasp them as the burns and abrasions were only on the back of his hands." Superintendent Clarke, who arrived on the scene just eight minutes after the body was discovered, tried to resuscitate McCurdy but to no avail. "The body, when found, was lying about twenty feet from the dynamo, but McCurdy's hat was near the machine, showing that he received the shock there." McCurdy, described as a competent and careful engineer, left a widow, his mother and a brother in National City.

As the 20th century began, the city of San Diego made plans for the future. The idea of an Isthmian Canal was widely discussed, especially when it was shown how difficult it had been for the U.S. Pacific Fleet to reach Cuba during the Spanish-American War. The war, which ended in August 1898, fulfilled the expansive notions of those who wanted the United States to become a world power. The Philippine Islands and Guam, along with Puerto Rico, were added to the American domain. The San Diego Chamber of Commerce and other Pacific Coast organizations were in favor of a canal through Nicaragua rather than the alternative Panama site. A naval coaling and repair station for San Diego, as well as a railroad connection with Imperial Valley, also became major objectives of local promoters. All of this activity meant an expanded base for the San Diego Gas and Electric Light Company.

RALPH L. CLARKE

Ralph L. "Dad" Clarke, a 22-year-old engineer trained by his father, went to work for the Jenney Electric Company on March 23, 1886. When the San Diego Gas Company took over Jenney and became an electric company as well, Clarke came as part of the package. Although he served in many capacities from lineman to fireman, Clarke was appointed chief engineer and superintendent of the Company by Dr. Powers.

As the Company grew and emergency work was required of employees, Clarke, who lived just across the street from the plant, was always the first to peel off his coat and start in. He answered trouble calls at night by horse and wagon, repaired lines during storms, fixed faulty armatures and steam fittings, and worked side by side with those under him.

When the Byllesby Company of Chicago took over in 1905, Clarke remained as general superintendent and became assistant manager in 1920. He died in November 1922, leaving his widow, Frances, and sons Frank and Arthur.

Where's the stadium? Where's the freeway? This view of Mission Valley and the ruins of Mission San Diego de Alcalá in the late 1880s shows the barren lands that covered most of San Diego before the coming of water. (Photo courtesy of the Seaver Center, Natural History Museum of Los Angeles County)

13 FT. STATION METER AN
EB. 6, 1907.
SAN DIEGO CONSOLIDATED

Chapter 3

1901-1910
Birth of a Metropolis

*County population based on census 10-year estimates

The turn of the century was indeed a turning point for San Diego. Significant population increases were recorded throughout the city and county, and continued growth seemed assured. New city builders included Louis J. Wilde, D.C. Collier, O.W. Cotton and Ed Fletcher—all of whom would contribute to the promotion and development of California's most southern city. John D. Spreckels bought out the *Evening Tribune* newspaper in 1901 and purchased the old Horton Bank Building at Third and D streets to house both *The Union* and his new acquisition. The City of San Diego, the building's current occupant, had to move its offices to Fifth and G streets. Steel magnate Andrew Carnegie donated $50,000 for a library and, after the inevitable controversy over a site, the city fathers laid the library's cornerstone on E Street between 8th and 9th avenues. The public library, with additional city funds, was completed in April 1902 with landscaping designed by Kate Sessions and paid for by George W. Marston. City planners also formed a Park Improvement Committee to landscape the city's extensive parklands.

The Chamber of Commerce began to think in terms of large-scale tourist promotion and set an advertising budget of $1,000 per month for three months. Spreckels opened a new summer resort called Tent City on the strand south of the Hotel del Coronado, and a steady stream of visitors admired the views along the beaches and bay of San Diego.

The San Diego Union of January 1, 1901, reported that the accident in the Company's powerhouse the previous summer had encouraged installation of duplicate machinery so the city would not again be plunged into several nights of darkness. The article pointed out that the plant at the foot of Ninth

< This 13-foot-diameter station meter and gauge board from 1907 were used to control flow of manufactured gas into city pipes. Gas-flow control was critical to successful operations, particularly as new, high-pressure pipelines began serving rural communities like La Jolla and East San Diego.

San Diego's first 500-kilowatt, vertical type, steam turbo-generator, installed in Station A in October 1906, was an innovation in power generation. Machines prior to this had been driven by belts connected to steam engines. (This Curtis machine was soon supplying 800 kw to a rapidly growing San Diego.)

A 1,500-horsepower Allis Chalmers horizontal cross-compound Corliss engine was installed in July 1909 to drive a new 1,200-kw generator. Unlike the turbo-generator, this engine used steam pistons to drive its generator.

Avenue was very complete and modern and, in addition to street lighting, kept several thousand incandescent lights burning in stores and residences. The plant also had a gas-holder with a capacity of 150,000 cubic feet, soon to be increased, that furnished gas to places of business, meeting halls and residences.

Unfortunately, just a few weeks later *The Union* reported a major fire at the plant. The gas works at the foot of Tenth Avenue had been "in imminent danger of being destroyed by fire" caused by "the overflowing of a crude oil tank in the retort house." The fire department had responded quickly, although by the time they arrived, flames were shooting out of the roof. No one knew who was to blame, but Superintendent Ralph Clarke, "after a hasty examination, said the loss was perhaps $300 or $400, unless the retort was damaged, in which case it would be much more." He was going to investigate the cause.

In February 1902, a feature story in *The San Diego Union* indicated that there was "favorable sentiment for city ownership" of public utilities such as gas and electricity. F.E. Van Haren, a citizen, thought that the city was paying altogether too much for its lighting service and urged that municipal ownership be considered. He told the city council that if it were necessary, "the citizens of San Diego can carry lanterns on the dark nights and get along with the aid of moonshine." He said this would be better than paying exorbitant rates for an inadequate system. Alderman Whitson explained that he favored municipal ownership of all utilities but that acquisition of the city hall and the water plant had reduced funds in the treasury. He proposed that it would do no harm to talk to the Company to find out what it would take for the system. The city council, upon Whitson's motions, authorized $500 to employ competent engineers to estimate the cost of acquiring and operating its own plant for 200 lights of not less than 2,000 candlepower. In the meantime, petitions were granted for new electric-light locations in Brooklyn Heights, at C and Front, H and Union, First and Date, 22nd and D, Fifth and Palm, 15th and L, 18th and G, and Fifth and Laurel; lights on Fifth and Quince were moved to Fourth and Quince.

At the end of March 1902, the San Diego Gas and Electric Light Company lowered the cost of 170 arc lights to $9.50 per lamp per month and agreed to furnish the incandescent lights at city hall for $20 per month or $240 per year. The total of $19,620 per year would be only slightly more than the $19,434 paid the previous year for 158 lamps and no incandescents in city hall. This lowering of cost seemed to calm those wanting municipal ownership, and one member of the Board of Public Works remarked that the new contract "isn't so bad." The board approved the contract on April 11 and

Visitors at Coronado's Tent City in 1904, a popular summer attraction, enjoyed telephone service, arc-lights and electric trolleys. After the Company completed a gas pipeline under San Diego Bay in 1909, up to 484 prepaid gas meters were installed each season. Until the early 1920s, however, electricity was provided by generators at the hotel's powerhouse (smokestack just right of trolley). (Photo courtesy of San Diego Historical Society–Photograph Collection)

MORTON B. FOWLER

Morton Fowler, a native Californian, was born in Santa Clara in 1878 and came to San Diego in 1895. He was graduated from the old Russ High School in 1897 and soon went to work for Dr. Powers in a combination job with both the Gas Company and the Bank of Commerce. At first he washed windows, ran errands and did other odd jobs, but soon the bank required his full time service as bookkeeper.

Fowler left temporarily to become secretary of the San Diego Flume Company but rejoined San Diego Gas and Electric Light Company in June 1904 as a one-man billing department handling collections, accounting, ordering, and the cash. On the side he sold gas ranges and filled in as janitor.

According to Fowler, the 50 electric consumers and 800 or more gas consumers did not receive bills in the mail. "The customers called at the office and were handed their bill from a little row of alphabetical pigeon holes. The bill was paid there and then. To locate a bill it was necessary to know the routing as few houses had addresses." When the Byllesby Company took over, Fowler became secretary and then treasurer of San Diego Consolidated Gas & Electric Company. He retired in 1945 after 41 years of service and died August 8, 1962.

moved on to recommend that Chief Cairnes of the fire department, whose hay contract had expired, be able to purchase the hay that he needed "wherever he could buy cheapest."

On June 12, 1902, the Company announced that it was prepared to offer 24-hour service on its electric light and power line. A 300-horsepower tandem-compound Atlas engine had been installed in 1898, and when the company purchased duplicate machinery after the McCurdy accident, it also dug a well 25 feet in diameter and 22 feet deep to supply water for the surface condenser. An additional 125-foot well sunk at the bottom of the large well doubled the water capacity of the plant. The Westinghouse generators were scrapped, and two small alternating-current generators of 150-kilowatt and 50-kilowatt capacity were installed for incandescent commercial light service and the power circuits of double pressure. *The San Diego Union* explained: "That is, it is of three wires so that connection from the center wire to either side gives a pressure of 110 while a connection from one outside to the other gives a pressure of 220." For this power circuit, better known today as 110 volts and 220 volts, the Company had installed "one of the prettiest little electric plants imaginable." The company had also put in a new gas-holder, known as "a relief holder," with a capacity of 10,000 cubic feet to regulate the pressure in the large holder of 150,000 cubic feet.

On September 13, 1902, *The San Diego Union* reported that the old powerhouse of the San Diego Electric Railway's Fourth Avenue cable line was sold to D.C. Collier, a man who would become known as the "creative genius" of the 1915 Panama-California Exposition. The big brick building, completed in 1890 and containing "the most modern cable power-house machinery," was set to be demolished. After the city had an electric line paralleling the cable line only 200 feet away, all the way to the powerhouse, there was no need for it. "When the upper piece of the road from the head of Fifth Avenue to Mission Cliffs was made standard gauge and the cars from the city ran through to the pavilion, there was no more use for the power house even as a car barn."

San Diego was definitely growing and planning for the future. The city council agreed to accept the bid of the San Diego Gas and Electric Light Company for 179 lights at 2,000 candlepower each at $9 per month each—a rate down 50 cents from the previous year. Fifty-three of the lights were on towers, 77 on iron arms, and 49 suspended at the center of the intersections. New buildings were going up as new banks were organized in the downtown area.

John Spreckels was actively promoting a rail connection eastward to Yuma while E.W. Scripps offered land and exhibits for a biological station, the origin of today's Scripps Aquarium in La Jolla. Scripps and others also gave donations for the landscaping of Balboa Park. On July 4, 1903, members of the Woodmen of the World celebrated by planting 1,000 trees, mostly eucalyptus, in the park's Pound Canyon. The transoceanic canal through Panama had been approved by Congress, and since San Diegans envisioned their port a logical terminus for increased trade, the city continued to request funds for the deepening and widening of the channel and improvement of the jetty.

Land was cheap when this photo was taken in 1910 looking east on University Avenue from Florida Street. Workers install tracks for the trolley system that was powered by electric motors. The direct-current motors received their energy from overhead wires suspended between the two rows of wooden poles.

San Diego grew so rapidly in 1903 and 1904 that the facilities of the local gas and electric company were greatly strained. As new districts opened in the suburbs, the Company could not immediately extend its system to serve them. Sufficient financing was unavailable to make important changes and additions, and rival companies made further threats of competition. In 1904 a new 370-kilowatt, Westinghouse alternating-current generator of modern design was direct-connected to a vertical cross-compound McIntosh and Seymour engine. The Company also made arrangements to purchase the generating apparatus that had lighted the World's Fair at St. Louis in 1904. The new 50,000-cubic-foot gas generator used oil for fuel, and coal-gas generation was abandoned. Gradually, new gas-holders and gas-purification machinery sent gas through 34 miles of street mains. Large extensions were made in the low-pressure systems in the downtown district. High-pressure gas was piped to outlying districts.

Nevertheless, a one-horse wagon drawn by a scrub California cayuse contained all the construction and service tools owned by the Company. Extensive plant expansion was needed to serve the 2,168 gas customers and 1,258 electrical hookups. The Company could not raise the amount of outside capital needed to build facilities for a growing population and still keep rates down. Even so, gas service, originally $5 per 1,000 cubic feet in 1881, had been reduced to $1.50, and customer cost of incandescent lighting had dropped considerably. The electrical distribution system consisted of about 30 miles of pole lines with a total of 1,375 poles in place. The arc streetlights were still operating on the "moonlight schedule."

Many of the Company's early work force appear in this 1904 photo, taken at the Station A gas plant. Dr. Robert Powers, co-founder, is seated at center in the first row. Many of the others in this photo went on to high positions and long careers in the Company.

GAS HOLDER

At 120 feet tall, the new 500,000-cubic-foot gas-holder was one of the tallest structures in the city when it was completed on October 18, 1906.

A gas-holder resembles a huge folding drinking cup, turned upside down. When empty, the holder telescopes together, like the drinking cup. When gas is forced into the holder, the lifts are raised in step with the volume of gas injected, the innermost section rising first. It has a roof or "crown"; the other sections are open at both top and bottom. The lower section of the holder, seen from the outside as the foundation, is a tank filled with water. When the holder is empty, the lifts are telescoped into this tank.

Gas-holders are filled at night or at other times of low demand, when the gas goes in faster than it comes out. As demand increases, the sections of the holder drop lower and lower until, when it is empty, all sections are resting in the water. Under normal use, a holder will not be completely emptied during a day's operation, and the low overnight demand gives the holder time to fill up again for the next day's supply. Before the 1920s, this filled gas-holder held enough gas to meet an average day's supply for the city of San Diego.

On January 1, 1902, Colonel Henry Marison Byllesby, a noted engineer and financier, organized his own company for the financing, designing, construction, operation and management of electric and gas companies. Byllesby had drawn plans in 1881 for the first steam-operated central station in the United States, which was installed by the Edison Company for Isolated Lighting in New York. He left Edison in 1885 to join the Westinghouse Electric Company as vice president and remained there until 1891. He then gained additional experience in developing water power and managing small utility companies whose futures seemed insecure.

Byllesby traveled to San Diego and, after thoroughly examining the city's potential, successfully negotiated with the Company owners for the purchase of its properties. He estimated the population at 28,000 in 1905 and indicated that in 1904 "new building permits aggregated $1,011,000." Byllesby reported that "the business section of the town is substantial, containing fine office blocks, bank buildings, mercantile establishments, etc." and that, with the completion of the Panama Canal and "the rapidly increasing oriental and South American trade," the port would "bring the city to a very prominent size and position in the commercial world."

In assessing the Company itself, Byllesby indicated that the utility, while having had large earnings, had paid only one dividend, since the balance of its net earnings had gone into "the improvement and enlargement of the property" and to the retirement of $125,000 of its 6 percent bonds. He found the plant to be "in absolutely first-class condition" with no machinery

Although a new century had dawned, the horse and wagon still provided transportation and support for these electric linemen in 1908. Horses and wagons often were superior to early motor vehicles on unpaved streets.

TRANSPORTATION

An old stable report gives the names of horses forming the backbone of the Company's transport system. There was Queen, a gray mare born in 1889, who hauled a meter wagon, and Jimmie, King, Frank, Duke, Night and Teddy, all foaled around the turn of the century and brought into the Company at an early age. Ditches were started by horse-drawn rooter plows and finished out by pick and shovel. A Hoot-Nannie was a two-wheeled cart used to lower pipe into a ditch. Instead of checking gasoline used every day, there was morning concern about bushels of oats and bearded barley, and tons of hay. Queen and her stablemates must have wondered about the first Orient trucks purchased just prior to 1906. Cost-report entries of harness repairs and new horseshoes began to yield to such entries as "engine overhaul" and "repair of broken wheels." And stablehands began to wonder if they could become mechanics.

Excerpt from a *News-Meter* article by W.E. Frazer in April 1941

A line crew pauses from line expansion work near 18th Avenue and H (now Market) Street sometime during 1906. Frank Chase sits on the end of the wagon, with most likely his brother Fred standing in the middle. This crew consisted of two linemen (with climbing spikes and belts), two helpers and a teamster (in white shirt).

needing to be replaced; average leakage of the entire gas system had been less than three percent for the previous five years. Byllesby examined the two-story brick office building and noted that it could eventually carry six stories. The building had cost, "exclusive of the real estate, about $24,000" and yielded annual rentals of more than $2,000. The Company's property, entirely surrounded by a brick wall and concrete sidewalk, occupied "an entire block of ground contiguous to the bay, having its own conduit from its plant to the bay for the purpose of bringing in condensing water." In addition to the steam plant, the Company had "a substantial and suitable coke and coal shed, submerged oil tanks, a fully equipped repair shop and storage rooms" with an interior court entirely paved with asphalt. The electric apparatus was "of the best class throughout" and the distribution system covered over 30 miles of lines with "the poles being handsomely painted and in the best condition." The gas distribution system represented a total length of 41.22 miles.

Byllesby was impressed by the "substantial cash in the treasury of the company, amounting on June 30th, 1905, to $102,000." He indicated that a modification to the gas generators by 1906 would make possible the use of crude oil to a larger extent than before in manufacturing gas and would "effect a net saving of not less than $10,000 per annum." Crude oil had dropped from 75 cents a barrel to 60 cents. Byllesby predicted that net earnings would be at least $95,000 in 1905 and not less than $115,000 in 1906.

The Company's impending reorganization as the San Diego Consolidated Gas & Electric Company, capitalized at $1.5 million, was announced by *The San Diego Union* on April 9, 1905. The new funds, mainly from Chicago, would be used to expand and improve facilities. Dr. Powers would remain as president with L.M. Arey as secretary. Although several new directors were from Los Angeles—especially George Chaffey of the new People's Company of Los Angeles who was long involved in promoting hydroelectric power—the Company denied rumors that there was any direct connection with the People's group. Other Los Angeles directors were Walter M. Newhall, J.W. Phelps and John O. Mossin, also directors of the American National Bank of Los Angeles. Law partners Lynn Helm and E.S. Williams joined the board with H.M. Byllesby. Plans were soon made to extend gas mains to University Heights and electric light lines to La Jolla, Pacific Beach and National City.

The new general manager, T.H. Creden, announced on May 11, 1905, that San Diego Consolidated Gas & Electric Company would reduce gas rates from $1.50 to $1.25 per 1,000 feet on July 1, and the charge for new service pipes would drop from $12.50 to $7 with no charge to the customer for hooking up stoves for cooking and heating. Creden also pointed out that the "price of electric lighting in the city would be reduced and compare favorably with figures in other cities which do not have their electricity made by mountain water power, and they are lower than the figures at Sacramento and Oakland, where they do have such electric power." He indicated that the

Colonel H.M. Byllesby, founder of Byllesby Engineering, which purchased the Company in 1905.

The Byllesby Engineering cornerstone for the powerhouse at Tenth Avenue and M Street (Imperial Avenue) in 1906. Byllesby's capital money infusions into the Company helped it meet the city's steady growth.

The Company's 935 Sixth Avenue office sported the latest in lighted advertising and decoration in an effort to boost electric sales. Kerosene lamps, gas lamps and candles gave electricity stiff competition in these early days. (Photo courtesy of Central Federal Savings and Loan Association of San Diego)

Company hoped to popularize the use of gas stoves and would be able "to show that at the present price of coal, the expense of cooking and heating by gas at $1.25 will be less than the expense of coal and kindling." Coal was not popular locally because it had to be imported, and wood, never abundant, had to be hauled in from the mountains.

The San Diego Union reported on November 28, 1905, that installation of a new gas plant with a capacity of one-half million cubic feet per day would be added to the existing facility at the foot of 10th Street. Early in 1906, San Diego's mayor requested that the Board of Health look into "the gas question" since there had been a number of complaints about the quality of the gas for lighting and heating and that others believed it might be injurious to a person's health. People seemed to be satisfied on the health question since it failed to make further news. On February 27, the Company announced a further reduction of gas rates to $1 and would later offer a cut in electric prices.

The old guard was slowly being replaced when H.M. Byllesby took over as president on June 27, 1905, and R.G. Hunt of Ohio replaced Dr. Powers as general manager on September 14. Times were changing throughout the city as old buildings were demolished to make room for modern ones. The historic Horton House Hotel was torn down in July 1905 to clear the way for construction of the U.S. Grant Hotel on the same site. Alonzo Horton, age 91, removed the first brick, followed by Ephraim Morse and W.W. Bowers, all of

CAPITAL IMPROVEMENTS

"On April 1st [1905] the property of the San Diego Gas & Electric Light Company was acquired by H.M. Byllesby & Company of Chicago [which] . . . immediately began extensive improvements in the generating and distribution of the plant. In the following succession, generator units were added to the power plant:

1. 500 kilowatt vertical General Electric turbine and generator.
2. 1,200 kilowatt General Electric generator driven by an Allis Chalmers cross-compound engine.
3. 2,000 kilowatt General Electric horizontal turbine generator set.
4. 4,000 kilowatt General Electric horizontal turbine generator set.
5. 5,000 kva horizontal General Electric turbine generator set.

All this necessitated condensing apparatus and auxiliaries, and a large supply of cooling water and a very thoroughly constructed concrete intake and outlet tunnel for salt water from the Bay was installed.

In the boiler room the old horizontal boilers were removed, and Babcock & Wilcox boilers were installed from year to year, as needed, until the present capacity of 15,060 horsepower. Step-up transformers from 2,300 volts to 11,000 volts of 1,890 k.w. capacity were installed, and a high tension distribution system built, which at present extends from Del Mar on the north to Tia Juana on the south, and from San Diego to Foster's and Lakeview on the Northeast, and Lower Otay Dam on the Southwest. The total generating capacity of the station at present is rated at 15,060, with an overload capacity of 25%. With the addition of 3 -1,000 k.w. step-up transformers, we have been enabled to carry the Exposition lighting load and all new businesses."

From *History of San Diego Consolidated Gas & Electric Company, and its Predecessors* by R.L. Clarke "with the assistance of Dr. R.M. Powers, president of the first Company, and M.B. Fowler, secretary of present Company [1911]."

whom were present at the laying of the cornerstone of the Horton House 35 years before. Downtown was changing, and the city, whose population had grown to 35,000, was expanding to the north and to the west. O.W. Cotton promoted Pacific Beach and East San Diego. Ed Fletcher, a young produce merchant from Littleton, Massachusetts, thought that water from the San Luis Rey River could be used to develop the coastal regions north of La Jolla. He worked for the South Coast Land Company, which, in addition to lands and existing water rights along the river, obtained all of the original settlement of Del Mar, more than 800 acres in Leucadia, 1,400 acres of Rancho Agua Hedionda, nearly all of Carlsbad and large holdings in Oceanside. By 1905, the Oceanside Electric Company was providing arc streetlights and incandescent lamps.

When San Diegans learned of the disastrous earthquake and fire that hit San Francisco in mid-April 1906, they offered aid to their stricken neighbor and sent $25,000 worth of food, clothing, tents, stoves and other supplies to the north by ship and rail. John Spreckels, who had retained his home in San Francisco until that time, decided to move permanently to the San Diego area. He began construction of a mansion, complete with pipe organ, across the street from his Hotel del Coronado. He continued to promote his various business interests and especially a direct rail connection eastward to Yuma.

After considerable improvements were made and plans to double the capacity of the gas and electric plant were complete, R.G. Hunt was called back to the Chicago home office in May 1906. He was replaced by C.E. Groesbeck, who arrived in July. According to an article in the "Prosperity Section" of *The San Diego Union* on July 13, 1906, "no more popular nor efficient man could have been chosen for the important post." The article described the Company's presently owned machinery, including a Curtis

Sitting on top of their work are linemen extending the Company's electric system to the rural areas of North Park and East San Diego.

Employees in 1905 included (from left, top row) Louis Tarpley, Sid Weir, Nate Blood, J.C. Elliott and Frank Clark. Center row: Bert Van Epps, Mike O'Neill, Erick Simms, and Louis Meredith. Bottom row: Bert Peck, Earl Starr, Andy Youngberg, Sam McGovney, Roy Thompson, Arthur Simpson and Jack Thornton.

CORONADO CHRISTMAS

At 7 p.m. on December 24, 1904, the inaugural lighting of a Christmas tree at the Hotel del Coronado took place "by the turning on of an electric switch." The 250 colorful lights took their place alongside traditional lanterns hung on the 50-foot-tall Norfolk island pine. Present at the first tree lighting in Coronado was Violet Jessop, the 22-year-old daughter of Joseph Jessop who would later become the wife of Asher E. Holloway, president of San Diego Gas & Electric Company from April 1949 to October 1951.

On December 28, 1904, *The San Diego Union* reported that there was "so much interest in the outdoor Christmas tree with its many electric decorations as to have it illuminated each evening from seven to ten for the rest of the year." Absent from the tree-lighting ceremony was Thomas Edison, whose presence at several Coronado "electrical" events is speculative. The first authenticated visit of Edison to San Diego and the Hotel del Coronado was in October 1915 during the Panama-California Exposition in Balboa Park.

steam turbo-generator with a capacity of 750 kilowatts, and the building of a new, 36-inch concrete tunnel from the power plant to the bay costing $30,000. The article also reported:

The housekeepers of San Diego bless the Consolidated Gas and Electric Company for much of the leisure that is theirs to spend. The housewife has been enabled to appear well and daintily dressed even while in the midst of preparing the meals for a large family. She is not cross and irritable through fatigue caused by standing over a hot coal range. The tired husband is greeted affectionately, is good-natured, enjoys a dinner well prepared and never scorched and unpalatable and altogether the whole tenor of the household hangs on the gas range. It is the arbiter of the domicile! In the book wherein we would enroll the benefits given mankind by thoughtful invention, the gas stove would be given the particular place of honor if the housewives of America were consulted.

During the spring of 1906, certain members of the community, organized by J.C. Woodward, joined with James T. Boyd, an engineer and former employee of the Edison Electric Company of Los Angeles, to form a rival company called the Municipal Electric Company of San Diego. They gathered together some businessmen from Los Angeles and San Diego, including Rufus Choate, W.H. Fraser and L.P. Swayne, to compete in the "generating,

At the turn of the century the Hotel del Coronado was a popular winter vacation spot for visitors from as far away as the East Coast. (Photo courtesy of San Diego Historical Society–Ticor Collection)

distributing and supplying of artificial light . . . manufacture and sale of electrical appliances . . . and the supplying of water for domestic and other purposes." Since Boyd had known Superintendent Ralph Clarke for a number of years, Boyd approached him to discuss the new company. After meeting with R.G. Hunt of San Diego Consolidated on April 7, 1906, Boyd stated that "for the sum of $1,000" he would "drop the scheme where it stands and agree to entirely eliminate Woodward." Boyd told Hunt that he did not want him to think of the proposition as "a hold up" since he was a businessman and "the matter could be handled in a businesslike way." On April 20, 1906, Boyd signed a receipt for $750 and Woodward for $250, both agreeing to cease their "efforts toward the organization, construction and operation of a competitive gas or electric plant" in San Diego. The Company heard no more from James T. Boyd.

Early employees often worked six or seven days a week, 12 hours a day. When they could relax, workers enjoyed team sports such as baseball. Based on evidence of the uniforms, the photo was taken between 1905 and 1910.

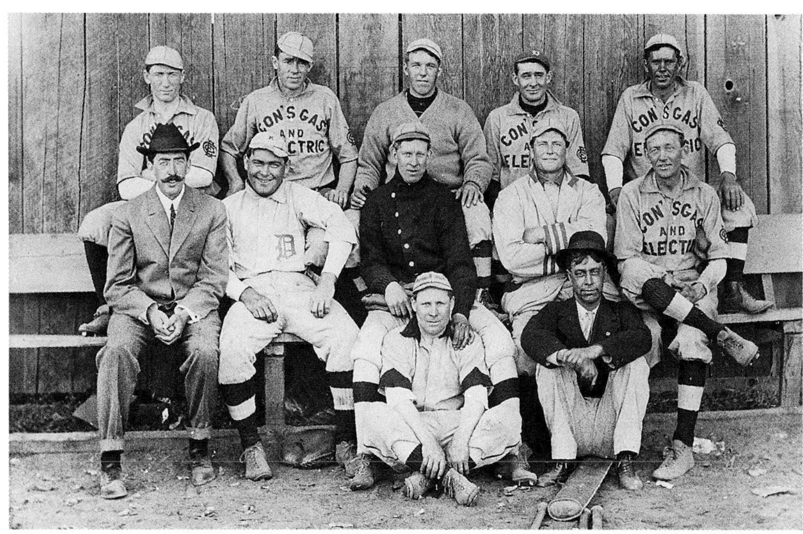

On September 22, 1906, San Diego Consolidated announced that it would build a bath house for its employees—a novelty for San Diego. The new building would be for the use and benefit of employees only and would be constructed of brick on the block occupied by the Company plant so that it would be "handy for all those desiring to make use of it." The cost was estimated at $2,500, and there would "be individual bath tubs as well as shower baths and a plunge tank of ample size." The water would be pumped from the bay for use in the steam condensers, and afterward the remaining warm and clear water would be ready for use. There would "also be fresh water for those who prefer it to salt water."

Gas crew from 1907, many of them responsible for digging and installing the gas line to La Jolla. They were not named in this photo, but their nationalities were recorded as (standing, from left) Greek, Pole, Bulgar, Yugoslav and Greek. Sitting: Montenegro, Saracen, White Russian, USA, Hungarian, Pole and Greek.

During late 1906 and early 1907 there were some discussions about who should pay for street lighting. Most people agreed that the lighting of downtown was a municipal affair, although some felt that in the suburbs, property owners should pay for poles and pipeline. The idea of municipal ownership of the utility had quieted down since the Company had promised

The continued electric-generation additions at Station A (in background) required the construction of a cooling water system into San Diego bay. This May 17, 1906, view at low tide shows workers laying a 24-inch-diameter pipe about 300 feet from the Santa Fe Railroad tracks. Today, this location is near the intersection of Harbor Drive and Eighth Avenue.

Station A in 1908 with workers constructing a smokestack. View is from Ninth Avenue and M Street looking southeast.

lower rates. On March 24, 1907, *The Union* praised the San Diego Consolidated Gas and Electric Company for spending "more than three-quarters of a million dollars" for improvements to its system under the management of the Byllesby group. The Company had been considerably handicapped in trying to get materials, since damage from the San Francisco earthquake and fire had diverted most building materials, pipe and machinery to that area. Nevertheless, gas mains had been extended to National City and other improvements made.

In October 1907, Company manager C.E. Groesbeck announced that on March 1, 1908, electric rates would be reduced by an average of 16.4 percent. Groesbeck had just returned from a conference in Chicago with Byllesby management and reported that the cut had been made primarily for the benefit of consumers using fewer than 100 kilowatts per month. This reduction would place San Diego on an equal basis with large cities and, with the installation of a new 520-horsepower boiler, the generating capacity would meet the city's rapidly growing energy needs.

To serve La Jolla, these workers and others in 1908 dug and installed pipe all the way from Tenth and University, across Mission Valley, around Mission Bay and up the coast to "The Village."

Plans were made in 1908 to extend gas service to both Coronado and La Jolla if the former could get 150 subscribers and the latter 200. According to *The San Diego Union* of August 29, 1908, "Col. James Wilson and other prominent La Jollans" had been "agitating for the proposition of obtaining gas in La Jolla for the past three years." The Coronado offer was made a few days previously to George Holmes, president of the board of trustees. He immediately began notifying prominent citizens and had mailed circular letters to interested parties. Plans were being made in Escondido by the Mutual Water Company to build a power plant in North County.

During this period, other changes were taking place to the east of San Diego. The California Development Company had made an unnatural cut in the Colorado River for an irrigation project in the Imperial Valley. Beginning in late 1905, flood waters had poured through the Colorado River bank for 16 months to wreak havoc in the New River channel and finally to create the Salton Sea. In 1907, Imperial County was formed from 4,089 square miles of San Diego County on petition of residents there who felt that the high Laguna Mountain range divided them naturally and it was a hardship to conduct county business in San Diego. In 1908 the cities of El Centro, as county seat, and Calexico, on the Mexican border, were incorporated.

ANNOUNCE BIG CUT IN RATES ON ELECTRIC CURRENT

Slash of From 6 to 27 Percent to be Made by Company March 1

SMALL CONSUMER IS GIVEN BIG REDUCTION

Newspaper articles featured electric costs during the early years.

Closer to home, William E. Smythe organized a cooperative farming community in 1908 in the Tia Juana River Valley with a campaign of a "little land and a living." Smythe raised money to purchase 550 acres of farmland

Arc lights continued to be used for street lighting in San Diego until 1915. Arc lights required daily replacement of the carbon rods that created the bright light.

Horse-drawn wagons are joined by one of the Company's first motor vehicles in this 1908 photo in front of the Sixth Avenue office.

and called his community San Ysidro. His followers, called "Little Landers," did their best to live a self-sustaining, idealistic life but suffered from inadequate irrigation and problems of marketing their produce.

In downtown San Diego, another idealist—city planner and landscape architect John Nolen—had been commissioned by the Chamber of Commerce to project the course of the city's future. The Nolen Plan for city development integrated San Diego's two central features: the bay and the park. Nolen designed a waterfront plaza with a tree-lined central mall with artistic shops and restaurants leading up a broad prado to Balboa Park. Another public plaza from Front to First between D (Broadway) and C streets would house a civic center with an integrated grouping of public buildings. Handsome transportation terminals and another plaza would be erected at the foot of Broadway to E Street. Unfortunately, San Diego did not seem to be ready for the Nolen Plan when it was presented in *The San Diego Union* on January 1, 1909. It was buried, coincidentally, along with San Diego's visionary founder Alonzo Horton, who died on January 7 at the age of 95.

As life moved on into the world of the automobile, the board of supervisors created a new county road commission of three millionaires—E.W. Scripps, John D. Spreckels and A.G. Spalding. With new roads being laid out or graded throughout the county, whose population had reached 60,000, San Diego Consolidated Gas & Electric had its work cut out in meeting demands for new service.

By September 1909, however, there were discussions among residents and within city government about the high utility rates. There was increased pressure by the city council to get a cheaper lighting contract since the five-year contract that had been signed when the Byllesby group came to San Diego would expire on June 1, 1910. The city was paying $7 per month per light and wanted to reduce it to $5 with the addition of 22 arc lights to the present 333. By advertising for bids, the city hoped to encourage outside capital to come in and erect a power plant.

A lengthy editorial in the *San Diego Sun* on September 14, 1909, had discussed a statement, in the form of an advertisement, in which C.E. Groesbeck, president and general manager of the Company, had attempted to outline clearly the manner in which rates were set and explain that the time for "better understanding" had arrived and that "the day of secrecy in the conduct of public utility companies" had passed. The editorial pointed out that Groesbeck's statements were "in part true and in part not entirely true" but congratulated him "upon his determination to engage in a discussion of the subject at all."

Downtown La Mesa in 1909. (Photo courtesy of San Diego Historical Society–Ticor Collection)

The editorial writer admitted that "laws never have been and never will be devised or enforced which will meet all the requirements of the case and insure a perfect adjustment of the bargain between the public and the public utility corporations" but that a major problem existed when the quality of the gas was inferior. "The public . . . knows that the price of good and poor gas remains the same, owing, of course, to the monopolistic character of the public utility corporation" which gives it "an immense arbitrary advantage." Also "the secrecy maintained by public utility corporations, or the deliberate misrepresentations as to its affairs, . . . as to the actual capital invested, and as to the actual earnings—prevent the public from acquiring any true knowledge in regard to the fairness of rates charged." But, "Mr. Groesbeck has taken a most commendable stand on the subject" and the result could not "fail to be a better understanding between the public and the utility corporation which he controls at least."

Despite the continuing discussions concerning rates, the Company moved ahead with its installations. *The San Diego Union* announced on April 13 that San Diego Consolidated was rushing work on extensions to the suburbs and expected "to furnish light and heat to La Jolla, La Mesa and outside towns" at the same rates as within the city.

During 1910, the issuance of $1.5 million in gas bonds for municipal ownership continued to make headlines in Spreckels' *San Diego Union* and E.W. Scripps' *San Diego Sun*. On April 19, 1910, *The Union* reported that socialist interests were demanding that the project be put on the ballot but

CIRCA 1910

Linemen and their wagon team pause by an early streetlight in downtown San Diego about 1910.

Some of the more interesting office equipment, right down to the telephone instruction book, in this 1911 view of the Investigating Department.

Ornate front office and payment booths of the Company's 935 Sixth Avenue location about 1910.

The Company's one-horse "trouble" car, as used about 1910 in the vicinity of First Avenue and Robinson Street. Fred Escher occupies the driver's seat.

that the legality of the proposition was being questioned. On April 21, the paper announced that City Attorney W.B. Andrews had rendered an opinion that the city could not vote on utility bonds and devoted three columns to Andrews' findings. The city attorney referred to court decisions that held that municipalities were prohibited from engaging in commercial lines. An article on May 10, 1910, quoted Superintendent Clarke's report that the Company was extending lines to all suburbs and erecting electric poles toward El Cajon and south to Chula Vista. He said that labor was both high priced and scarce and answered other charges that rates were too high.

The *Union* supported the Company's position on gas bonds. The two newspapers continued their rivalry over other issues of public and private ownership, while Spreckels and Scripps vied for power over the city and its development. Fortunately, their combined efforts on the County Road Commission provided for the extension of graded roads through the El Cajon Valley and north to Santee, Lakeside, Ramona and Julian; northward from Fallbrook and up the San Luis Rey Valley through Pala to Warner's Hot Springs, and from there to Santa Ysabel. Escondido was connected to Oceanside on the coast by a route through Vista, and automobiles were able to go to Los Angeles by way of Del Mar, Encinitas and Oceanside over six bridges along the route.

Company's early mapping and records office, seen.here on November 30, 1910, is in some respects not that much different from today's office, except for the telephone, which would now be a priceless antique. Employees at work are Sam McGovney (seated, left), J.S. La Sha, A.S. Akin (standing at map), Ray Cavell and W.C. Beatty.

With new businesses starting in the city and the building of new homes throughout the county, San Diego Consolidated Gas & Electric Co. faced increasingly complex issues. A summary history written by Ralph Clarke and R.M. Powers in 1911 showed how successful the Company had grown after its acquisition by the Byllesby Company of Chicago in 1905. It listed the machinery added, improvements made and extension of service. Electric rates for arc lights had gone down from $18 per lamp per month in 1887 to $7 in 1905 and to $5 in 1910. The total number had reached 856 city arcs, 492 block lights, and posts containing 3,255 lights. There were 473 miles of pole line, 331,809 duct feet of underground cable lines and services, and 19,028 electric consumers. The gas plant, with a total capacity of about 4 million cubic feet per day, served 21,700 gas consumers through 433 miles of gas mains. There were 10,098 ranges, 2,524 hot plates, 5,000 water heaters, 2,260 space heaters and 2,410 other appliances. These included electric irons, foot warmers, night lamps and hair curlers, all of which had been sold by the Company since 1909.

The first electric stove sold in San Diego, in 1911, was purchased by a resident named Holt. Employee H. Cooper Ayres sits at desk just behind the stove. Although gas stoves had been sold since the mid-1880s, electric stoves and electric appliances were being invented and marketed in the twin efforts of building electric load and saving the homemaker time and effort.

Residents of Escondido celebrated their city's illumination on March 5, 1910, when Seth Hartley, president, and Charles C. Glass, manager, of the Escondido Utilities Company, stood by as California Governor James Gillett in Sacramento touched a button that started the new electric system. San Diego sent a large delegation to the ceremony, which was accompanied by fireworks and a banquet for 175 guests.

In San Diego, the U.S. Grant Hotel was completed and opened for business on October 15, 1910, at a cost of $1.1 million. Furnishings had cost $250,000, and the cost of operation was estimated at $1,000 a day. It had two swimming pools and a top-floor ballroom. Opening-night festivities attracted 400 visitors from Los Angeles and 100 from Pasadena. Across the street, Louis Wilde, part owner of the hotel, presented the city with a fountain designed by architect Irving Gill that was illuminated by electric lights with 15 color effects. It featured the portraits of Juan Rodríguez Cabrillo, Junípero Serra and Alonzo Horton. The year 1910 came to a close on an optimistic note as the number of new automobile deliveries reached 325. San Diegans, although looking toward the suburbs, planned for a fair in Balboa Park that would enhance the city's reputation throughout the state.

Workers in February 1909 lay 4-inch-diameter, flexible cast-iron gas pipe across San Diego Bay from a barge to bring gas to Coronado, in background. Laying gas pipe underwater was tricky with this early technology, but the boost in sales made the effort economical.

Horton Plaza fountain, designed in the classic style by architect Irving Gill, featured cascading waters illuminated by colored electric lights.

2
3

Chapter 4

1911-1920
A Decade of Optimism

The official program at the July 19, 1911, groundbreaking for the Panama-California Exposition, boasted that the "fourth epoch of California" had begun with the "rebuilding of San Diego" during the "marvelous progressive movement in Southern California and the awakening of imperial enterprise throughout the Southwest." It would close, according to the exposition's promoters, with the completion of the Panama Canal and the San Diego & Arizona Eastern Railway, "thus concentrating the traffic of a continent and the commerce of a great ocean in the harbor of San Diego . . . the first port of call in American territory north of the canal."

1911

Population*
61,665

Electric

Customers
9,885

Sales in kwhr
6.8 million

Average cost / kwhr
5.64 cents

Gas

Customers
13,061

Sales in therms
1.9 million

Average cost / therm
18.73 cents

SAN DIEGO COUNTY
PALA
BORREGO SPRINGS
OCEANSIDE
ESCONDIDO
JULIAN
LAKESIDE
TECATE
MEXICO

Service Territory

*County population based on census 10-year estimates

Such optimism was not misplaced. The population of San Diego in 1910 had again reached 40,000 and would climb to 75,000 by the end of the decade. The number of people served by San Diego Consolidated Gas & Electric Company would grow from 51,750 in 1911 to 122,000 in 1921, with the number of electric customers increasing from 9,885 to 30,983 and gas customers from 13,061 to 29,651. When the Byllesby group took over the Company in 1905, there were 53 employees; in 1911 there were 261 and by 1921, 701.

Although plans for San Diego to become a heavily utilized commercial port failed to materialize, the harbor would soon develop into a major naval base. The city, in its plans for new military installations, looked toward the skies as well as the sea. On January 26, 1911, Glenn Curtiss made aviation history as he took off from the mile-long waters of the Spanish Bight between Coronado and North Island to fly the world's first successful seaplane. The

< The great 1,200-kva Allis-Chalmers steam engine was installed at the San Diego Electric Railway power plant in 1911. This engine operated DC and AC generators to power the electric trolley cars. It was purchased along with Station B in 1921 but dismantled in the mid-1920s to make way for more modern electric-generation machinery.

This panorama from the top of the Company's gas holder shows Station A and the San Diego waterfront, about 1912. The original gas plant occupies the foreground of the Station A facility, with newer gas facilities in the left and center background. The electric-generation building is in the right corner. The thin smokestacks vented the boilers that supplied steam to the generators. The piers and docks in the bay occupy the area now taken over by the San Diego Convention Center and other harbor businesses.

Navy provided the Curtiss School of Aviation on North Island with its first pupils and encouraged William Kettner, a charter member of the Aero Club and U.S. Congressman from San Diego in 1912, to promote the area as a naval base. The only military activity at this time, however, came as a result of the Mexican Revolution of 1910 when a number of conspirators began shipping arms across the border into Baja California. These were not mainstream revolutionaries but members of a Marxist Liberal Party who had received help in Los Angeles from the Industrial Workers of the World. A group of these rebels was captured and taken to Fort Rosecrans, where they were temporarily detained.

The cruiser *California,* a 14,000-ton warship, successfully entered San Diego's harbor in 1911 "at low tide and at night with no difficulty," but the entrance needed dredging and other improvements. The State Legislature voted to turn over to the city the control of the bay's tidelands from National City to Point Loma in exchange for San Diego's promise to approve $1 million in bonds for major improvements, including reclamation of 50 acres of tidelands, installation of a 2,500-foot seawall, and construction of an 800-foot pier. A $1 million bond issue passed almost unanimously in November

1911, in an election where women voted for the first time. Women were also joining the labor force and were fighting for equal pay.

At San Diego Consolidated, the enlargement of Station A to accommodate a 2,000-kilowatt turbo-generator was completed in May 1911. On Christmas Eve, 1912, a 4,000-kilowatt generating unit was installed, and exactly two years to the day later, another 4,000-kilowatt unit was completed to mark the last addition to Station A. Since the process of manufacturing gas from crude oil had been greatly improved during the preceding several years, the Company also installed six additional gas generators to meet the increased system load, which had just surpassed 1 million cubic feet in 1909. The two largest were each capable of generating 1,350,000 cubic feet of gas per day, and by the end of the decade, the total daily capacity reached about 6,250,000 cubic feet. On April 12, 1911, *The San Diego Union* reported that the Company had been issued a permit to build a $125,000 gas holder with a capacity of 3 million cubic feet. The steel-and-concrete holder would be 175 feet high and contain four lifts, each 140 feet in diameter.

While carrying on an extensive program of new construction and providing service to the growing population of San Diego, the Company also

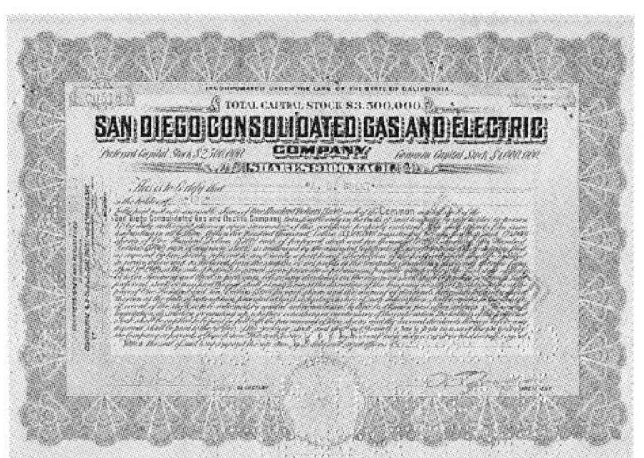
SAN DIEGO CONSOLIDATED GAS AND ELECTRIC COMPANY

Early stock certificate, issued in 1911. Selling stock to raise capital became an important source of money during the decade from 1911 to 1920.

extended its gas and electric distribution system to the surrounding communities. Gas service was made available to Chula Vista in 1911 and to La Mesa and Lemon Grove in 1912. In 1908, transformers had been installed in the electric plant to increase voltage to 11,000 volts and make possible the extension of lines eastward to Grossmont, El Cajon, Lakeside, Santee and Spring Valley in 1911 and to Bostonia in 1912. The lines to the south reached Sunnyside, Bonita, Nestor and Palm City in 1912, then Imperial Beach and San Ysidro in 1913.

Electric line workers in a very early line truck pause at Station A before another day's work installing the Company's ever-expanding electrical system.

These electrical generators, the last additions at Station A, were installed in 1911, 1912 and 1914, and had a total generating capacity of 10,000 kw.

A line introducing electricity to La Jolla was completed January 2, 1911, but the Company had difficulty obtaining customers. They preferred the "nice white light" given off by gas and did not want electric poles on the streets. Some of the residents signed a petition to keep the lines out and tried to frighten the construction workers, but to no avail. The first four people to sign up for electric service were Jesse Smith, Mission Cottage; A. Rhoades, Marine Street and La Jolla Blvd.; I.H. Tanner, Girard Avenue; and A. Brewer, Prospect Street.

The extension of gas and electric lines into rural areas followed the pioneering sales efforts of two young engineers who, working together in 1911, toured the back country to persuade owners of farms and ranches to sign up for electric service. One of these, Laurence M. Klauber, joined the Company in January 1911, after receiving an electrical engineering degree from Stanford University and working for two years at Westinghouse Electric and Manufacturing Company in Pittsburgh. Klauber later recalled that he "first sold electric signs around town—those blue signs with white letters" and "solicited for new gas customers in Chula Vista so that the Company could afford to extend its gas lines . . . and I also solicited for electric lighting customers in El Cajon, which at that time we did not serve."

The other young man, Asher E. (Doc) Holloway, had been an all–Big Ten halfback for Purdue University in 1910 and started with the Company the next year. The two extolled the virtues of electric motors rather than gasoline engines for pumping, and showed how electric lights were superior to kerosene lamps. During those trips, Klauber liked to "fool around with rattlers" during his lunch hour and was bitten twice. When he was reassigned to downtown San Diego, he kept up his interest in snakes and later helped develop an anti-snakebite serum at the San Diego Zoo. Later, Klauber and Holloway both became presidents of the Company.

As the Company busily expanded its own Station A, the original south building of the future Station B was constructed in 1911 as a power plant for the San Diego Electric Railway Company. The electric rail cars required direct current to operate. This view is from the corner of Kettner Boulevard and E Street. (Photo courtesy of San Diego Historical Society–Ticor Collection)

In 1910, the San Diego Electric Railway, a Spreckels Company, decided to tear down the old carbarn of the San Diego Street Car Company at the southwest corner of Arctic (later Kettner Boulevard) and Broadway (formerly D Street) and erect a large, new, reinforced-concrete building. The plant, designed by Eugene Hoffman of New York in classical revival style, was finished in 1911. The interior contained a 1,200-kilowatt Allis-Chalmers direct-current generator driven by a vertical reciprocating steam engine about 25 feet high. It exhausted to a low-pressure steam turbine that drove another 1,000-kilowatt direct-current generator. The other machines were turbine-driven alternators or direct-current generators ranging from 500 to 5,000 kilowatts in size. All of the streetcars had direct-current motors; it was inefficient, however, to transmit large amounts of direct current very far, so the railway

The San Diego Electric Railway Company's power plant, when completed, housed the generator pictured at the beginning of this chapter. The building's original entrance on Kettner Boulevard remains essentially unchanged today.

EXCERPT FROM THE SAN DIEGO UNION, AUGUST 8, 1911

The investigation which . . . E.W. Scripps urged against the San Diego Consolidated Gas and Electric company for furnishing a poor quality of gas to consumers has resulted in a complete vindication for the company.

After some days of "first page" agitation . . . Edward W. Jewell, city electrician . . . who made a thorough investigation of all complaints, reports the quality of gas as "excellent."

"I wanted the facts," said Mr. Jewell privately, after the report had been read to the council yesterday afternoon. "I am not employed by the gas company and don't care for it in any way, but I wanted to see justice done and conducted my investigation with only that purpose in view."

A new rectifier for which the gas company recently paid $15,000 was the source of all trouble. The machine had been placed in the open and when the sun warmed it, the plates being steel, the napthaline, which under proper conditions would have been neutralized, escaped into the air as vapor and when striking cool pipes would congeal and clog the sides. As soon as the source of trouble was discovered, the new rectifier was discarded. . . .

W.W. Bowers, former congressman, who sent a long letter of complaint [to the *Sun*], was one among several whose houses were inspected by Mr. Jewell. It was found that the pipes leading into the house were clogged with napthaline and that the burners of an excellent stove were screwed down so tight that the gas could not get out. After the pipes had been cleaned out and the burners adjusted, there was plenty of gas and plenty of heat.

Mr. Bowers at once sent a full letter of explanation: "Editor Sun: Please allow me to say in the Sun that last Saturday afternoon, . . . a number of the company's employees, accompanied by city electrical inspector Jewell, came to my residence with the auto steamer, detached my supply pipe, forcing a strong jet of steam through it, and then adjusted my gas range and I am happy to say that since that visit we have had an abundant supply of gas at all hours, and we trust it will so continue. We celebrated the event with a dinner with hot biscuits and strawberry short cake—as suggested by Mr. Jewell—and we feel thankful for that visit, hoping other complaints may receive and acknowledge a like benefit."

company also produced alternating current and transmitted it out to remote substations where it was converted into direct current and delivered to the trolley wires. San Diego Consolidated bought the land, building and equipment in December 1920. Early in 1921, the structure was renamed Station B to distinguish it from Station A at Tenth and Imperial. Station B continued to sell power to the electric railway company and, with later extensions, would become the Company's principal generating station until the 1940s.

Interior of the Company's main office facing Sixth Avenue. Employees in this November 1910 photo are (from left) C.C. (Cliff) May, Gus Keller, George Leach, an unknown employee, Fred Ladd and Stella Springer. A power substation occupied the building's basement.

The Company became involved in what may have been its earliest environmental case in 1913. On January 25, *The San Diego Union* reported that the game warden, at the request of the San Diego Rowing Club, had filed charges against San Diego Consolidated for allowing oil to escape into the harbor. The Company denied the charge and blamed the San

Diego & Arizona Eastern Railway. Harbor master A.J. Foster referred the matter to the city council on February 15, and Charles H. Delacour, special representative for the Company, said the matter was being addressed. City councilman Daniel K. Adams, who supported the Company's position, commented that the harbor master had "oil on the brain." Apparently the problem was solved since no more articles appeared about the leaking oil. Councilman Adams began working for the Company in June 1915 until he retired in May 1941.

At the same time, the burden of heavy debts for new equipment and expansion of services caused the Company to petition the California Railroad Commission, then in charge of regulating all public utilities, for authority to increase its bonded indebtedness. On March 13, 1913, the Company was granted permission to use $106,000 to pay its debts, and in June the Company asked to issue 5 percent bonds.

In November 1913, the Company announced that it would voluntarily cut electricity rates 20 percent while maintaining the minimum charge of $1 per month. Customers using less than 100 kilowatt hours a month (kwh/m) for lighting, according to *The San Diego Union,* would benefit from the reduction. "As the average householder uses only thirty kilowatt hours a month, a man paying an average bill of $1.25 or $1.30 will hereafter pay the minimum charge of $1." The Company explained that there were 16,000 electric meters in San Diego homes but that only about 450 used more than 100 kwh/m. The rate to the remaining customers was to be dropped from a 10-cent gross and 9-cent net charge per kilowatt hour to an 8-cent gross and 7½-cent net charge. Company officials reported that there were about 325 consumers who used from 100 to 1,000 kwh/m, and their rate would be reduced to a 4½-cent minimum; no change was planned for those using more than 1,500 kilowatt hours per month.

The summer of 1914 was marked by news of the assassination of Archduke Franz Ferdinand of Austria in Sarajevo on June 28. Problems of the Mexican Revolution took second place to the threat of an impending global conflict. Despite local interest in the military ramifications of the fighting in Europe, the spark that set off World War I was overshadowed in San Diego by completion of the Panama Canal and by plans for the opening of the Panama-California Exposition in Balboa Park on January 1, 1915.

Titled "The office girls at Tent City, Coronado, in the summer of 1911," this photo shows the Company's first female employees. At top is Olive Brand; the next three, from left: Stella Springer, Nell Molloy and Maude Schofield; bottom row, from left: Georgia Ann Bourke, Ann Trezise, Louise Oppenheimer and Elizabeth Allen.

CARL WIGGINS

Wiggins' first acquaintance with the "electric light works" was watching Sam McGovney climb to the top of a 125-foot steel mast near his home to trim the arc lamps. After several interviews with Superintendent Ralph Clarke and General Manager Dr. Robert M. Powers, Carl Wiggins landed a job on September 30, 1893. According to Wiggins, his first job did not carry a title unless it might have been "laborer." He received a salary of $30 a month and was excited to be working "in a very fascinating business."

Since the schedule for residence lighting was from sundown to midnight for street arc lights, the power-plant force—consisting of Clarke as chief engineer, John Starr, assistant, and James McInness, fireman—worked most of the night. Wiggins started out cleaning the plant after the crew went to sleep, taking care of lubricating oil and getting in coal for the night's run.

In a few months, McGovney was promoted, and Wiggins took over his job of climbing a dozen 125-foot masts and trimming arc lamps at $60 a month. When the fireman quit, Wiggins assumed his job of shoveling coal or coke and a few years later took over Starr's job as assistant engineer. In 1905 the Byllesby Company placed Wiggins in charge of the power plant. He remained as superintendent of electric production until his death in January 1940.

Members of Local 465 International Brotherhood of Electrical Workers prepare a horse-drawn float for the Labor Day Parade of 1915. Their float included several arc lights and even an early telephone operator's setup. (Photo courtesy of San Diego Historical Society–Ticor Collection)

Chief architect Bertram Goodhue of New York had designed several buildings that represented the Spanish colonial style popular in Mexico. Goodhue's first assistant, respected local architect Irving Gill, had a different style in mind, so Goodhue hired Carleton M. Winslow, also of New York, to help carry out the Hispanic theme. The Baroque buildings, tree-shaded prado and open plazas suggested a typical Spanish city of the 17th century. As visitors approached the park across the Cabrillo Canyon Bridge, they were impressed by the breathtaking view and Goodhue's re-creation of Spain's Mediterranean and Moorish styles.

The Santa Fe Railroad demolished its Victorian-style station in downtown San Diego and built a new depot in Mission Revival style to honor Southern California's Hispanic past. The station, just across the street from the Electric Railway building at Kettner and Broadway, was dedicated on March 7, 1915, to handle the increased traffic expected for the fair in Balboa Park.

San Diego Consolidated provided all of the special lighting effects for the Panama-California Exposition, which officially opened at the New Year's celebration of 1915. President Woodrow Wilson, from the White House in Washington, D.C., touched an electric button that turned on a light suspended by a balloon to open the festivities in Balboa Park. The guns at Fort Rosecrans on Point Loma and those on ships in the harbor fired simultaneous salutes to signal the event. A fireworks display at the Spreckels Organ Pavilion portrayed a replica of the Panama Canal, from which the prow of a ship labeled "1915" emerged. The phrase "The land divided—the world united—San Diego the first port of call" was outlined in flame. Visitors—including Theodore Roosevelt, William Jennings Bryan, and then–Undersecretary of the Navy Franklin Roosevelt—came to San Diego from all parts of the country. One of

Thomas A. Edison (center, with flowers), joined his good friend Henry Ford (at Edison's left) at San Diego's 1915 Panama-California Exposition in Balboa Park. (Photo courtesy of San Diego Historical Society–Ticor Collection)

The Cabrillo Canyon bridge and the road that became Highway 163 as they appeared during the 1915 Panama-California Exposition. The Balboa Park clock tower and other structures had just been finished. (Photo courtesy of San Diego Historical Society–Ticor Collection)

This glass-plate photo shows the lighting display at the 1915 Panama-California Exposition. Electric lighting was still a novelty outside of major cities, so displays like this attracted considerable interest and increased business.

the most impressive buildings from an electrical standpoint was the Alhambra Cafeteria on the Prado with its many twinkling lights.

Domination of California politics by the Southern Pacific Railroad Company and widespread corruption in local governments after the turn of the century brought about the formation of a progressive organization called the Lincoln-Roosevelt League in 1907. Election of the league's candidate for governor in 1910, Republican Hiram Johnson, together with control of the legislature, gave the movement power to institute certain governmental reforms such as the direct primary, initiative, referendum and recall. California residents took a renewed interest in labor laws and control of large corporations. Philosophical differences between municipal and private ownership of public utilities and other political issues were discussed openly in leading newspapers up and down the state. In common with a national trend, California extended the authority of the State Railroad Commission in 1912 over all public utilities, with power to fix rates and regulate service, and created a Water Commission to control the state's unappropriated water.

The San Diego Union of May 23, 1915, ran a long article by T.H. Inker titled "Plain Talks for Plain People," which explained the regulation of gas and electric companies in relation to the prosperity of the United States in 1915. The author noted that in California, as a result of investigations held by the railroad commission, gas and electric-light rates had been reduced, and in some cases rather dramatically. He believed that even with reductions

The employee baseball team in June 1916 featured spiffy uniforms and a well-dressed coach. Organized employee sports teams continued well into the 1960s.

. . . public utility men would rather be controlled by a commission of standing and experience than be left to the tender mercies of a supervisor or councilman who makes a political issue of water, gas or electric rates, and carries his platform pledges into a court of which he is one of the judges and in which court he is supposed to act with even-handed justice and absolute impartiality. . .

Laws are being passed in our various legislatures increasing the burdens of all public utilities. Juries of late years have shown a disposition to give large verdicts against public utilities because of the general feeling of hostility on the part of the people toward all corporate interests. Some juries seem to feel they should render large verdicts as a punishment just because a corporation is involved, and it is a popular idea that all corporations are rich or dishonest in some way or another. But jurymen lose sight of one important fact—that all damages that have to be paid and all other burdens that have to be carried by the public utilities must inevitably be passed on to the people for payment. It is the ultimate consumers, or the common people, who finally pay the bill. . . .

Inker thought that in contrast to former times, there was a general feeling running through public enterprises in 1915 that they wished to deal as fairly and justly with the public as they knew how and that the old idea of "the public be damned" was gone for good.

The tendency of the managers of these enterprises is to get in as close touch with public opinion as they can and to give to the public as clean-cut and as square a deal as is possible and consistent with the safe operation of the investment and first-class service to the people. . . .

Finally, Inker thought that utilities would always be more expensively run by politicians than by private owners. Municipal ownership under the present political system, he concluded, "is vastly more expensive and unsatisfactory than what we have." Those in favor of public ownership, however, would gain support in later decades.

A hearing to establish proper rates to be charged by the Company was held

A worker tests a gas meter for leaks at the meter shop in 1911. The meter was tilted as part of the test. This photo, like many others of early Company activities, was taken by the well-known photographer, Herbert R. Fitch.

The gas main and service department personnel on July 9, 1916. Top row (from left): Vito Grazio Orsino, caulker; Earl E. Silk, pipe wrapper; Francisco Angeles, Tomacio Galasso, Frank Zentella, James Mastro, Nicholas Gusta, Nichelo La Florenza, Nicholas Orsino and Dominick Verrano, laborers, and Howard W. Elder, estimator. Middle row: R.A. Chambers, fitter; William Symons, draftsman; Nicholas Bruno, laborer; Christopher Radolovitch and Nicholas Costa, pipe wrappers; Thomas Hawley, welder; H.E. Kimmel and Edward Surghnor, helpers; Angelo Athens and Pasquello Costa, laborers. Bottom row: E.W. Jones, S.E. Corwin and Frank Allwardt, foremen; Fred Harritt, superintendent–gas manufacturing; James Whitelock, foreman; A.R. Gittings, superintendent–gas mains and services; D.J. Young, superintendent–gas department; W.A. Lambert, inspector; George Stacy, foreman; J.W. Trader, dripman; Wolf Volk, foreman. Seated at bottom are Joseph Mastro and Lowell Gittings.

on August 2, 1916, before the California Railroad Commission. San Diego Consolidated engineers estimated that operating expenses would be $59,490 more in 1917 than in 1915, or a total of $732,294. Other costs—plant maintenance, taxes and a fair return to the Company for its investment in the utility—would be added so that the commission could fix proper gas and electric rates as requested. Company President Henry H. (Hal) Jones, principal witness at the hearing, testified that he expected less than 1 percent growth in San Diego's population during the next two years. The Company introduced an exhibit "in the form of a great book of 2,872 typewritten pages" showing the valuation of its property at $4,285,244.44. The exhibit was "sufficiently detailed to include every gas-cock or bit of wire belonging to the Company, 1-cent entries being conspicuous among those of thousands of dollars." The exhibit cost $48,000 to compile, and "the commission was not left without a suggestion" that it was to some extent responsible for an expenditure that "consumers probably will pay in the course of events."

Company's counsel at the rate hearing were Allen Chickering of Chickering & Gregory, San Francisco; John H. Reiner of Chicago for H.M. Byllesby &

Line work, like this pole-raising in 1916, required a lot of muscle power. This pole was part of the system that served the dams at Otay Lakes.

Company; and A.H. Sweet of Sweet, Stearns and Forward, for the San Diego Company. Present in addition to City Attorney Terence B. Cosgrove of San Diego were city attorneys F.M. Andrews representing Chula Vista and F.G. Blood representing East San Diego. C.J. Noel, president of the Taxpayers' Protective League of East San Diego, also attended.

Less than a month later, on August 31, 1916, the Company was authorized by the State Commission to purchase 1,819 shares of stock of the Oceanside Electric & Gas Company at $14 per share, "provided the price paid therefore shall not be urged as a basis for rate fixing." The revenues of the Oceanside company, established in 1905, did not appear to warrant the price paid for the stock, but the commission felt that San Diego Consolidated could supply Oceanside's 234 customers (162 residential, 65 commercial, 1 municipal and 6 agricultural) "far more economically" and would be able to effect a reduction in rates with considerable improvement in service. The electric plant, valued at $24,644, had operated at a net loss of $361.50 in 1915, but the bath house, valued at $3,823, had a net income of $1,301 during the same year. San Diego had to extend its transmission line from Del Mar to Oceanside at a cost of $37,000 to improve service.

In December 1916, the Company began negotiations with A.W. Wohlford, president of the Escondido National Bank, for the purchase of the Escondido Utilities Co. owned by his daughter, Mary K. Wohlford, a college student. According to the *San Diego Sun* of February 16, 1917, the railroad commission had authorized the sale of the North County facility for $40,000

Henry H. Jones, Company president and general manager from 1912 to 1924.

The great flood of January 1916 wrecked quite a few of the Company's power lines. This is the San Diego & Arizona Eastern Railway yards somewhat inundated. (Photo courtesy of San Diego Historical Society–Ticor Collection)

Electric transmission across Mission Valley, probably to Camp Kearny, began at this high point above one of San Diego's water-pumping facilities.

permitting "the San Diego company to issue $30,000 first mortgage, 5 percent bonds and $10,000 preferred capital stock to Mary Wohlford as the purchase price."

The Escondido plant was built in 1910 and failed in 1915. It defaulted on a promissory note, and possession passed to the Los Angeles Trust and Savings bank and then to Mary Wohlford. The plant had continued in operation under an agreement with the Escondido Mutual Water Company, which had supplemented lighting and power to Escondido in 1914 by developing hydroelectric power on the San Luis Rey River. San Diego Consolidated planned to build a 22,000-volt, 13-mile transmission line from Olivenhain to Escondido at a cost of $21,000 and an 11,000-volt, 13-mile line from Vista to Escondido costing $114,141. These lines, when completed, joined the main transmission lines north from San Diego through Del Mar and Oceanside.

By April 1917, the United States had declared war on Germany and become involved in World War I. Congressman William Kettner sponsored a bill for a federal takeover of Rockwell Field on North Island for a permanent Army and Navy aviation school. Seventy employees of San Diego Consolidated Gas & Electric Company left for war. Five of these joined the Italian army, two were killed in action and one died of influenza. Eight employees—H.K. Anderson, A.E. Atkins, John C. Campbell, Harold M. Coleman, Thomas E. Hartigan, Earl R. Justice, Clarence H. Morris and D.H. Perkins—returned after the war to work for the Company.

The U.S. Army established Camp Kearny on the mesa north of Mission Valley in May 1917, based on the Company's guarantee of gas and electric service. The task of extending electric lines and gas mains to a location 15 miles north of the city, across the San Diego River bed and over rough terrain beyond the bluffs of Mission Valley, gave San Diego Consolidated a tough assignment. Since there were no gas mains within 10 miles of the camp, it became necessary to start the gas-line extension from Tenth and University in the Hillcrest area. Construction began June 30 and was completed on schedule August 5 at a cost of $133,628. A total of about 10 miles of distribution mains were laid in the camp area, and 350 service connections were made.

Gas was used for cooking and baking in 238 mess halls, for heating water throughout the camp, and for heating in the hospital units and general offices. The estimates on receipts from Camp Kearny were, according to the *San Diego Sun* of February 16, 1918, "based on contingencies. If the camp should remain for three years, the company should be able to amortize the capital required less salvage, and secure a return on the investment. Otherwise this would be impossible, of course." Even though the war ended on November 11, 1918, Camp Kearny continued in existence until 1920. A portion of the land was set aside for a Marine Corps installation in 1937, but the Navy took over the site and built Camp Elliott during World War II. The marines were transferred to Camp Pendleton. Some of the original construction-crew members were on hand 24 years later to upgrade the gas and electric lines for wartime use.

Bill Oseno (left), an unidentified helper and foreman Fred Corwin with the gas meters they installed for the new Camp Kearny during World War I. A 10-mile-long gas and electric line extension had to be constructed to serve the camp.

Because of World War I, the price of oil had more than doubled and was expected to reach "$1.62 per barrel against 75 cents, the old price." The report of the consulting engineer for the Railroad Commission showed a return of 8.62 percent on the base rate during 1917, but with an increase in taxes and the cost of labor, the Company was asking for a gas-rate increase from 90 cents to $1.10 net per 1,000 cubic feet of gas to yield a 7.7 percent return in 1918. The military continued to be a substantial user of gas and electricity and, in addition, Congress approved the establishment of the Marine Corps Recruit Depot, completed in 1919, and the Naval Hospital in Balboa Park, which opened in 1922.

The construction of the Company's first high-voltage transmission line in 1918 further extended service and provided the first direct link to another major electric utility. This 66,000-kilowatt line extended 75 miles north from San Diego through Del Mar and Oceanside, and then beyond the county line to the then-rural farm community of San Juan Capistrano, tying in with the transmission system of Southern California Edison. The Company then had access to a source of hydroelectric power to supplement the capacity of its own steam-electric generating plant.

The point of interconnection initially provided for the transfer of a maximum of 5,000 kilowatts, equivalent to 43 percent of the Company's

Raising power poles, on the transmission line to San Juan Capistrano in 1918, involved getting a little wet where the line crossed the lagoon at Del Mar. This photo is part of the Del Mar Historical Collection.

The Kerckhoff power plant at Del Mar, about 1917. The building supplied electricity, steam heat and hot water to the Del Mar Inn. Many Del Mar city residents continued using oil lamps until the mid-1920s.

installed generating capacity. Ironically, the first major transfer of power was from south to north. A severe drought in the summer of 1919 created an emergency shortage of hydroelectric power in the Edison system, so San Diego sent north all the electric power it could spare. The interconnection, which today provides for the exchange of 1.2 million kilowatts, was for many years the Company's only tie with other member utilities of a statewide power pool.

The city of Del Mar had a small powerhouse built by the Kerckhoff Company in 1914 to supply the Del Mar Inn with electricity, steam heat from radiators, and hot water. A brick structure, 50 feet by 75 feet with a square smokestack, was located just south of the beachfront plunge, which it also heated. With the passage of the new transmission line through Del Mar in 1918, Kerckhoff contracted with San Diego Consolidated to have electricity brought in for the hotel, beach and hill areas. Residents in the village, however, used kerosene lamps until the late 1920s.

The San Diego & Arizona Eastern Railway, begun in 1906, was finally completed to Yuma in 1919, providing a direct link to Campo, El Centro and other points east. Los Angeles, however, continued to remain the major commercial port in Southern California, and San Diego's mountainous back country did not develop significantly. The *San Diego Sun* reported on December 22, 1919, that the city council had voted to enter into a contract with San Diego Consolidated to build a power line and furnish power for the construction of Barrett Dam near Campo. This closed "a long controversy originally opened by the water commission, as to whether the city should deal with the gas company." The Fairbanks-Morse engine company had put in a bid for the job but backed out when they saw the gas company's lower figures. The West Coast Engine Company, another possibility, said they could not handle the necessary peak load, so that left only San Diego Consolidated Gas & Electric Company to complete the job.

William B. Dyke, in a review of the Company's history to 1962, summed up the major gains made from 1905, when the Byllesby group took over, to 1920. During this time the Company expanded its facilities to serve more than four times the population of 1905. The annual electric peak load rose from 450 kilowatts to 11,400 kilowatts, and daily gas deliveries from 336,000 cubic feet to 5,541,000 cubic feet. Electric-generating capacity increased from 770 kilowatts to 11,750 kilowatts. Investment in plant and property grew from less than $1 million in April 1905 to more than $8 million at the close of 1919.

Dyke wrote: "As the calendar turned to 1920, a steeper rate of community growth was under way. . . . That which some forecasters had only recently asserted would never happen in their lifetime was already happening. Station A generators were being overloaded to carry the system demand. Space was not available . . . for additional generating units, so the company negotiated for the purchase of San Diego Electric Railway's power plant, acquired it in January 1921, and immediately began to remodel and enlarge it as Station B."

The 1920s would usher in a decade of continued expansion and new construction. The Company would have its hands full in juggling the needs of the city, the demands of the city council and the requirements of the California Railroad Commission.

By 1920, the Company's horsedrawn vehicles had become motorized, as this lineup of Company service and emergency troubleshooting trucks at Station A shows.

THE BLEDSOE CO.
FURNITURE
HOTEL
CECIL
U.S. GRANT HOTEL
GARAGE
POTTER

Chapter 5

1921-1930
A Time of Progress

1921

- Population*: 112,248
- **Electric**
  - Customers: 30,983
  - Sales in kwhr: 58 million
  - Average cost / kwhr: 3.83 cents
- **Gas**
  - Customers: 29,651
  - Sales in therms: 6.5 million
  - Average cost / therm: 23.65 cents

Service Territory

*County population based on census 10-year estimates

As the decade of the 1920s began, civic boosters and businessmen were disappointed that the federal census showed San Diego's population lagging far behind that of Los Angeles, the state's most populous city. Although the number of city residents had reached nearly 75,000, the figure paled in comparison to the 576,000 of San Diego's northern neighbor. Nevertheless, the feeling of optimism experienced during the previous decade continued as plans to enlarge and modernize the port for commercial activity received a high priority. The end of World War I brought some military cutbacks, although banking, manufacturing, the canning industry and agriculture continued to thrive.

The San Diego–California Club, formed in 1919 with Oscar W. Cotton as secretary, carried on a program of advertising in the Midwest and East to market San Diego's delightful year-round climate, scenic beauty, clean air, orange groves and seaside resorts. Slowly people responded, and by 1923, the city's population, with the adjoining communities of East San Diego, Coronado and National City, had grown remarkably. A rapid increase in automobiles brought improved back-country roads and paved streets within the city. An early "flight to the suburbs" began, and San Diego's prosperity seemed assured.

Certain problems—such as developing an adequate supply of water, maintaining a proper balance between civic, cultural and business interests in downtown, providing adequate public transportation, and preserving the buildings in Balboa Park—commanded the attention of San Diego's leaders. During this period, Henry H. (Hal) Jones directed the affairs of San Diego

< Downtown San Diego at night shows how popular electric lighting had become by the time this photo was taken January 7, 1929, from the top of the recently completed El Cortez Hotel. The searchlight beam is radiating from the top of the San Diego Trust & Savings Bank building, at the corner of Sixth Avenue and Broadway.

Ditch digging uphill on Date Street, between Ninth and Tenth avenues, in May 1924. Equipment like this track-mounted wheel digger allowed much quicker work with less labor. Compare this photo with the one in Chapter 3, page 47, of the digging crew on its way to La Jolla in 1908, only 16 years before.

Consolidated Gas & Electric Company as it expanded to keep pace with the growing city. One of his major concerns during the early 1920s was the Company's changeover from horse-drawn wagons to motor vehicles in all operations. Another was the purchase of new machinery for Station B at Kettner Boulevard and Broadway. The extension of gas mains and power lines outside the city also commanded the attention of management.

For the employees, an innovative feature was the beginning of "The Company Magazine" in November 1921, with a $10 prize offered for the best suggestion for a name. Examples from other companies ranged from the catchy "Fumes and Flashes" or "The Volt" to more standard names such as "Edison Topics" or "Sierras Service Bulletin." The monthly magazine, edited by Ray C. Cavell, would feature "valuable articles on educational and entertaining subjects" and acquaint readers "with facts that are generally known only to those in immediate association with the subjects under discourse." The name chosen out of 755 entries was "Glow," and the prize went to Charles L. Lawrie of the Record Department.

With the 1920s came a new era in employee communications. The monthly employee newsletter *Glow,* started in 1921, later became known as *News-Meter* and has continued since the 1980s as *UpDate.* More than 40 volumes of published employee communications fill a four-foot shelf. (See sidebar on page 82.)

Laurence M. Klauber, the Company's general superintendent, wrote the first article detailing the improvements at Station B that would provide a 200 percent increase in output. Roy E. Thompson, chief engineer of the station's operation, directed the installation of the latest models in generating equipment. Five new steel-encased Babcock & Wilcox boilers, the largest so far installed on the Pacific Coast, were put in place along with necessary accessory equipment and boiler-room auxiliaries. The new turbine was a 15,000-kilowatt 1,800-rpm machine of the most recent General Electric–Curtis horizontal design.

IMPROVEMENTS TO STATION B

The first 15,000-kilowatt, horizontal turbo-generator of modern design was placed in operation at Station B in 1921, just 35 years after the first belt-driven electric system began feeding the city's arc lights. Steam entered the turbine through the large pipe at left. The spinning turbine (in center housing) was coupled directly to the generator (under cover at right).

Station B's north turbine room under construction in late 1928. Workmen carefully unload a generator stationary armature from a railroad flatcar.

Station B, after construction of the new north wing in 1928. The Broadway side of the building (right) contained switching gear and a substation for service to San Diego's downtown area.

INSULATORS

The confinement of electric current to its designed path necessitates the use of supporting structures of a non-conducting nature, which are generally classified as insulators. In electrical construction of all classes, the insulator is one of the most important parts. . . .

Insulators for different purposes are made in many shapes and sizes. They must be strong, not easily broken or punctured, shaped for proper division of voltage and mechanical strength, and assembled to prevent injury from stresses. Porcelain which has been correctly manufactured and which does not absorb moisture is everlasting.

. . . In the short period of approximately twenty years, voltages of transmission have been raised from 10,000 to 220,000; conductors from telegraph size to one inch diameter; supporting structures from small wood poles to steel towers weighing up to three and one-half tons; and insulators from the size of a large apple to a length of over six or seven feet requiring nearly 600,000 volts to flash over. This wonderful progress was made possible due to the advancement in the manufacture of the insulator.

Excerpt from a 1927 *News-Meter* article by William H. Talbott, superintendent, Electric Meter Department.

A lineman works to connect insulation strings on a high-voltage power line. Insulators anchor wire to this "deadend" pole, causing the insulators to stand almost straight out. On other poles, insulators carrying only the weight of the wire usually hung straight down.

According to Klauber, the considerable addition to the steam-generating capacity at Station B necessitated important modifications in the switchgear:

As the new unit will tie directly to our 11 kv. [kilovolt] system by way of two separate 11 kv. lines to Station A, transformers will become necessary at Station B to take care of the railway load. For this purpose the nine air-blast transformers now at Station A, with a total capacity of 6000 kva. [kilovolt-amperes], will be moved to Station B and will be located at the north end of the gallery. At the south end . . . will be a new 11 kv. switch structure, containing oil switches controlling the turbine, the transformers and the outgoing 11 kv. lines.

In a more practical sense, this equipment had made it possible for new homes in the suburbs to feature electric lamps and vacuum cleaners, electric kitchens and fireplaces, and other modern conveniences. Even the U.S. Marine Corps base had converted to electric irons.

Early in 1921 it became apparent that the Company needed an electrical facility or substation closer to the center of town. A site at the corner of Fourth and Ash streets was selected for Station C, which would furnish all commercial direct current within the city and alternating current to the underground and overhead district north of Broadway and west of Balboa Park, including portions of Golden Hill, University Heights and Mission Hills. The building, constructed from the plans of architects Richard Requa and Herbert Jackson, was a steel-frame structure with plastered tile walls appearing from the outside as a two-story residence in the Spanish Romanesque design popular during that period. Many of the details were taken from a palace in Salamanca, Spain, of about 1350 and featured large arched entrance doorways, small windows with wrought-iron grilles, French windows on the second-story opening on to wrought-iron balconies, carved stone panel shields and moldings, and a parapet of Granada tiles.

In order to minimize noise and vibration, all ventilation and natural illumination would come through large skylights, since the decorative windows did not actually pierce the pinkish-tan sandstone walls. The interior of the building was furnished with a floor of red quarry tile and cream-colored walls. Station C, fed from either Station A or Station B, was divided into a transformer room and switchboard room with the initial transformer installation consisting of four 2,000-kilovolt delta and four 4,000-volt Y transformers, three transformers in active service and a fourth set aside as a spare.

During the summer of 1922, San Diego Consolidated Gas & Electric Company completed a 16-mile-long, 88,000-volt electric power line from the Escondido Mutual Water Company's power plant on the Rincon Indian Reservation through the San Luis Rey River canyon to the construction site of Henshaw Dam. From the summit of the Rincon grade, the line, held in place by W-type poles, ran through the barren lands of the Cuca and Potrero Indian reservations, paralleling the river through the most picturesque, rugged and seemingly inaccessible country, up to the dam site. The Record Department's surveying crews, under the leadership of Emery D. Sherwin, put in strenuous work all through the daylight hours laying out the course of the power line. Then at night they had to work on the maps, calculations and reports.

Station C at 4th and Ash streets, the Company's first substation, as it looked shortly after construction. Today, it is almost completely covered by trees and ivy. Substations act as local electrical-distribution hubs, with distribution lines radiating out from the hub into nearby commercial and residential areas.

Kirk B. Ayres, superintendent of distribution, had estimated six weeks for the project to be completed. In his log of May 22, 1922, Ayres wrote:

Have found labor plentiful here among the Indians and have increased our digging crew until now we have 25 men on the job. On Friday, the 19th, went up the San Luis Rey River and selected a site for Camp No. 2 about four and a half miles below Henshaw Dam. Expect equipment for this camp tomorrow (Tuesday, May 23). Will shift the digging crew to this camp as soon as it is made ready. At present have 60 holes completed. The Indian laborers we have found very satisfactory. They do not seem to be inconvenienced by the heat. One white laborer was compelled to lay off yesterday on account of the excessive heat.

After several weeks of cutting brush, digging holes, wrestling with 49 reels of wire weighing 84,899 pounds and putting in 80 50-foot poles, the crew was held up by Native Americans from the La Jolla reservation. According to Ayres, a delegation of Indians arrived on June 17 to protest against construction of the line. They agreed to stop work until Mr. Ellis, the Indian Agent at

Extension of electric service to Henshaw Dam in 1922, one of San Diego County's vital water reservoirs, eased the difficulties of construction in remote areas of the county. In addition, nearby communities and farms often benefited by securing electric service from the initial line extension.

Survey work, to set the course of future power lines, required living in the brush-covered hills and valleys of eastern San Diego County. This survey crew in September 1923 worked in the Boulder Creek area, near Descanso. Work camps were frequently used in the 1920s and 1930s, as roads and vehicles did not permit employees an easy drive home at the end of the work day.

Riverside, could meet with Sherwin and Lester A. Wright, the Company's district agent at Escondido, to discuss the matter. The situation had to be taken up with officials in Washington, D.C., so nothing could be done until July 1, when Ellis arrived with the necessary permit from Washington to proceed with the work across the La Jolla reservation.

"We proceeded with the work immediately," Ayres noted. "Saturday Mr. Wright and I practically settled with the Indians one by one." He reported that they had employed 30 Indians and paid them a total of $4,728.49 during construction or an average of about $160 apiece. By the time work began again, the temperature had risen to higher than 110 degrees. "It was so hot that we could not tell just how hot it really was. Our thermometers only read up to 110 degrees and it was over that in the shade."

Major General George H. Harries, U.S. Army retired, a member of the World War I Armistice Commission, was president for a short time in 1924.

Poles and wire for the line were shipped by railroad to Fallbrook and transported to camp by truck via Bonsall and Pala. Hardware was brought in from the storeroom and shops in San Diego. Provisions and meats were purchased at Rincon and Pala. Vegetables were bought from Indian farmers when possible. For the 56 days of construction, an average of 74 men were fed a total of 12,382 meals for the entire job.

An interesting sidelight of the job was their collection of 20 to 30 snakes of several varieties, including red racers, gopher, king, ribbon and others. Only five or six rattlers were seen, wrote Ayres, "and they were killed." The future of the line after completion of the dam was uncertain, but officials of the Company believed that the dam never could have been built without the aid of electricity.

The year 1923 stood out for the Company's record of accomplishments. A total of $3,685,255.04—the largest amount so far spent in one year—represented a variety of improvements. The greatest number of new customers was added, amounting to 3,270 gas and 4,572 electric, or an average of a new customer every 17 minutes of the working day; and the largest number of new stockholders was recorded. Also that year, San Diego Consolidated began operations at Station C, completed the 15,000-kilowatt turbine at Station B, and constructed a 6-million-cubic-foot gas holder on the block bounded by K and L streets, 12th and 13th avenues. By the end of 1923, the total number of gas customers had reached 35,829 and for electricity, 40,717. Although only one section of transmission line was put in—between Del Mar and Escondido—a considerable extension of pole line was made to Alpine, containing one of the longest spans supported by wooden terminal structures in the country—4,437 feet across a deep canyon near Flynn Springs.

The Company's new headquarters, the former Timken Building, shortly after it was purchased and remodeled in 1923. The building continued to serve the Company until the mid-1960s.

Of major significance was the Company's purchase of the Timken Building, designed by Harrison Albright, at 6th and E streets. It was renamed the Electric Building and became the new general offices. The Company had been leasing the basement of the building since 1920 and had installed two pairs of modern bowling alleys for departmental team competition. Billiard and pool tables were also provided, and the basement was made into an employees' club.

The Company's accounting department in the early 1920s. All records were maintained by hand. This location is on the second floor of the Timken Building.

More than 100 workers carefully lower 320 tons of steel floor of the Company's newest gas holder onto its foundation in 1923. The plates could not be laid directly on the foundation for assembly.

The Company also acquired the property of the United Light, Fuel and Power Company of Coronado in August 1922 and moved a staff of employees under William J. Lambert into a new office building in Coronado at Tenth Street and Orange Avenue in January 1923. A 4-inch cast-iron gas main had been placed under the bay in 1909, and another, also 4-inch cast iron, was placed into service in December 1921. Both of these measured about 3,500 feet in length. Two steel-armored submarine cables were laid in 1922, one to serve the military installation at North Island and the other to upgrade electric service to the community of Coronado. The Hotel del Coronado received electricity from a power plant operated by the Coronado Beach Company.

These years brought considerable military development to San Diego. The Navy Hospital in Balboa Park was dedicated in 1922, and the first permanent building of a naval supply depot was commissioned that year in the tidelands area. In 1923, with the beginning of the Naval Training Station, there were 10 Navy or Marine Corps bases being built or authorized, and nearly $4 million were being spent on the Naval Air Station at North Island and Ream Field in the South Bay area.

The 11th Naval District planned administrative offices, a fuel depot, radio station, destroyer base and submarine base. On March 12, 1925, a total of 120 ships, including scout cruisers, battleships, destroyers, submarines and auxiliaries, entered the harbor and headed for moorings in the channel. The 15 commanding admirals and their subordinates were entertained throughout the city, firmly marking San Diego's identity as a "Navy town."

Workers and construction activities proceed on the gas holder as sheets of steel are riveted together to make the sides.

"The Fair Fifteen visit the Plant" in early 1928. Members of the Women's Committee toured the storeroom, shops and 32nd Street yard. "The trip was a revelation to most of us who had never seen these activities before and all voted the meeting a distinctly interesting and instructive one," reported one participant.

During this period, women employees of San Diego Consolidated Gas & Electric Company began to be heard. In 1924, the Pacific Coast Electrical Association formed a women's public information committee, and Rose Risley of the business department was selected to attend the first meeting at the Edison Building in Los Angeles. In January 1925, women employees took part in a visit to the electric plant and set up weekly groups of six to eight women each to tour the gas plant.

Women's activities would continue to be important, and J. Frances Emans, chairman of the Pacific Coast Section Women's Division of the National Electric Light Association, told local women employees that they should "be prepared to answer all questions of general interest concerning [their] company ranging from queries regarding service to operation of various electrical appliances." As more women became employed throughout the Company—60 in March 1927—the Women's Committee, as it came to be known, continued to grow. Nell Molloy served as the first local chairman, and Ruth Creveling, *News-Meter* editor, became a member at large of the Pacific Coast Women's Division.

Robert J. Graf, an executive from the Chicago office of the Byllesby Engineering and Management Corporation, became president on May 24, 1924. Graf's entire career had been with the late Colonel Byllesby, first in the capacity of private secretary and then, with the formation of the company in Chicago in 1902, in full charge of the books, accounts, issuance of securities, and other executive matters. Although he made periodic visits to San Diego, Graf's residence remained in Chicago. Former president Jones was moved to the Northern States Power Company in Minneapolis and then to the Western States Gas and Electric Company in Stockton. Major General George H. Harries, U.S. Army retired, became general manager in San Diego from May to September 1924.

THE PASSING OF GLOW

The magazine *Glow* came to an end in June 1925 and was replaced by a redesigned publication called *News-Meter*. The Byllesby company had decided that the format of all company magazines would conform to a standard size and be more newspaper-like in character. A review of names originally suggested in 1921 brought forth *News-Meter*, suggested by Walter T. Newman of the Bookkeeping Department.

San Diego Consolidated Gas & Electric Company

NEWS METER

Published Monthly in the Interest of its Employees

EL CORTEZ San Diego's Distinguished Electrical Hostelry

The cover of the first issue of *News-Meter*, the replacement publication for *Glow*, featured the new "electrically furnished" El Cortez Hotel. This photo shows the hotel before its famous outside glass elevator was installed.

Morton B. Fowler continued as secretary-treasurer and predicted a prosperous year in 1925. On January 1, the Company was supplying 40,012 customers with gas and 46,495 customers with electricity—a gain of 10,061 or more than 13 percent over the year before. The largest daily gas sendout in the history of the Company occurred on Christmas day, 1924, and totaled 10.097 million cubic feet. Because of previous activity, little construction was planned. Nevertheless, by the end of the year, Substation F, located on El Cajon Boulevard between Iowa and Boundary, was proposed for completion in 1926.

To blend in with the neighborhood, Substation F was designed as a lovely Spanish-style two-story structure with arched windows, a red-tile roof, extensive landscaping and a broad entryway with an ironwork balcony. The massive wooden doors were held in place by brass hinges, and the inside contained huge banks of circuit breakers, relay switches, electrical controls and meters. The only giveaway was that the "residents" chose the busts of Thomas Edison and Benjamin Franklin to adorn the façade.

A few miles farther to the east, the area of Kensington, first developed in 1910, was experiencing a boom. The Kensington Land Company had installed curbs, sidewalks and ornamental streetlights and formed an architectural board headed by Richard Requa. The minimum requirement for most homes was 1,500 square feet, and by 1926 a number of Spanish colonial–style homes overlooked Mission Valley. San Diego Consolidated was kept busy with street lighting and individual gas and electric hookups.

Robert J. Graf, president from 1924 to 1931, had previously been Colonel Byllesby's private secretary.

Station F, a substation, was designed to blend into its neighborhood on El Cajon Boulevard. The busts of Thomas Edison and Benjamin Franklin are located directly below the square windows.

Smiling 1926 Company PBX operators are Mrs. Rex Davis (left) and Belle Christopher. The Company's PBX was fourth largest in the city at that time. The two daytime operators handled 1,800 calls a day and 109 Company phones. The 11 p.m. to 7 a.m. operator was Rowan Cooley, who joined the Company in 1909, but had to give up his gas department job when he became totally blind.

The Commonwealth Building at Fifth Avenue and B Street housed the Pantages Theater, where the new "talking pictures" attracted throngs of viewers.

Also in 1926, a fifth branch office of the Company was opened in La Mesa to serve the 2,500 gas and electric customers in the communities of La Mesa, Grossmont, Spring Valley, Lemon Grove and surrounding territory. Edward R. Hollingsworth, formerly of the billing department, headed the office with the assistance of Mary White and Albert Kessler. A new branch office was also built in La Jolla, and by fall 1927, plans were made to serve an elegant residential community in Rancho Santa Fe consisting of 230 separate estates. Electricity not only provided all the amenities for the Spanish-style homes and civic center but ran four powerful pumping stations on an estate owned by Douglas Fairbanks and Mary Pickford to lift water up to a large man-made lake and dam.

The number of telephones had increased substantially since the opening days of the Company. The employee handling the standard switchboard, a series of plugs with extension cords attached, was called a PBX—Private Branch Exchange—operator. Each call had to be manually plugged into a socket to make the connection to the central exchange. The Union-Tribune had the largest exchange with 14 trunk lines, the U.S. Grant Hotel and the County Courthouse both had 13, while San Diego Consolidated Gas & Electric was fourth with 12 main lines serving 109 telephones. A report of September 1, 1926, showed that the local exchange handled from 1,600 to 1,800 calls daily or an average of more than three calls a minute. During peak times, each operator, all female, handled about 200 calls an hour. Most of these were for new orders, the electric distribution department, or the trouble department.

Because of the demand for electricity in all phases of business and residential life, San Diego Consolidated Gas & Electric Company was intimately associated with almost every major activity in the city and county. Radio broadcasting had begun in 1926 with station KFSD located on the roof of the U.S. Grant Hotel on Broadway. The generating room for the station resembled a miniature power plant and housed two direct-current generator sets driven by the Company's alternating current. Electricity was involved in every aspect of transmission and broadcasting from the studio. It was estimated that there were 6,000 "receiving sets" in San Diego County in 1926 and that radio sales were increasing rapidly.

> Street and store lighting had always been one of the Company's principal early businesses. This view is of Sixth Avenue after installation of the new lighting system in 1926.

Theater lighting had evolved from lanterns, candles and even torches to the sophisticated electric footlight and backlight illumination produced during the 1920s. The motion-picture industry also had become dependent on electricity for indoor lighting and then for "talking pictures." The use of sound revolutionized motion pictures both as an industry and as an art. Because of their commanding position in the field of radio and sound, corporations such as American Telephone and Telegraph, Western Electric, Westinghouse and General Electric became dominant factors in this multi-million-dollar industry. Spectacularly lit theater marquees brightened San Diego's streets.

By 1928, neon tube lighting had become tremendously popular and was finally available for outdoor use. Gustav H.P. Dellmann, writing for the August 1928 *News-Meter,* explained that clear glass tubes, approximately one-half inch in diameter and usually 16 feet in length, were equipped with an electrode at each end, exhausted of air and filled with neon gas. When an electric current of high potential—12,000 to 14,000 volts—was passed through, the neon glowed with a rich orange-red light. The average current consumption of neon tubes was 8 watts per foot, or about 250 watts for a sign reading BOOKS, significantly less than the 800 watts used for 10-watt incandescent lamps. The color of neon could be changed by adding other elements such as mercury for purple or blue, or by changing the color of the tube.

Because it could stand out even in the daytime, neon was fast becoming the element of choice in all types of advertising. According to Dellman, "one Pacific Coast manufacturer has developed animation in the form of discs with various shaped tubes mounted thereon. When these are revolved rapidly and tubes turned on and off by a flasher, they make many everchanging patterns of a kaleidoscopic effect."

"STREET LIGHTS"

During 1926, approximately 1,300 new street lights were installed, a 30 percent increase over the previous year. Of the new lights, 1,092 were of the ornamental type illuminating the business centers of San Diego, Encinitas, Escondido and National City. Oceanside signed a five-year contract for 144 street lights, giving that city a 600-candlepower light at every intersection. La Mesa also contracted for 79 ornamental street lights in conjunction with an extensive street-paving program.

Ornamental street lighting, like this one at Fifth Avenue and G Street in December 1927, was widely employed after removal of the city's arc lights in 1915. Many different designs were used.

Gas stove and refrigerator displays at local home shows attracted considerable interest from the public.

Not to be outdone by all of the advances made in the uses of electricity, the Gas Department continued to serve in innovative ways. Many ideas in gas refrigeration were being developed, but gas refrigerators had not been publicized in San Diego. The *News-Meter* promoted the idea of equality among both departments and pointed out that since each had their partisans and advantages, it was useless to speculate about whether gas or electricity was better.

In 1927, the "side of electricity" received a boost when it was shown that "electricity, generated by the San Diego Consolidated Gas & Electric Company, helped construct the *Spirit of St. Louis* at Ryan Aircraft Company." Credit for Charles Lindbergh's successful solo flight to Paris spilled over to all contributors, from the paint contractors to the manufacturers of the plane's rubber tires. The electrical metalworking and other machinery were, however, of utmost importance, and the success of Lindbergh's Ryan plane brought additional capital to Ryan for the installation of improved electrical equipment.

The Gas Department also achieved success for its role in the manufacture of an all-metal, tri-motored, 7-passenger transport airplane by the Prudden–

Charles Lindbergh and the *Spirit of St. Louis*. "I am proud to have done it for America. . . . " (Photo courtesy of San Diego Historical Society–Ticor Collection)

Appliance sales through the Company's Electrical Happiness Stores were featured on many billboards, such as this one at 16th and Island. Refrigerators were a popular item, since the traditional icebox required almost daily visits from the iceman.

Electrical Happiness salesmen enjoy waffles and "little pig sausages" to demonstrate the benefits of new gas and electric appliances.

San Diego Airplane Company. According to Ralph J. Phillips of the business department, "Where accuracy of temperature control is so vital in the heat treatment of duralumin for aircraft manufacture, gas fuel has proved to be indispensable." Reliability, economy and safety were the key factors. "No furnace which is not absolutely free from fire and explosion hazard should be considered in a modern industrial establishment. Properly designed equipment using gas fuel entirely eliminates these dangers."

Duralumin, an alloy of aluminum and copper, had to be heated to 920 degrees Fahrenheit. As a material for aircraft construction, it was ideal, and when properly treated gave far greater strength in proportion to weight than any other known material. The gas furnace used was a circular pot type consisting of a steel outer shell containing insulation material and fire brick lining. Four tunnel-type burners fired tangentially into the combustion chamber around the pot.

While the sale of gas and electricity had always been its major activity, the Company had for many years recommended and sold gas stoves, electric ranges, water heaters and other household appliances. Experts were employed to answer questions by telephone and look after customer interests in the home. In May 1927, the Company entered into the field of electrical appliance merchandising and opened six stores, called "Electrical Happiness Stores," in connection with district offices in Oceanside, Coronado, La Jolla, La Mesa, Escondido and Chula Vista. In June 1928, a seventh and main store opened at Sixth and E in the Electric Building. With the increased availability of such appliances as toasters, waffle irons, percolators, spot heaters, electric fans, curling irons and vacuum cleaners, the stores became immediately successful. The Company instituted the "little by little" plan where customers could purchase "electrical servants" and pay off the cost monthly with

Salesmen also competed in selling light bulbs, as this "score bulb" from October 1929 shows.

Workers ready the wrecking ball for the old Los Banos plunge in January 1928. The plunge, a popular attraction for decades, was removed to allow the expansion of Station B, seen in the background. Photo was taken on Broadway, looking south.

their light bill. According to Edwin W. Meise, superintendent of merchandising, "the principles of the 8-hour day and the deferred payment" had revolutionized the world of commerce and industry. "Time payments make it possible for the average worker to enjoy the luxuries and conveniences of modern living [and] the 8-hour day gives him an opportunity to enjoy those comforts and conveniences." The Company had arranged a liberal employee discount and urged workers to buy through the merchandising department.

While most activities of the Company were received favorably by the community, some advances were met with sadness. One of the favorite swimming establishments in San Diego was Los Banos, a mammoth plunge that for nearly 30 years had provided recreation for aquatic fans and aspiring swimmers. An average of 5,500 persons used Los Banos each month, but it stood in the path of the city's progress. It was torn down in January 1928 to make way for the extension of Station B between E Street and Broadway on Kettner Boulevard. The new portion of the building, designed by William Templeton Johnson, seemed to be a modified art-deco style featuring Spanish/Moorish influences. Completed by the end of the year, it was designed to house the Company's four turbo-generators, including a new 28,000-kilowatt machine, and contain space available for another similar installation.

> When finished, the new addition to Station B housed this 28,000-kilowatt steam turbine and generator (foreground). The original plant building and generators are located at the rear.

The 5,000-kw frequency changer at San Juan Capistrano in 1928. Because the Southern California Edison system operated at 50 cycles per second instead of the Company's 60 cycles, the change of frequency was necessary to allow transfer of electricity. SCE adopted the 60 cycle standard in 1948.

On the main floor of the old building were one 6,000-kilowatt and two 15,000-kilowatt turbo-generators and five motor-generator sets for supplying direct current to the street railway.

The new section of Station B featured a basement and six floors with the east gallery containing the station offices and switchboard room on the second floor. The north gallery, without windows, was used primarily for storage of tools, fittings, spare parts, bearings, valves, cable terminals and other parts essential to the operation of a power plant. The east gallery, easily located from the outside because of its numerous windows, contained some storage vaults in addition to lockers, wash rooms, station transformer banks and battery rooms. Station B, situated where practically all arrivals by boat, train or motor vehicles had to pass, was the Company's principal generating station.

The four-story Service Building across the street from Station A. It was hailed as one of the most modern utility warehouses and parts-distribution systems in the country when it was completed in 1930. Today, the building serves several utility operations.

Because Southern California Edison maintained a system frequency different from most other West Coast utilities (50-cycle vs. 60-cycle), it was necessary for the Company, in July 1928, to purchase a 5,000-kilowatt-frequency changer station from Edison to operate in Orange County. A new district office and appliance store was established at San Juan Capistrano in the Capistrano Hotel Building to serve customers there and in Dana Point, San Clemente and two communities called Coast Royal and Serra. Colonel Byllesby had become personally interested in southern Orange County when he passed through the area while riding the train from Los Angeles to San Diego. George A. Ferguson was named district agent at this office when it opened July 20, 1928.

The *Missionite,* Capistrano's local paper, indicated that San Diego Consolidated Gas & Electric Company had "shown rare foresight and excellent

The massive crystal chandelier in the casino at the Agua Caliente Hotel in Tijuana, Mexico, was one of the most beautiful electric-lighting fixtures on the West Coast. (Photo courtesy of San Diego Historical Society–Ticor Collection)

judgment" in reaching out to the north end of its territory, since the area was a growing agricultural district with electric power as a prime requisite. The paper's editor, Raoul Cyr, happened to be the brother of Bill Cyr, former editor of *Glow* and *News-Meter.*

The Company also extended its influence to the south by selling electricity to the Companía de Teléfonos y Luz Electrica in Tijuana for use at the new and palatial Agua Caliente Hotel. All of the lighting fixtures were made especially for the hotel. The casino's massive crystal chandelier, one of the largest and most expensive on the continent, had an illuminating capacity of more than 2,500 watts. The hotel also had an electrically operated ventilating system, an electric dishwasher and many other modern electrical appliances to handle the crowds traveling south of the border for horse racing and gambling. The heyday of Agua Caliente ended in the mid-1930s when Prohibition was repealed in the United States and Mexican President Lázaro Cárdenas prohibited gambling in Mexico.

With the coming of the motor vehicle, the inevitable "car-pole contact" was not far behind. This accident occurred at Pringle and Titus streets, near Mission Hills, in April 1927. In the background is a clear morning view of Point Loma and the Marine Corps Recruit Depot.

The Service Building at Station A could accommodate tons of supplies for the electric and gas construction crews. The freight elevator (behind the door at right) could actually lift a vehicle to the upper floors.

"ELECTRIC CANDY"

A little publicized but important use of electricity was reported from the Showley Brothers Candy Factory at 8th and K streets, which in 1926 produced 30 different types of bar candy including Cluster Ruff, Pacific Spray, Cherry Sisters, English Nut Loaf, Almond Caramel Bar and Creme de Menthe.

Electricity was used with greatest effect in the chocolate-dipping room where the hand-mades were dipped and the finished goods hardened. This room housed a number of electrically heated tables and a large electrically driven Enrober or chocolate coating machine. A large electric ice machine aided in maintaining a constant cool atmosphere in the dipping room as well as for refrigeration elsewhere.

Other electrically driven machines were used for stirring and separating candy from molds. Showley Brothers turned out 210,000 pounds of Easter eggs between January and April 1926.

As the county's population grew steadily, the ninth district office was established in National City. The tenth office and "Electrical Happiness Store" opened in Orange County in San Clemente on March 1, 1930, under the supervision of George Ferguson, whose duties included all Company activities of the Orange County service area. Even though the number of residential customers in the area numbered fewer than 1,000, proportionately more homes were completely electric than in any other territory served by the Company. All of the new small appliances were popular and easily sold.

One of the final construction projects during the decade of the 1920s was the new $350,000 four-story Service Building occupying the south half of an entire block on Imperial Avenue between Ninth and Tenth. Opened in the fall of 1930, it had all the modern conveniences, including a 10- by 25-foot elevator of 30-ton capacity—the largest in San Diego—that could lift a loaded truck to either the second or third floors. The building housed approximately 20,000 square feet of stockroom for materials used by the gas and electric distribution departments. Stored here were tools, hardware, pipe fittings and thousands of other items ranging from Lily cups to ponderous anchor chains, and from tiny rain gauges to pole jacks. Eight racks 10 feet high and 27 feet wide contained 2,634 bins and 352 drawers or a total of 10,230 square feet of bin frontage.

The system of shelf labeling and recordkeeping, long before the advent of computers, was described as "foolproof." An electrically operated 1-ton-capacity crane on an overhead monorail moved material from any location inside to trucks spotted on either side of the building. Along the entire south side was the gas-loading platform; electrical equipment was loaded on the north.

The second floor contained wire, cables and other heavy electrical material, a gas-fitting test room and a vault with operating department records. The third floor held materials such as fire brick, heavy gas fittings, camp equipment and supplies, and major electrical appliances. The offices of more than 40 "sedentary" and 70 "migratory" employees were located on the fourth floor, along with a 300-seat auditorium, dressing rooms, showers, a kitchen and a large room where refreshments could be served. The building was hailed as an immediate success.

Not to be outdone by the men's sports teams, the Company's first women's basketball team was organized in 1929. Members were (standing, from left) Margie Myrick, Ella Dockings, Harriet Harrington and Vivian Kirkpatrick. Kneeling (from left) are: Pat Palmer, Margaret Currier, Peggy Coleman (team captain), Josephine Ramsey and Ruth Gorton.

In the meantime, Women's Committee activities continued to expand. On October 27, 1930, Philip L. Gildred, chairman of the Chamber of Commerce's civic committee, spoke to the group in support of a bond issue to build a new civic center on the waterfront. The Gildred brothers had completed construction of an entire block, from Seventh to Eighth avenues between A and

The office at San Juan Capistrano in 1929 was one of several expansion offices opened in the Company's service territory in the late 1920s. The office, the farthest north in the service territory, featured a full "Electrical Happiness" store and customer services.

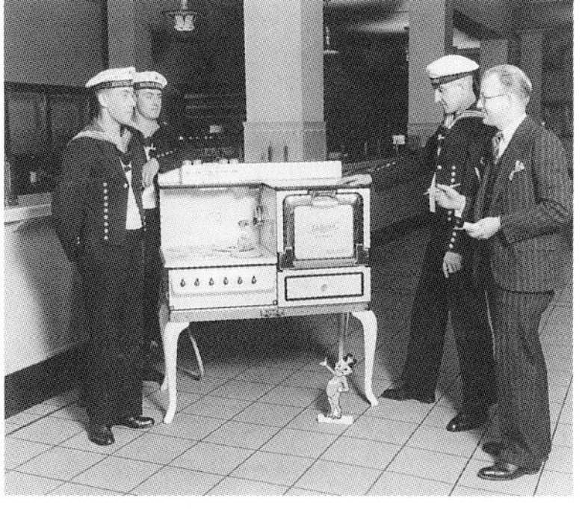

Appliance salesman Earl P. Warren tries to interest new foreign friends in a Hotpoint "electric servant." These visitors to the Company's Electrical Happiness Store at 6th and E in September 1929 were crew members of the German naval cruiser *Emden*, which was making a port visit to San Diego at the time.

B streets, which featured the spacious 2,900-seat Fox Theatre. According to Nell Molloy, Gildred illustrated his talk with "a very interesting movie of the city and county offices scattered in many different locations." Company vice president William F. Raber announced the appointment of OrLynn McKoane as the new chairman of the Women's Committee, replacing Molloy, who had served since its founding in 1926. McKoane, a home economics major at the University of Michigan, had been with the Byllesby company since 1922 in charge of home service units and had been doing follow-up work on electric refrigerators in San Diego.

The 1920s saw some changes in San Diego's leadership. Both John D. Spreckels and E.W. Scripps died in 1926, and Dr. Robert Powers, a Company founder and early president, died in 1927. Colonel Ira C. Copley of Aurora, Illinois, bought the San Diego Union-Tribune Publishing Company, along with Spreckels' 20-room mansion in Coronado, and became a force in the community. George Marston helped found and became first president of the San Diego Historical Society on December 13, 1928. He donated the Serra Museum and Presidio Park to the city on July 16, 1929, San Diego's 160th birthday.

Mission Beach and its boardwalk were popular tourist attractions as far back as this day at the beach in July 1925. The original casino is at left, with the roller coaster behind. The building at right is the Plunge and bath house, and the small building behind is the skating rink. Beyond the beach is Mission Bay, before its development.

It took several months for the effects of the stock-market crash of October 29, 1929, to be felt in San Diego. By the early 1930s, however, land promotions collapsed, the number of building permits dropped, and bankruptcies ran high. Fortunately, certain federal and state projects for water development, harbor improvement and highway construction eased unemployment in the county. A year after the crash, as of October 31, 1930, the Company Employees' Association financial report showed a membership of 999 with cash on hand of $1,130, Company stock worth $2,200, and Byllesby Company stock valued at $1,538. On November 4, 1930, San Diego Consolidated Gas & Electric Company bought the South Coast Gas Company serving Carlsbad and Oceanside and installed distribution systems at Del Mar, Solana Beach and Encinitas. The decade of the 1930s would bring new challenges.

The Company's first logo, designed by an employee, was used on everything from buildings to uniforms and service pins.

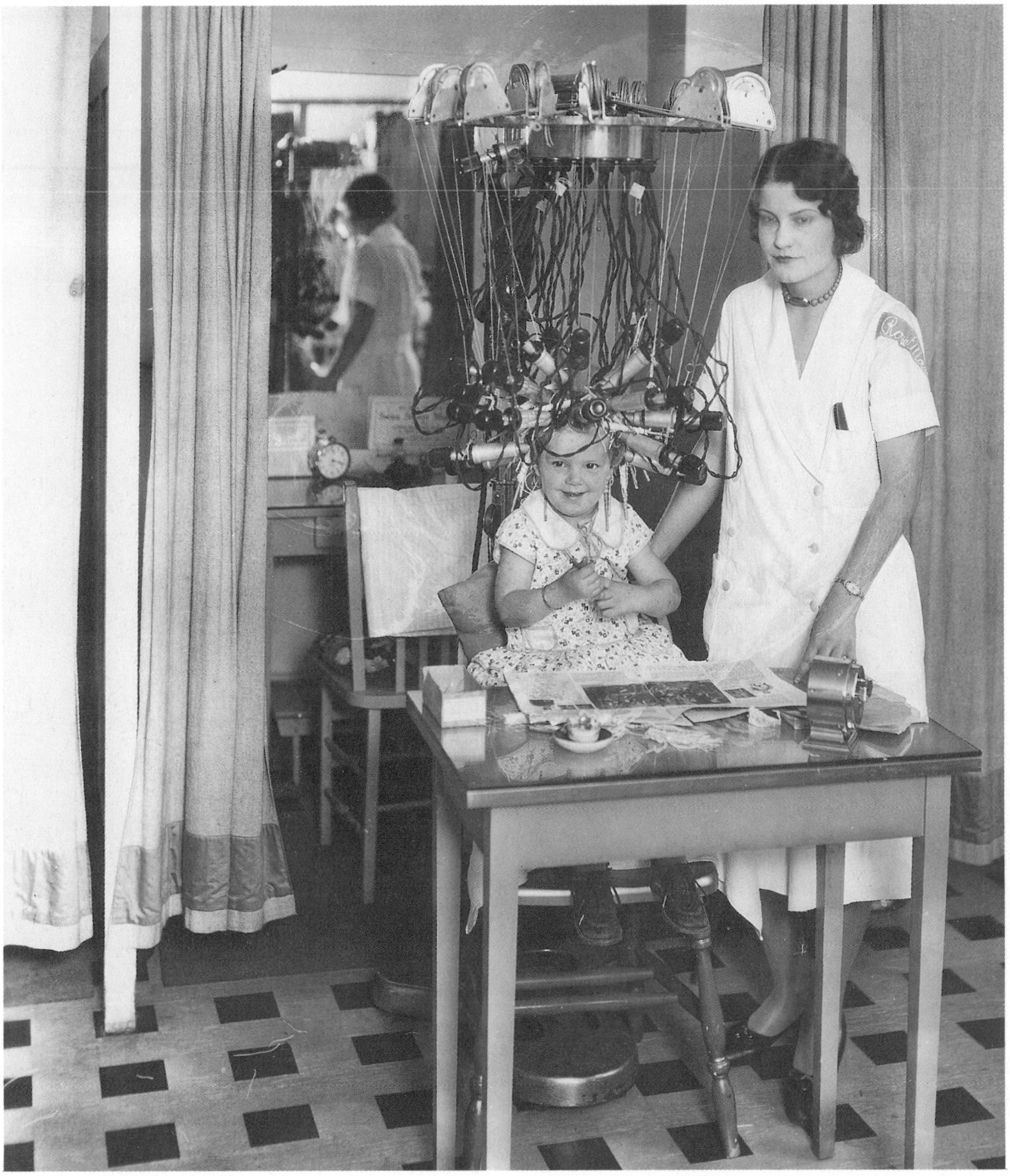

A younger member of the beauty set gets the latest in electric-powered hair curling in this late 1920s photo from the Rose Marcele Beauty Shop in San Diego. (Photo courtesy of San Diego Historical Society–Ticor Collection)

Joslyn Company
of California
FACTORY
DISTRICT BLVD.
LOS ANGELES
DISTRICT OFFICE
RUSS STREET
SAN FRANCISCO
1932 AUGUST 1932
Sun. Mon. Tue. Wed. Thu. Fri. Sat.
1 2 3 4 5 6
7 8 9 10 11 12 13
14 15 16 17 18 19 20
21 22 23 24 25 26 27
28 29 30 31
COMMERCIAL GALVANIZING
RODER
INSULATED
OFF ON
OVEN

Chapter 6

1931-1940
San Diego Fights the Depression

Fortunately for San Diegans, several governmental projects, such as harbor dredging, expansion of Lindbergh Field, and construction of a highway through Rose Canyon to replace Sorrento Valley's winding road, kept the local economy moving through the early years of the Depression. The Chamber of Commerce moved to a new site at the corner of Broadway and Columbia streets, and members planned a goodwill tour to Mexico with an airplane convoy. A city bond issue provided $300,000 for recreational projects, including a golf course and tennis courts in Balboa Park. A new city charter approved in April 1931 initiated a plan whereby a city manager would have authority over fire, police, health and certain other city departments. The six-member city council would be nominated by districts and elected at large, while the mayor, nominated and elected at large as a seventh and presiding member of the city council, would be the ceremonial head of the city. A new San Diego State College campus 10 miles east of downtown was dedicated in a three-day ceremony in May 1931. Its Spanish-style buildings accommodated 2,000 students and a curriculum of 200 courses.

On January 17, 1931, the largest single gas-main project ever undertaken by the Company was completed. It took three months to lay 26 miles of transmission pipe to send

1931
Population*
209,659
Electric
Customers
73,658
Sales in kwhr
163 million
Average cost / kwhr
2.93 cents
Gas
Customers
58,302
Sales in therms
13 million
Average cost / therm
20.29 cents

PALA
SAN DIEGO COUNTY
BORREGO SPRINGS
OCEANSIDE
ESCONDIDO
JULIAN
DEL MAR
LAKESIDE
PINE VALLEY
TECATE
MEXICO

Service Territory

*County population based on census 10-year estimates

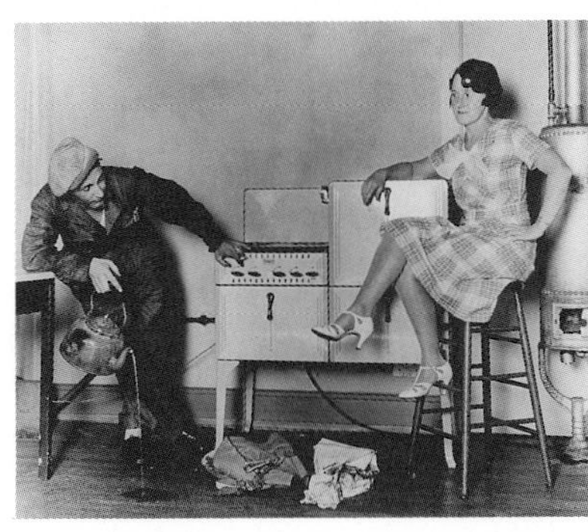

< The change to natural gas in 1932 required adjusting the burners in every appliance in the city. To train the more than 700 temporary workers that would do in-home appliance repairs, George Sullivan and Dot Hughes enacted a "playlet" of the proper (left) and improper (right) gas-company-employee behavior. The playlet was staged in the Service Building.

Workmen wrap pipe in a protective coating of tar and paper during the 1932 installation of a gas line between La Jolla and Huntington Beach. The line allowed the Company to tap into clean-burning natural gas from Los Angeles and the San Joaquin Valley.

gas from the La Jolla high-pressure holder northward to Carlsbad and Oceanside. The pipeline, protected from corrosion by a new wrapping method, followed the state highway over Torrey Pines grade. After the pipe was welded into long sections and tested for leaks, it was placed over the trench, cleaned, and painted with a primer coat. Next came a coat of asphalt followed by wrapping with asbestos felt applied spirally by a recently developed hand-wrapping machine traveling along the pipe. Crews applied a second coat of felt and then wrapped the pipe with kraft paper for protection during laying and backfilling operations.

Another significant development for the gas distribution department was a vote by the city council in June 1931 to employ a competent gas engineer to make an independent check of natural-gas sources and supply costs. The council also asked the Company to do the same thing and further agreed to meet with representatives from an unidentified oil company in the Kettleman Hills field north of Bakersfield. The oil company was eager to deliver natural gas to San Diego.

On July 24, William F. Raber, vice president and general manager of San Diego Consolidated Gas & Electric Company, was promoted to president, an office that he would hold until August 24, 1941. Raber reported that net earnings of the Company for the year ending July 31, 1931, were $3,776,765, compared with $3,494,094 for 1930. According to *The San Diego Union,* these figures reflected local stability since the net earnings for the parent, Standard Gas and Electric Company, had declined by about 2.12 percent for the year. Raber explained

William F. Raber, president and general manager of the Company from 1931 to 1941, inspects a new "electric eye" sensor at a local display.

Workers in November 1931 conduct a line-extension survey in snowy Pine Valley. Power lines were extended to many east San Diego County locations during this period.

that dredging work in the harbor, which had been done electrically, and general expansion in the county had accounted for the increase.

As the year came to a close, *The Union* reported on December 6 that the city had filed a formal complaint against the Company alleging that its utility rates were excessive and that it was reasonable for San Diego to bring in natural gas. City Attorney C.L. Byers stated that the complaint was "en route by air mail to San Francisco" where it would be acted upon by the State Railroad Commission. Company officials answered that negotiations for natural gas were well under way.

On the local level, electric lights were turned on in Julian on Saturday, January 16, 1932, at 7 p.m. Work on the 21-mile transmission line from Ramona had begun on November 5, but the frequent rain and snowstorms had made work difficult. The event was celebrated with a banquet and ball. Much of the rest of the mountain area to the east continued without electricity for several years more.

The long-awaited news that natural gas was coming to San Diego broke on March 15, 1932. "Contrary to the ambiguous propaganda of local politicians," reported the *News-Meter,* "this Company has been in favor of the introduction of natural gas in San Diego, provided a satisfactory rate schedule could be arrived at and this has now been accomplished." The Company had begun negotiations with Southern Counties Gas Company two years previously and had agreed upon a price of 25 cents per 1,000 cubic feet.

Application had been made to the Railroad Commission for distribution, but while it was pending, the gas pressure in the Los Angeles basin had decreased to the point that gas could not be supplied to San Diego County. Instead, gas was obtained from the combined fields of Kettleman Hills, Ventura, Santa Barbara and the Los Angeles basin, and made available at a

Groundbreaking for the natural-gas pipeline occurred in Oceanside on June 6, 1932. Construction work went on at several points at the same time, allowing the $1 million pipeline to be completed in only four months.

Welded steel pipe is lowered into a ditch on Highway 101 in the Rose Canyon area of La Jolla during work to bring natural gas to San Diego in 1932.

somewhat higher price. Southern Counties Gas Company began construction of a pipeline south from Long Beach paralleling the coast highway to Rose Canyon, where it would be brought in to Company lines.

Since natural gas contained nearly twice as much heat per cubic foot as manufactured gas, the same amount would cook nearly twice as many meals or keep the home warm for nearly twice as long. It would also cost the customer half as much, which would require a rate adjustment to offset the loss of Company earnings. To the contrary, reported *News-Meter,* some "bubbling politicians, whose reverse prowess as public utility experts has afforded no end of astonishment during the past few months," were claiming that since natural gas occurred in nature, it should be given free, or nearly free, to customers.

Employee personal cars authorized for use during the changeover to natural gas fill the parking space between the Station A Service Building (left) and the Station A garage (right).

The changeover from manufactured gas to natural gas necessitated the readjustment of every gas appliance served by the Company. The openings through which the gas flowed into the burners had to be reduced to allow only about 60 percent as much gas to enter. Approximately 400 men were trained for two to four weeks in appliance work to be able to carry out the changeover, which required about six weeks to complete. Several thousand cubic feet of tanked natural gas was brought to San Diego by truck for demonstration purposes. An artificial odorant was added to give the odorless gas a distinctive aroma.

The Company also made plans to supplement the supply with manufactured gas in case of a natural-gas

"And everywhere the army went, this trailer was sure to go." In this case, the army was the Company's appliance adjusters. This field headquarters served as a base of operations for the workers from dawn to long after nightfall. As one area was finished, the mobile headquarters was moved to the next neighborhood.

A COMMUNICATIONS CHRONICLE

Acquainting customers—residential, commercial and industrial—with the contrasting characteristics of manufactured gas and natural gas and how they would have to change their use habits and techniques involved an extensive, long-range communications program.

It started in March 1932, when the ditcher began churning up the turf around Oceanside. Parallel radio and newspaper announcements kept all customers advised of construction progress. There was one full-page advertisement in the newspapers to announce the beginning of the project.

Next came a monthly publication, mailed to all customers, called "Natural Gas News," in which articles briefed readers about the men who would be calling on each customer, their attire, their expected deportment, a history of the Company's gas service, how each fuel behaves under identical circumstances, how to use the new fuel in various appliances, backgrounds on the men who were supervising the changeover, information about the tools, equipment and vehicles being used.

TOMORROW MORNING

Natural Gas

Will Be Turned Into the District Shown Below

Between Alabama and 30th Sts from Upas St to El Cajon Ave and between Alabama and Arizona Sts North of El Cajon Ave to Mission Valley

CAUTION If you live in the district shown above, TURN OFF ALL OVENS, WATER HEATERS, ROOM HEATERS, PILOT LIGHTS and other gas burners before midnight **tonight** and leave them off until the Gas Company adjuster arrives at your house.

Use only the TOP BURNERS of your gas range till the adjuster arrives.

These precautions are necessary. The Company regrets the inconvenience and will appreciate your patience and co-operation.

All gas appliances must be adjusted properly to burn the new gas. Gas Co. adjusters will do this for you without charge. If you do not live in the above district, watch for a notice by post card and the newspapers.

San Diego Consolidated Gas & Electric Company

As pipeline construction progressed, large ads kept the public informed about events. A small portion of each ad was devoted to telling readers how proud the Company was to be providing the most modern, clean and efficient fuel for their use. Within that portion was another paragraph describing some new development in San Diego such as "... the new San Diego State College now being housed in a group of new buildings one mile north of El Cajon Blvd. at the end of College Ave." Or that "San Diego has been chosen by the U.S. Government as the site of the largest naval operating base on the Pacific Coast."

A map appeared in the newspaper almost daily, showing the borders of each section to be worked on two days hence, and each customer in that area received a one-day notice by post-card.

Grocery ads at the same time would give pause to shoppers today: coffee, 15 cents per pound; toilet tissue, 4 rolls for 15 cents; avocados, 2 for 25 cents; apples, 6 pounds for 25 cents. Tickets to motorcycle races were 50 cents.

To mark the changeover's completion in October, a full-page ad was taken to thank all customers for their time, patience and cooperation, and to pledge the Company's assurance of superior natural-gas service in the future.

Before and during the changeover to natural gas, this specially built truck carried compressed gas in the long cylinders on the back. The gas was used to test the operation of industrial boilers or, as in this case, the ovens of the Continental Bakery.

> Butane, held in these tanks at the Station A gas plant in January 1932, increased the heating value of manufactured gas to match the heating value of natural gas. This allowed manufactured gas to supplement natural gas during periods of heavy demand.

shortage due to transmission failure, earthquake or other causes. Because natural gas contained approximately 1,100 Btu per cubic foot in comparison to 550 Btu for oil gas, it would be necessary, after the appliance changeover, to build up the oil gas to approximately the same heating value and specific gravity. J.A. Harritt, superintendent of gas production, developed a method whereby butane vapor, with a heating value of about 3,000 Btu per cubic foot would be blended with the oil gas. Butane storage capacity would be increased from 75,000 gallons to 225,000 gallons.

The advantages of natural gas—cleaner, quieter, faster for cooking—and the competency and efficiency of employees effecting the changeover prompted many letters of gratitude from customers. For the Company it caused a difficult rate situation. At the outset of the natural-gas discussion, it was contended by some experts that the loss in the domestic load would be compensated for by an increased demand in the commercial and industrial fields. San Diego, however, was not an industrial center, and the Company began to study ways to build the residential load by encouraging homeowners to install gas heaters and other gas appliances. Two top executives from the Central Arizona Light and Power Company of Phoenix spent several days in

J.A. HARRITT

A pioneer in the manufacture of gas from fuel oil, J.A. (Fred) Harritt became a national figure in the gas industry. He shared in a gold medal award from the Pacific Coast Gas Association in 1932 for his part in developing a high Btu gas from diesel oil that could take the place of natural gas in case of a shortage.

As superintendent of the gas production department, he wrote a sad little epitaph for manufactured gas in the November 1932 *News-Meter.*

The Death of Manufactured Gas

In the little village of San Diego in 1881 a spindling infant was born under the auspices of Dr. R.M. Powers, et al. Though he showed but little promise for the future, he was carefully nurtured by the idolizing parents, through sickness, misfortune and vicissitudes which would have daunted any hearts but theirs.

At the age of 24 years he was adopted by H.M. Byllesby & Company and by their careful tutoring was developed into one of the most conspicuous residents of the then thriving city of San Diego.

He continued to grow in magnitude as the community grew. His usefulness to the citizenry widened apace. . . .

He gave his best and it was good. It can truly be said of him, "Well done, thou good and faithful servant."

He was cut down in the prime of life, at the age of 51 years, having been asphyxiated by Natural Gas on October 24th, 1932.

Those who knew him best and longest loved him most, and to these particularly our hearts go out in sympathy.

Billboards like this sold the idea that heating water on the stove for the Saturday night bath was no longer necessary.

Streetcars carried posters advertising the low cost of gas heating in an effort to build the gas load.

San Diego in October 1933 to gather data and advice on their changeover to natural gas.

During the early 1930s, the general economic slowdown and tightening of belts caused people to look for ways to save money, especially in taxes. One popular proposal was municipal ownership of public utilities, which reportedly would result in lower taxes. The Company gathered statistics showing that in contrast to having lower taxes, the average per-capita property tax of municipal ownership cities was 19.7 percent greater and the per-capita cost of government 24.5 percent greater than in cities with privately owned public utilities. In 1930, the general per-capita cost of government in certain comparative municipal and non-municipal electric utility ownership cities was as follows: Los Angeles $62.38 vs. San Francisco $46.22; Seattle $48.66 vs. Portland $39.91; Long Beach $47.48 vs. San Diego $37.61; Tacoma $32.73 vs. Spokane $31.95; Pasadena $55.88 vs. Berkeley $39.13. The average per-capita tax of seven cities having municipal ownership was $46.96 versus an average of $37.72 for seven cities not having municipal ownership. Nevertheless, the city council continued to propose that municipal ownership would result in lower rates and tax savings.

In the midst of economic problems, the southern part of the state was severely jolted on the evening of March 10, 1933, by a devastating earthquake centered in the Long Beach area. The supply of gas there was turned off within a few moments after the shock, but electrical service was interrupted for only two or three minutes. San Diego, which had no damage, sent needed supplies to the stricken city. The Seal Beach station of the Los Angeles Gas and Electric Corporation suffered considerable damage, although the Long

Beach plant of Southern California Edison Company escaped with only minor problems. Six Edison linemen repairing power poles, which carried an 11,000-volt circuit, rode out the quake in their safety belts on the crossarms of 60-foot poles. Exactly two months later, Laurence Klauber and nine officials of the Company forwarded a lengthy report to President Raber on the potential earthquake hazard in San Diego with suggested action to be taken.

The 1933 Long Beach earthquake was the first significant tremor to hit modern power-generating equipment. Based on damage to facilities in the quake area, the Company remodeled its plants to be more earthquake-resistant.

On January 31, 1934, *The San Diego Union* reported that the local utility hearing had opened with a "city attack on rates and management." The Company figures were challenged by investigators who claimed that "the historical cost of the company's properties is $35,334,812, instead of somewhere around $37,000,000 as claimed by the company." Gilmore Tillman, assistant city attorney, was prepared to prove that San Diego rates were probably higher than in any other city of comparable size. The city also charged that Station A was maintained principally as a standby to provide emergency service for the Southern Sierras company and should be written

The vehicle fleet at Station A, 1932, with the regular force of gas troubleshooters. The gas holders behind were used to maintain pressure in the system, even after natural gas came into use.

off. In addition, the city complained, users of gas, electricity and steam "should not carry the burden of promotional investments in back country utility lines."

City expert witness T.A. Hopkins also charged that "any services rendered by the Byllesby management for the 2.5 percent of gross receipts it collects from the company are unnecessary and the fee should be eliminated from operating expenses." Company counsel Evan Williams asked whether Hopkins meant that the fee should be eliminated but that Byllesby management should continue to pay President Raber's salary. Hopkins replied in the affirmative but asserted that the local payroll was sufficient to pay for all executive expenses in comparison to the amount charged by other companies. Hopkins also challenged the amount of $400,000 for the natural-gas changeover having been charged to the consumer, since the Company had still been making an adequate return on its investment.

Confessing that the city was unprepared to proceed with its case, F. Von Schrader, special city counsel, asked that the hearing be continued until February 20. At that time the city's goal was to have the commission reduce the Company's yearly charge for gas, electricity and steam by $1,634,889 and limit the Company's return to 6.5 percent on the city's valuation, which was more than $2 million below the last known Company valuation.

Pine Valley Picnic—This cartoon illustration by Wilson Cutler of the Record Department's 1934 picnic depicts only a few of the many fun activities experienced during this event.

Despite claims to the contrary, the Company's rates were not among the highest in the country and, in fact, after March 1, 1935, when rates dropped from $7.88 to $6.73 per 100 kilowatt hours, they were among the lowest. In January 1935, San Diego ranked 30th out of the 75 cities rated, but in March, when rates were changed to a basis that would allow a fair rate of return on capital invested, San Diego ranked 16th. The cities with the lowest rates either had an abundance of water power readily available, such as Tacoma, Seattle and Buffalo, or a high volume of sales because of business and manufacturing, such as Kansas City, Cincinnati and St. Louis, or a water and power bureau operated as one, with water bearing a great part of the cost of power, such as Los Angeles.

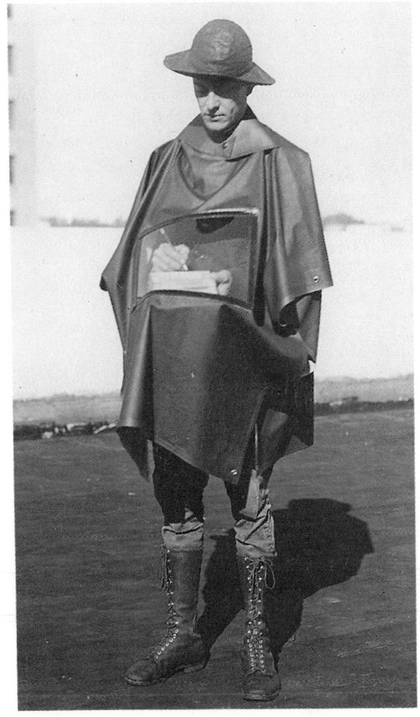

Innovative ideas were always important in the utility business. Since rain could easily soak meter-reader books, chief meter-reader J.H. Bivens developed a rubber poncho with a celluloid window to keep customer records dry. Drying wet records required hand pressing with an electric iron.

San Diego was primarily a Navy, residential and tourist city rather than the site of any large industries. Government census figures showed fish canning to be San Diego's leading business with five canneries having a combined annual payroll of $605,000. The local fishing industry, including the tuna fleet, had an estimated total value of $10 million but required very little power; second came printing and publishing, while the third largest business was the manufacture of ice cream. Later in the decade, military demands would increase, and industries such as Consolidated Aircraft, which moved to San Diego from Buffalo in 1932, would become significant components in the city's economic base.

On the bright side during the early 1930s was San Diego's plan to open its second major fair in Balboa Park—the California Pacific International Exposition—scheduled for May 1935. The purpose of the event was to honor the past by depicting four centuries of development in the West, and salute the new era of prosperity expressed in such construction projects as Boulder Dam in Nevada, the All-American Canal in Imperial Valley, and the San Francisco Bay bridges.

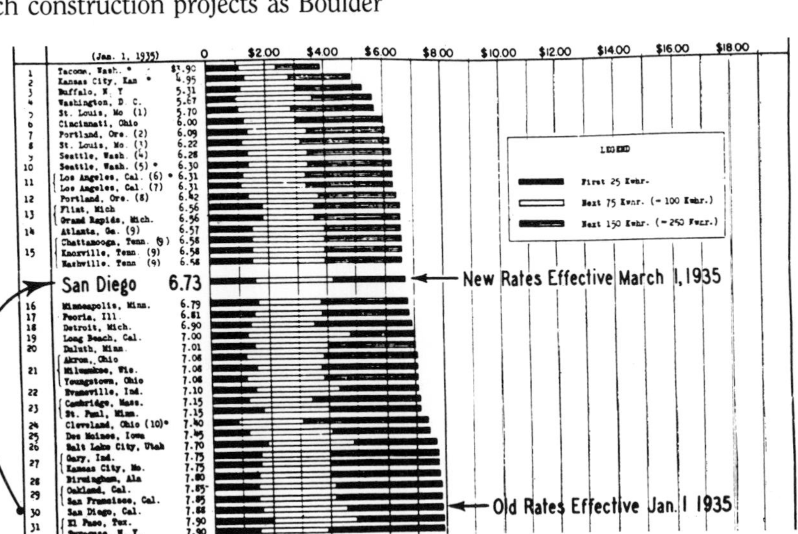

Charting the Company's relative cost of power compared to other utility companies from the electric rate survey prepared by the U.S. government.

Plans for the Company's electrical and gas service to the Exposition were completed in early March. Crews were on the job in April to build two transformer substations. One was east of the railway station at Laurel Street, with a capacity of 2,700 kilowatts, and one down in the palisades behind the Ford Building, with a capacity of 6,000 kilowatts. Both stepped the current down from 12,000 to 4,000 volts, and two independent 12,000-volt circuits were built into each station with automatic switching to give continuous service. Forty electric meters were placed in the park and eight on the zoo grounds. The

Balboa Park at the beginning of the 1935-36 California Pacific International Exposition. The Ford Building and the structures near it represent the new Exposition construction. The original 1915 Exposition buildings are in the middle. At top is Florida Canyon and North Park.

NELL MOLLOY

Nell Molloy, first to chair the Women's Committee, started working for the Company in June 1910 as a stenographer and within a few years became secretary to the president. An efficient, popular employee who "never lost her poise, patience or perseverance," Molloy was well remembered by all with whom she came in contact.

At her 25th anniversary with the Company in June 1935, Vice President Laurence Klauber wrote the following tribute:

You hear about executives,
Vice presidents and other stiffs,
And all the pompous effigies, who
think they set the pace;
But these brass hats are scenery
Or, better, call them greenery,
Because it is our little Nell, who
really runs the place.

Nell Molloy retired in August 1951 and died in February 1974.

Exposition management installed their own distribution system and ran it until 1968, when SDG&E took over its operation.

The Company's gas crews installed nearly two miles of main to ensure ample gas service. Of this, about 1,600 feet of 1½-inch high-pressure main was a permanent installation to serve the buildings south and west of the Organ Pavilion, including the Ford Building, Palace of Travel and Transportation, the Federal Building and the State Building. In addition, all restaurants would utilize gas for cooking, including the large Cafe of the World seating 900 people. Gas would also fire the glass-melting furnace for the Venetian glassblowers' exhibit and provide fuel utilized in the Ford exhibit and the Coca-Cola bottling display. As Gene Adler, gas sales engineer, pointed out, "The nudists in Zoro Gardens are afforded the benefits of gas refrigeration and gas cooking, but as yet rely on the sun for heat."

The architects for the international fair augmented the 1915 Spanish-colonial theme by combining ancient Mayan styles with Indian Pueblo,

Besides constructing electric and gas extensions to serve the Exposition, the Company displayed the latest in home and industrial appliances and equipment. Gas heating was used by Exposition displays to run furnaces and to vulcanize tiny rubber models of Ford cars.

introducing buildings with modern lines, and putting in a variety of landscaping. A Japanese garden with small pools and stone lanterns, native California vines and blooming flowers, and replicas of Moorish gardens in southern Spain graced the outdoor areas. Individual exhibitors, the U.S. government, the State of California and others spent millions to participate in the Exposition, which continued for two years.

The Exposition closed in the fall of 1935 and reopened the next spring. A new Palace of Electricity took the place of the previous year's water and transportation palace. According to President Raber, the Company had "gathered a display of everything that is modern and new in appliances" and had also provided a number of Edison's first inventions to serve "as a vivid reminder that his work is the very foundation of all that we have today in electrical equipment."

The controversy over public versus private ownership of utilities continued as an important theme during the difficult economic times of the 1930s. The local *San Diego Sun* of August 30, 1935, promoted municipal ownership with such loose claims as "Savings of millions of dollars per year to consumers hinted in addition to cutting investment costs." A city electric engineer, W.D. Stark, estimated that a third of the cost of street lighting could be saved if the city had its own plant. If this same reduction were applied to the domestic bill of private consumers, he claimed, another $1 million could be saved.

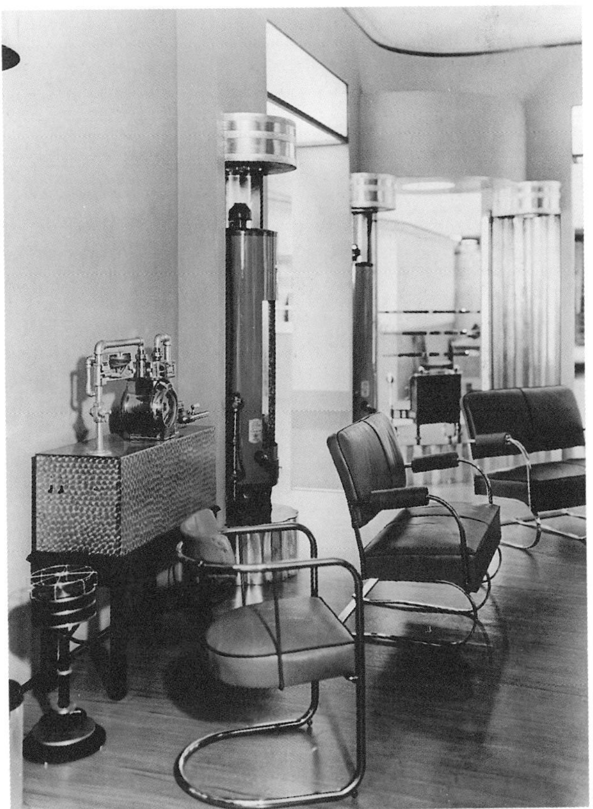

Interior of exhibit shows a hot-water tank at left and a polished gas meter.

The Company's announcer for its Exposition display was a young Art Linkletter, seen here at the mike for radio station KGB on December 3, 1935.

City engineers estimated that the first unit of a municipal plant would cost about $350,000, and $1 million would pay for diesel plants to light all the city's streets. Proponents of municipal ownership were backed by Professor Harry C. Steinmetz of San Diego State College, who had been a candidate for mayor. Steinmetz, labeled a "radical" by *The San Diego Union,* was eliminated in the primary, and Percy J. Benbough, a local mortician, was elected to the top position. The city continued to look into municipal ownership during the 1930s but without success.

By October 1935, San Diego's economy was recovering. Company sales in San Diego had increased remarkably. Electric appliances, gas heating installations, new line extensions and lighting sales had made considerable gains over the first eight months of the year. August sales of electric refrigerators had tripled over the previous year, and electric-range sales had almost doubled. The 38-billion-gallon El Capitan Dam east of Lakeside was dedicated that year, but because the reservoir's elevation was relatively low, the falling water could not generate hydroelectric power and still reach its destination in San Diego.

Company salesmen worked hard to extend electric lighting to commercial businesses, such as this Union Oil Products service station downtown on West Broadway. Good lighting attracted customers and displayed products clearly.

Local movie theater marquees displayed spectacular lighting by the 1930s.

Just a year later the Company revealed plans to expand Station B by installing a new electric generator of the steam turbine type, having a normal capacity of 35,000 kilowatts. President Raber was quoted in *The San Diego Union* of October 25, 1936, as stating that even though "hydroelectric energy might some day be delivered to San Diego at prices no higher than the cost of steam-generated energy, the requirements for continuous service are such that steam generators are necessary for standby, regardless of any other normal source of supply. A community the size of San Diego cannot be dependent on the uncertainties of transmission lines from distant points but always must have available local machines having a capacity sufficient to furnish all the electricity a community may require." He also added that no major generating capacity had been added since 1926.

During 1937, a $423,000 cut in gas and electric rates helped the Company's public relations and kept local electric rates in line with those nationwide. Operating expenses had increased because of higher prices for materials purchased and an overall wage increase for employees of approximately 9 percent. Added revenue, however, had resulted from new gas and electric extensions into rural districts and extremely cold weather during January and February. Fifty miles of electric lines and 12 miles of gas main had been laid during the year. Local business activity improved with a general increase in population and a healthy tourist trade in San Diego.

Demonstration kitchens, like this one with Mildred Kier, helped customers learn more about cooking with gas and electricity, as well as the safety and convenience of refrigeration.

The dedication of Station B's last major generator in February 1938 was broadcast live over radio. At the switch throwing were Carl Wiggins (left), superintendent of electric production; Percy J. Benbough, mayor of San Diego; R.M. Alvord, General Electric Company; George Phythian, superintendent of construction; T. LeRoy Richards, chairman, San Diego County Board of Supervisors; W.F. Raber, president, and L.M. Klauber, vice president in charge of operations.

According to *The San Diego Union* of July 4, 1937, the previous 18 months had seen "perhaps the most ambitious program of dwelling construction in the city's history. At the beaches, in the foothills, in established subdivisions and older residence districts . . . carpenters' hammers have raised a clamor as new construction brought San Diego housing up to population gains." Dealers in the Company stores reported the sale of 8,625 electric refrigerators, 4,600 automatic gas water heaters and 5,572 gas room heaters, while a "Two Radios Per Home" advertising campaign had encouraged the sale of 12,625 radios. A total of 3,492 new electric customers and 2,508 new gas customers during the year bought many of these appliances, but residents of older homes also wanted to take advantage of the new merchandise.

The new construction had placed a huge demand on the Company's electrical production equipment. Approximately $2 million was spent by the Company for Station B's new 35,000-kilowatt turbo-generator with an overload capacity of 60,000 kilowatts for emergencies. In addition to the new turbine, two new boilers were installed to increase steaming capacity of the station by about 60 percent. Production capacity was increased from 64,000 kilowatts to 99,000 kilowatts to provide for future growth in the city. The improvement was indeed timely, since a 59,800-kilowatt peak load was carried on December 8, 1937, and the new generator went into operation with an appropriate ceremony at Station B in February 1938.

At the dedication, Mayor Percy Benbough congratulated San Diego Consolidated Gas & Electric for its foresight and faith in the community since "from the standpoint of investment, [the machinery] represents twice the cost of our Civic Center and four times that of our new Post Office building." Less well known was the fact that the Company had become the largest taxpayer throughout the territory it served.

Sadly, on March 3, 1938, at 7:49 p.m., veteran superintendent Carl Wiggins threw the switches for the last time to shut down Station A at Tenth and Imperial. "I can't forget," said Wiggins, "that for 50 years this station never has failed for a single day or night to perform its duty." The three original generators at Station A were sold for scrap. Just a few months later, on July 15, the Hillcrest Substation at the corner of Front and Robinson streets was officially opened to become the Company's latest addition to meet new residential demands.

Veteran employee Carl Wiggins shuts down the generators of Station A for the last time, just a few days after the dedication of the new Station B generator. Wiggins had worked at the plant since he joined the Company in 1893. He died a year later, while still on the job.

Employees during this time had celebrated the 20th anniversary of the Employees' Association in October 1935, and had expanded the scope of their participation in the Company. Work-related activities included cooperation with merchants selling gas and electric appliances, periodic contacts with electrical contractors, plumbers and architects, and participation in cooking schools and appliance shows.

In June 1937, in conformance with national guidelines, they decided to form the Gasco Federal Credit Union. Membership, limited to employees, was $5 plus a 25-cent entry fee, paid in cash or through payroll deductions in semi-monthly installments. A member could subscribe for as many $5 shares as the credit union directors might permit, but each member would have only one vote. The new credit union would encourage savings and provide dividends, which at that time were at a maximum of 6 percent.

For many years, the Company undertook serious support of individual and team sports and hobbies. Athletic director Lee Waymire, who established the Golden Hill playground before being hired in 1919 to manage the bowling alleys, maintained a well-rounded sports and recreation program for employees. They competed individually and as groups in golf tournaments. The Gasco Golf Club's May Medal Play Tournament at Balboa Park in 1938

The scoreboard at Balboa Stadium was donated by the Company.

brought out 49 employees with 8 handicapper Ed McKnight winning with a net 68. There were 17 competitive bowling teams with 25 employees achieving scores over 200 during May 1937. Eight softball teams played during the summer of 1937 for the W.F. Raber Championship trophy, won in 1936 by the meter readers. In addition to the women's basketball team, four female employees rowed for the Southwestern Girls Rowing Club and worked out in the bay on Sundays. There was also a camera club and weekly ice skating.

While employees carried out Company services, the California Railroad Commission concerned itself with electric rates. On November 22, 1938, the commission ordered reductions ranging from 2 percent to 6 percent beginning January 1, 1939, which would save San Diego electric customers $168,000 yearly. According to *The San Diego Union,* "the reduction was effected through joint negotiations by officials of the company, the city of San Diego and members of the railroad commission." Laurence Klauber, vice president in charge of operations, and Asher Holloway, vice president in charge of sales, represented the Company, and rate consultant Walter W. Cooper represented the city. Those benefiting the most were small commercial and domestic users in San Diego, Coronado, National City, Chula Vista, La Mesa, El Cajon, Oceanside and Escondido, as well as San Clemente in Orange County.

Team sports included this women's bowling team in April 1936. From left: Verna Kirkman, Mary Hurley, Margaret Fitzpatrick, Marge Albers and Betty Loop.

Commissioner Ray L. Riley commented that this rate reduction, the fifth since 1935, illustrated that a policy of continuous investigation and adjustment made it possible to keep rates equitable. "Close cooperation between representatives of the city, the company and the commission had resulted in a reduction of more than 25 percent in the rates for the small domestic consumers during this period." No change was made in lighting rates for unincorporated areas or for industry or agriculture, since a reduction had been granted in rural territory on March 15, 1937.

Humor was not unknown to help make a point about keeping safe working conditions. In this November 1937 photo, "Ozzie" (Francis Cobb of the gas-meter shop) demonstrates how to get "tied" up in your work. Anyone making a safety mistake in the shop had to wear the "Ozzie" hat until he learned his lesson.

In early February 1939, in compliance with the Rural Electrification Administration's instructions, members of the newly formed Mountain Empire Electric Cooperative took the necessary steps to obtain $60,000 in federal aid for construction of a 50-mile power line from Potrero to Jacumba. The 100 members of the cooperative group met at Campo to elect directors and make plans for obtaining rights of way and easements. To complete federal requirements for a survey and cooperation in the field, they had to obtain 40 more members. The government would advance the money as a loan, repayable over 20 years, and figure a rate base so that the project would be self-liquidating. Power would be purchased from San Diego Consolidated Gas & Electric Company at wholesale and resold to consumers in the district.

The year ending December 31, 1939, had witnessed continued economic recovery throughout Southern California. The outbreak of war in Europe as Germany marched into Poland caused the United States to move into a program of military preparedness. Navy activities, with personnel numbering 38,000, and the aircraft industry, with approximately 9,000 employees, had contributed substantially to San Diego's prosperity.

The number of Company employees reached 1,282, of which 1,193 were members of the Employees' Association. The Women's Committee included all 110 female employees who met monthly throughout the year to discuss

REDDY KILOWATT AND LOTTA HOTTA

Reddy Kilowatt, developed in 1934 by Ashton B. Collins of the Alabama Power Company, was a nationwide symbol of the electrical industry. Collins permitted only investor-owned power companies to use Reddy for any purpose. Beginning in 1937, San Diego Consolidated used Reddy Kilowatt on Company vehicles, in advertising handouts, Company property signs, potholders, aprons, paper napkins and on parade floats.

According to *News-Meter,* September 1937, Lotta Hotta was created in February 1937 by artist Ted Rockwell, Record Department, who credited Vivian Kirkpatrick with inspiring him to fabricate a gas personality comparable to Reddy Kilowatt.

Lotta's expression of perpetual surprise was caused by amazement at her own growing popularity, particularly in the heating systems of San Diego homes.

San Diego juveniles were much interested in artist Tony D'Orazi's radio show in 1937. D'Orazi taught drawing over-the-air, with listeners sending in their results for judging. Winners were used in Reddy Kilowatt newspaper ads. Participants also became members of the Reddy Kilowatt Club, receiving a membership card, a button and a book of rhymes.

"Lotta is all-gas, from her stubby foot to the peak of her flaming head . . . her neck is a burner, and the . . . skirt a circular gas gauge recording chart. The gal is Hot Stuff. . . ."

Commercial lighting of store interiors had been promoted since the very first gas lamps, since merchants knew good lighting would increase sales. The prices in this late 1930s grocery may never be seen again, but the principle of good lighting is very much in effect today.

various issues. In cooperation with the Vocational Education Departments of the public schools, employee classes included elementary electricity, gas-heat engineering and practical psychology.

During 1940, the Company approached a significant milestone in its history. Through a series of stock and security transactions, ownership of San Diego Consolidated Gas & Electric Co. had previously passed from H.M. Byllesby Engineering & Management Company to Standard Gas & Electric Company, a subsidiary of Standard Power and Light Corporation, a registered holding company. As early as 1912, Standard Gas & Electric held 27,132 shares of San Diego Consolidated's common stock out of 27,150 outstanding shares, although the Byllesby Company continued to provide the Company with engineering services.

After 1900, and increasingly during the 1920s, public utility holding companies had proliferated throughout the country and extended wide control over utility service in geographically unrelated communities. While these holding companies were instrumental in expanding utility services to the public, they tended to be overcapitalized and extremely complex corporate organizations. As a financial investment they became speculative. Con-

Two door greeters from Beech-Nut gum welcome employees to the Company's main headquarters building in June 1938.

gress passed the 1935 Public Utility Company Holding Act (PUCHA) to require holding companies to integrate and coordinate their systems, and to divest themselves of control of these operationally unrelated properties. In this way, Congress intended to rejuvenate local utility management and restore effective state regulation.

Pursuant to the PUCHA, the federal Securities and Exchange Commission, in March 1940, ordered Standard Gas & Electric, which held 34 utility companies operating in 22 states across the country and in two states of Mexico, to present a plan to comply with its requirements. The plan, which was reviewed and approved by the SEC in August 1940, required Standard Gas & Electric to divest itself of ownership of 99.07 percent of the Company's outstanding common stock. The remaining .93 percent was held by individuals.

Escondido residents crowd into a Company cooking class in May 1939 to learn the latest dishes and cooking methods.

To do this, Standard Gas & Electric offered its own holders of notes and debentures 58 shares of San Diego Consolidated's common stock at $10 par for each $1,000 par of its own notes and bonds. Standard Gas & Electric's exchange offer resulted in a broad market for the Company's common shares. For example, at the annual meeting of Company shareholders on April 23, 1940, while Standard still held 99 percent of the common shares, there were 100,325 common shares issued and outstanding, which included those held by Standard. On December 31, 1941, after the divestiture, there were 1,250,000 common shares of Company stock issued and owned by 9,953 stockholders.

As a result of the SEC's order, San Diego Consolidated's stock was widely disbursed among persons and entities who were interested in a safe, rather than speculative, investment. When the stock ownership change took place, the Company's board of directors, at a special meeting on August 16, 1940, eliminated the word "Consolidated" from its name. At the same time, as the federal government's emergency program for national defense made San Diego one of the fastest-growing cities in America, a new era dawned for San Diego Gas & Electric Co. or, as it would be commonly known, SDG&E.

In the last tranquil months before World War II, San Diego enjoyed a return of prosperity after the Depression of the early 1930s. This view shows Fourth and Ash streets in the foreground, with the Company's Station C covered with ivy. At left is the Center City building, and just beyond are the smokestacks of Station B.

Chapter 7

1941-1950

War!

The bombing of Pearl Harbor by the Japanese on December 7, 1941, catapulted the nation into World War II overnight. Attempts by the United States to remain out of the war in Europe from 1939 through 1941 ended with the Japanese air attack, and the United States was pulled into the terrible conflict. Knowing that war was probably inevitable, the military had planned for that possibility and expanded all aspects of its operations during the first years of the European phase. When the conflict shifted to include a Pacific theater, the war zone directly affected the San Diego region.

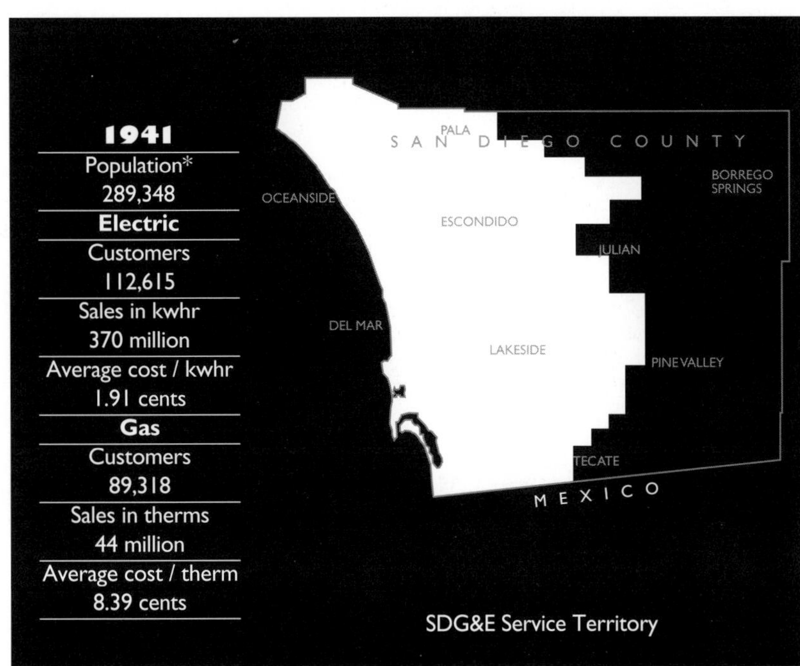

*County population based on census 10-year estimates

World War II created a multitude of diverse changes in both the city of San Diego and San Diego Gas & Electric Co. as the nation strove to meet the challenge of war. The city emerged forever from its reputation as a small, sleepy town on the edge of the Pacific Ocean and became a vital defense location critical to the war effort. The population would swell due to a massive influx of military personnel and defense workers eagerly seeking jobs in the rapidly expanding defense industries. The resulting increase in energy needs placed large-scale demands on SDG&E facilities and employees. At the same time, the Company was facing a labor and materials shortage due to staff members joining the armed forces. SDG&E met the challenge so effectively that the U.S. Navy presented its Citation for Meritorious Wartime Service to the Company in 1943. The award was accepted by SDG&E President Hance Cleland on behalf of the 496 employees then in the armed forces and the employees at home who continued to maintain the type of service that won the citation.

< Although actual fighting in World War II never came to San Diego, military concerns caused increased security at Company substations and power plants. These two guards were among nearly 60 soldiers pulling Company guard duty, in this case at the Mission substation in Mission Valley.

LINDA VISTA

Linda Vista, known in its early stages as Defense Housing Project No. 4092, was sponsored by the National Housing Authority of the U.S. government. The $14 million project covered an area of 1,459 acres. Ground was broken on February 23, 1941, and work was begun on the original contract, which called for the construction of 3,001 houses in 200 days. The houses were completed in November, and all were rented to defense workers and military personnel by April 1942.

The Company office was initially located in one of the small housing units, then later shifted to a two-story home nearby. The sign "San Diego Gas & Electric Company, upstairs, please" alerted customers to the new location. As the housing project quickly took shape due to the war emergency, dozens of customers came into the makeshift office to apply for service. Many of the new residents were first-time users of gas and electricity, providing a challenge for the small office staff of Fred Wright, Mary Hatcher, June Wilcox and Elizabeth Urbach. It was hard to convince one woman that her home would not burn up due to the small pilot light on her water heater.

In May 1942, another contract was let for the building of 1,846 more units, and in December 1942, the first utilities were turned on in the new section. The family homes were built on large lots with paved streets; four schools were constructed in the immediate vicinity. A full-scale shopping center was delayed because of wartime priorities, but residents did not mind—they were helping the war effort.

During 1940 and 1941, San Diego's military centers underwent large-scale expansion in expectation of the significant role they would play in wartime activities of the Pacific theater. As a major West Coast port, San Diego experienced a rapid increase of military personnel and defense-industry workers during the early years of the decade. San Diego's climate was ideal for the year-round training of Army, Navy and Marine Corps personnel. All branches of the military selected sites within SDG&E's service territory to establish training units to supplement the home bases already in operation. With 22 miles of landlocked harbor, San Diego had long been recognized as a major naval center. By 1940, $42 million had already been invested in San Diego by the U.S. Navy, with future contracts totaling more than $29 million. The Navy represented more than $2.5 million to the community in monthly payrolls and expenditures. The presence of the military had enormous impact on the growth of the city.

In response to orders from the military for aircraft, the local aeronautics industry greatly enlarged its production facilities and work force. Consolidated Aircraft Corporation, one of the world's largest aircraft plants, instituted round-the-clock shifts to produce flying boats and multi-engined land bombers. Ryan Aeronautical Company multiplied its plant facilities to meet the demand for monoplane trainers. Two manufacturers of essential parts, Solar Aircraft Company and Rohr Aircraft Company, also expanded their operational bases.

Attracted by the urgent demand for skilled labor, thousands of families poured into the San Diego metropolitan area. During the first two years of the decade, the population rose by 37 percent, bringing the total number of people in the city to 250,000. Major problems facing local governments at this time were the need for adequate housing, expanded water and sewer systems, improved transportation networks and more extensive educational facilities to accommodate the new arrivals. Large-scale housing projects, both military and private, changed the face of the city and county as new areas were developed.

Paralleling the enormous community growth, San Diego Gas & Electric also expanded during the decade of the 1940s. As a provider of key services for new residents in the city, the Company was one of the first local businesses to feel the impact of the change to a wartime economy. In 1940, customer gains exceeded the previous year's record-breaking totals; electric sales

By early 1943, many Company facilities were heavily fortified, such as these revetment walls for bomb splinter and blast protection around the Old Town Substation. One of the many barrage balloons that protected San Diego can be seen above the substation. Fortunately, the protection was never needed, and the walls were removed after the war.

increased 27 percent, and the electric system peak jumped 24 percent.

Because of the change in Company ownership during late 1940 and early 1941, SDG&E completed its process of growth from a small-town utility company to a modern, efficient corporation, geared to meet the needs of a large metropolitan area. By December 1941, upon completion of Standard Gas & Electric Company's sale of common stock to nearly 10,000 individual investors, the Company became an independent organization, locally managed and largely locally owned.

Another significant event in the Company's history took place when William F. Raber resigned the position of president on August 25 and was succeeded by Hance Cleland. From 1931 to 1941, Raber held the position of

Employees of the Company's Record Department practice gas-mask drills on June 1, 1942. Extensive preparations that were made in the event of local conflict were never needed.

HANCE H. CLELAND

Hance H. Cleland came to San Diego from Washington state when he was offered the position of president of SDG&E in 1941. Cleland was born in Campbell Hill, Illinois, and graduated from Central Normal College in Danville, Illinois, in 1906 with an LL.B. degree. Prior to his work in the energy field, Cleland served as assistant attorney general of the State of Washington from 1916 to 1919, and served as a member of the Washington Public Service Commission from 1919 to 1924. Before coming to San Diego, Cleland had served as president of the California-Oregon Power Company and was well known in the utility industry for his work as a valuation and rate expert.

Upon his arrival in San Diego, Cleland took an active interest in local affairs in addition to his role at SDG&E. As the Company's wartime president, he carried on the morale-building program of corresponding with each and every employee serving in the armed forces. Cleland served as president from 1941 to 1946 and as chairman of the board from 1946 to 1949.

In 1943, he was elected president of the San Diego Chamber of Commerce. During his tenure, he was largely responsible for the Chamber-sponsored Day and Zimmerman Report, an authoritative analysis of San Diego's economic life. Cleland also became president of the San Diego–California Club and the Pacific Coast Electrical Association.

SDG&E president, after serving as vice president and general manager for the previous seven years. Raber's career encompassed more than 50 years in the public-utility industry. He had held a variety of positions in Ohio, Oklahoma, Iowa, Arkansas and Colorado before joining SDG&E in 1924.

Cleland also brought a diverse background to the position of president, which he held from August 25, 1941, until December 9, 1946. He began his career practicing law in Oregon and Washington, served on public-utilities commissions in the area and, prior to coming to SDG&E, served as president of the California-Oregon Power Company. Cleland took the position at a time when major changes were facing the Company and successfully guided SDG&E through the difficult war years.

The first challenge Cleland met was the change in corporate status, one of the single most important events in the Company's history. It came at a time when increasing responsibilities were being thrust upon the Company and its management. There was a pressing need for more than $4 million in additional capital to finance construction of a new high-voltage transmission line from San Diego to San Juan Capistrano, and new electric plant facilities. The 132,000-volt transmission line linked the substation at San Juan Capistrano with the new Mission substation on the north rim of Mission Valley.

This line helped to establish a 35,000-kw-capacity interconnection with Southern California Edison Company and immediately proved invaluable as electric system requirements increased 30 percent in 1941. (The total length of the line from Southern California Edison Company's Chino substation to Mission Valley was 105 miles.) In December 1940, Edison built a new 30-mile transmission line between Chino and Capistrano that connected SDG&E's system with Boulder Dam's power output. The capital to finance SDG&E's new construction projects was obtained through the sale of preferred stock in September and common stock in November 1941. These successful sales took place at an opportune time because a few short weeks later on December 7, 1941, Pearl Harbor was bombed by the Japanese. The sale would have been impossible in a wartime situation and came when the Company was facing an enormous dual responsibility to meet the crucial emergency needs of the military and provide services to the rapidly growing population.

The outbreak of war directly affected the daily operations of SDG&E personnel. Many employees were called to serve in the military, and those who remained worked long hours to meet growing customer needs. All new utility extensions were put on a priority basis, to be approved by the War Production Board, since copper wire and steel pipe were in short supply. The WPB was designed to be a "superagency," controlling government purchases of war materiel and supervising the allocation of goods and manpower. Over the next two years, electric and gas system requirements increased by about 30 percent. Despite the wartime restrictions and shortage of manpower, the Company was able to extend its services to 17,290 new gas customers and 21,269 electric customers during the war years.

San Diego Gas & Electric provided collection depots for used rubber and metal products. Employees were encouraged to conserve gasoline and tire wear on vehicles by using public transportation whenever possible. Other changes were evident because of the pressing needs of wartime. U.S. Army infantrymen were ordered to guard the substations in January 1942 against possible Japanese attack until concrete revetments, 10 feet high and 6 feet deep, could be constructed around each facility.

A total of 509 employees, including five women, saw military action during the war. Three men became prisoners of war, and four men were killed in action. During that time, copies of the Company's newsletter, *News-Meter,* were filled with information about the activities of SDG&E employees who were fighting in the war. Everyone in the Company viewed the men and women in uniform as "family" and were intensely interested in their activi-

R.F. Oddo, shops, and Len Surber, transportation, with some of the more than 4,000 pounds of rubber that employees had collected by June 1942. Employees also collected scrap copper and other vital war materials for recycling.

PATROLLING THE HIGH LINE

Carl Helm patrolled the Company's high-voltage transmission line between the San Juan Capistrano and Mission substations on horseback during the 1940s. Coverage of the 75-mile stretch over rugged country would not have been possible without the aid of Goldie, a combination Thoroughbred/saddlehorse born on the Flynn Springs ranch of Al May, assistant commercial manager. The first patrol of the line by airplane was done in 1941, but this method had to be abandoned due to military and security reasons during the war. So Carl and Goldie were called into action.

Carl was well known among ranchers and back-country people because his family were pioneers around the Warner Ranch and Montezuma Valley areas. He trained horses for the San Ysidro stock farm at one time and also worked for several years on the Rancho Santa Margarita y Las Flores.

Helm rode for two days to travel from Capistrano to Oceanside, and then another two days were necessary for the section to Mission Valley. Horses were kept for him at these three places, but his headquarters were on the Lawrence ranch in Oceanside.

"A PERIODIC PUBLICATION FOR ALL GASCO EMPLOYEES IN THE UNITED STATES ARMED FORCES"

SHORTS and Flashes
San Diego, California

Vol. 5 JANUARY 1946 No. 1

The Atom and the Army

Though our atomic bomb has startled the world, the Army probably will take it in stride. Nothing can ever quite disintegrate the Customs of the Service.

Shorts and Flashes was the Company's link to employees serving in the military during the war. The publication's staff in 1944, with Les Kobler, editor, at right. It was mailed world-wide to more than 1,600 subscribers in the various military branches.

ties and safety. SDG&E President Cleland personally corresponded with employees on military duty, and kept scrapbooks with photographs and clippings from the soldiers. He also presented a billfold containing a $100 bill to every employee entering the service.

Les Kobler, staff photographer, took pictures of family members to be sent to uniformed employees at their duty stations. Regular contact was maintained with employees on military duty by direct correspondence and the publication of a special monthly bulletin called *Shorts and Flashes.* A company welfare committee was created to assist the families left behind. Employees were assured of returning to their former jobs at the end of the war.

A WWII aircraft-spotting tower in April 1943 used to identify airplanes in the days before radar. The tower was built on a hill on the Encanto area property of employee E.W. Meise, at left, with wife Peggie Meise, chief observer, and W.S. Rockwell, observer.

Due to the increased demand for services by military, residential and commercial customers, a 48-hour workweek was instituted during the war in July 1943. The Company did not return to the standard 40-hour week until August 1945. As an industry vital to the war effort, SDG&E was mandated by the government to work extra shifts to assure a steady supply of energy to critical areas. Employees also contributed to a request by the government to have 10 percent of their pay deducted to purchase war bonds. A booth was set up in the Electric

The Company's first women meter readers, Peggy Waltner (left) and Esta Hill, went on duty in January 1943 when hundreds of male employees were on military duty. They flank veteran Joe Sanchez, who had been reading meters since April 1908. Hill began at the Company as an elevator operator.

Building at Sixth and E streets where customers and employees could purchase war bonds and stamps. SDG&E employees volunteered to serve as air-raid wardens, auxiliary firemen and policemen, fire watchers and nurses' aides. Red Cross classes were popular with the staff, and many women employees volunteered to work four-hour shifts at night at the U.S. Army's aircraft-warning service center.

SDG&E employees experienced a number of changes as duties traditionally assigned to men were shifted to female staff members. The Company's first women meter readers, Peggy Waltner and Esta Hill, went on duty in January 1943. The first "girl" draftsman was Alyne LeGrand, who had started with the Company in 1942 as a messenger and received a promotion in April 1943. Four years of art training and an aptitude for difficult lettering won her a job in the Record Department as a gas-map recorder.

Alyne LeGrand, the Company's first woman draftsman, started as a messenger in November 1942. She drew gas-pipe maps, and cartoons for *Shorts and Flashes* and the Women's Committee publications.

The work force also expanded to include married women on a permanent basis. In the years before Pearl Harbor, the Company did not hire married women unless they had been employed prior to the Depression, when this ruling went into effect. (The rule was never applied to widows.) When the war was over in 1945, the decision was made to allow married women to keep their positions in the Company. The women had proven to be capable and diligent in their new responsibilities and constituted a significant force within the Company.

Facilities were upgraded to meet the new expectations dictated by the war effort. Several floors of the Electric Building, which housed SDG&E's main office, were remodeled to relieve overcrowding. A new house turbine and additional boiler capacity were installed at Station B power plant, the main generating station, to bring the unit to its 102,000-kw limit of production potential.

In June 1942, the prestigious Charles A. Coffin Award was presented to the Company in recognition of its achievements during the initial months of World War II. The following paragraphs appeared in "Insignia," a nationally circulated U.S. Navy publication:

Although the spotlight of production has been entirely on the spectacular war industries, the community services which had to keep pace in order to avoid a complete breakdown of living standards, as well as aiding materially in the war effort by keeping up with the new heavy demands of industry working night and day, quietly performed miraculous feats of their own.

Consider, for instance, the problems dumped into the laps of public utility concerns of a city such as San Diego, which grew from 203,341 in the 1940 census to approximately 350,000 in two and one-half years. Failure to meet the electric and gas power needs of both industrial and home consumers would have crippled the war effort of such an important production center. Because the San Diego Gas & Electric Company was able, through wise foresight, to anticipate the demands on it, the Charles A. Coffin Award, most honored symbol of accomplishment in the electric light and power industry, was conferred on it during the past year, 1942. Thus, those who serve on the sidelines have their "E" awards, too, on the home front.

During the war years, 1941-1945, the annual electric-system peak load

OLD TIMERS ASSOCIATION

The Old Timers Association was founded in 1942 by Hance Cleland, SDG&E president. His purpose was to recognize employees, both active and retired, who had been employed for more than 25 years at SDG&E. He compiled a constitution and by-laws and organized the first series of meetings. After World War II, when servicemen returned and the employee work force returned to normal, the organization came under the operation of the employees.

Active and retired employees comprise the group's membership roster, now totaling more than 1,000 retired members and more than 700 active members. The annual dinner meeting features a program and a door prize. In the early years, the door prizes were usually something useful, such as an appliance. But Cleland was known for his sense of humor, and sometimes rather unusual gifts were personally selected by him for special guests.

Many of the retired employees have moved away, so reservations for the annual dinner come from all parts of the country. A chance to see old friends and remember the good times is an important occasion for employees, and the dinners normally welcome 1,000-plus guests. Once a member of the SDG&E family, always a member!

The first Gasco Old Timers Association meeting in January 1942 attracted more than a hundred employees and guests.

The Charles A. Coffin award was given to the Company for its achievement during WWII.

Silver Gate Power Plant, in late 1942, shortly before the first generation unit was completed. The plant was built under special War Department priority to supply electricity to San Diego's war industry.

increased 55 percent, reaching 169,000 kw in 1945. Each of the peaks exceeded the Company's generating capacity, and SDG&E had to rely on purchased power obtained through existing interconnections with other systems. By 1942, these interconnections were furnishing 53 percent of the power, and Station B, operating at peak capacity, was generating 47 percent of the total kilowatt-hour requirements. Bay dredging, associated largely with defense projects, accounted for increases in the sale of power. Three electric dredges consumed enough energy to equal the needs of a community of 12,000 people. The dredging would not have been possible without the increased capacity created by the expansion of facilities.

Fortunately, while facing possible wartime restrictions and the demands on its generating capability, SDG&E had decided to build the Silver Gate power station at the foot of Sampson Street, two miles up the bay from Station B. Construction of the plant was started well before war was declared on December 8, 1941. Continuation of the project was given wartime approval and priority. Without the power plant, there certainly would have been a critical shortage of electric power during the remaining years of the war.

Construction of the $4 million first unit of the Silver Gate generating station was completed in January 1943 and contained a 35,000-kw turbo-generator. The turbo-generator was rated at 35,000 kw but generated approximately 44,000 kw in actual use. The 3,600-rpm hydrogen-cooled turbine was fed by two Babcock and Wilcox boilers with steam supplied at a pressure of 850 pounds per square inch and a temperature of 900 degrees Fahrenheit. Over the next several years, three more units were constructed until the facility was completed in 1952.

Generator and steam turbine of the Silver Gate Unit 1. This unit was the first of the now-standard boiler and turbine-generator design to be constructed by the Company. All the boilers and generators at Station B were constructed in a "ship" design, meaning the steam from almost any boiler could be piped to any generator. A modern power-plant unit has one boiler driving one turbine-generator set.

Bill New, electric repair shop, paints out part of a streetlight in June 1942 as part of the military dim-out campaign for coastal streetlights. Later in the war, New was a B-17 co-pilot and was shot down over Germany in November 1944. He was taken prisoner but was liberated in May 1945.

Several features made Silver Gate a breakthrough in technological production. The station used salt water for condensation of the turbine exhaust steam. The salt water was brought from San Diego Bay through twin tunnels approximately 750 feet long. The traveling water screens were located immediately outside the station, instead of in a separate screen house at the waterfront, like Station B.

The station building was one of the few windowless power plants in the United States at the time. Air for ventilation and combustion was provided by electrically driven fans. The administration building, with a few windows, provided office, laboratory and storeroom facilities. The turbine itself was located on an "island" (a separate section of the floor in an open space) to prevent the transmission of vibration to the rest of the station.

To save essential ground space, the station's companion Sampson substation was built on the common roof of three underground fuel-oil storage tanks. Specially constructed concrete columns built within the tanks supported the weight of the 50,000-kw substation.

Customers benefited from the increased capacity created by the opening of Silver Gate but found their usage curtailed due to wartime dim-outs and blackouts deemed necessary by the U.S. government. San Diego, along with all other coastal cities of the United States, was subject to these orders. Blackouts were necessary to prevent the silhouetting of ships against lighted land areas, thus making them more visible to the enemy as night targets. The naval order required that all lights that could be seen from the ocean be shielded so as not to cast direct rays seaward or upward.

Thousands of street lamps had to be partially blacked-out with paint, in varying degrees, while at the same time saving as much light as possible for public convenience and safety. The top half of car headlights had to be painted over, and speed limits on city streets were substantially lowered because visibility was lessened from the streetlights and headlights. "Groundglow" and "skyglow" were words that became very familiar to San Diegans as they attempted to comply with federal regulations. The dim-outs were estimated to be more than 90 percent effective during the critical years with a high level of local cooperation.

Consumers found it almost impossible to purchase new appliances because the production and sale of electric and gas appliances was extremely limited. Appliance factories were converted to manufacture war materials, and metal and rubber were used to produce needed war supplies. The

Company closed its own appliance sales rooms and diverted its remaining stock to other appliance dealers. The entire appliance sales department was then converted into a customer-service organization. People were encouraged through advertising campaigns and promotional brochures to keep their appliances in good working order because no new ones were going to be available for consumers until the war was over. It was readily apparent to Company executives that with no new appliances being produced, residential revenues would soon decline unless customers kept their existing equipment in usable condition.

Betty Lewis sews another star onto the Company's Minuteman flag in 1944. The flag symbolized war-bond participation by more than 90 percent of the employees.

Newspaper ads were used to tell customers how to care for and use appliances properly. This publicity was supplemented by class instruction and circulation of a consumer textbook. Information on how to perform simple tasks, such as reading meters, replacing burned-out fuses and repairing electric motors, helped customers keep their appliances functional. The sales department familiarized customers with governmental orders limiting their use of services, meter setting, extension of lines, dim-outs and blackouts, and which price regulations would be enforced to control the sale and repair of appliances by dealers.

All these activities were considered necessary to keep home appliances functioning at a high level. Inoperable appliances would not only affect the overall revenue of the Company due to lack of energy sales but could possibly impair the health and safety of the public. Many advertising campaigns conducted by the government advocated the need for nutritious meals and a

Every effort was used to push the war effort. A float carrying a mock billboard at the March 1944 War Show was the Company's contribution to the show's "Stay on the Job and finish the Job" theme.

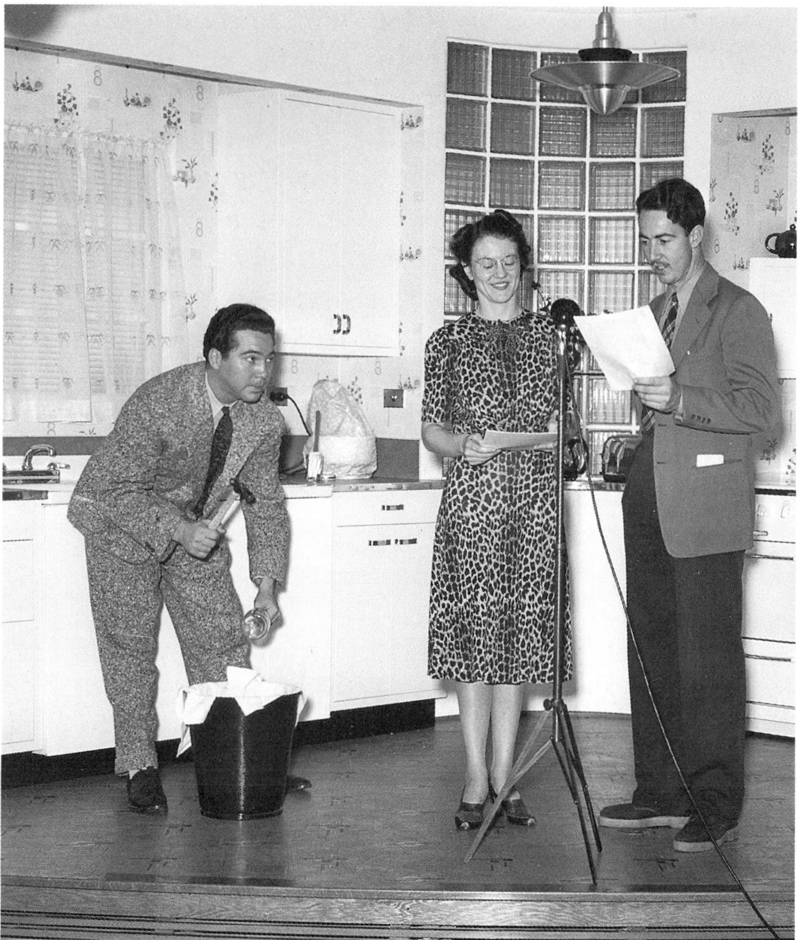

The Company's Diets for Defense radio program was broadcast for much of the war from the Company's kitchens in the Electric Building. Company home economist Mildred Kier Townsend was aided on the air by sound-effects specialist Jim Gibson (left) and Terry O'Sullivan, both of radio station KGB.

safe home environment to keep war workers healthy, thus maintaining maximum efficiency at the defense plants.

In addition to providing customers with appliance information, the Company offered homemakers classes in new techniques in canning, food preservation and nutritional information through its Home Economics Department. Weekly demonstrations held by Mildred Kier Townsend, Company home economist, and her successor, Lucile Grant, in the Company's model kitchen drew capacity crowds. Help was available by telephone for those who could not attend in person.

Because of rationing of items such as meat, sugar, butter and other staples, housewives found themselves limited when they turned to the cupboard to prepare dinner for their families. Many families planted victory gardens to grow wholesome, inexpensive food for their table and benefited from the advice given to them by SDG&E's home economists. Women could always find a "friend" at SDG&E to assist them in finding ways to stretch a limited food dollar and fix appealing, nutritionally sound meals for their families in times of rationing and shortages.

On January 30, 1943, a $262,900 reduction in both gas and electric rates was announced for the San Diego area. The largest cut was in gas rates—

residential customers would save about $158,700; industrial and military users, $42,500. Electric-rate reductions amounted to $61,700—$59,000 for military establishments and $2,700 for shipbuilders.

Despite the drop in rates, the gains in the number of customers and in the resulting energy sales brought an increase in profits to SDG&E in 1944. The easing of government restrictions on electric extensions, coupled with increased production by factories, boosted electricity sales. Many new customers were connected in the urban and rural areas. The farming districts were encouraged to produce more food, which increased the demand for power for irrigation.

Because of increased water needs in the area, the San Diego County Water Authority was organized on June 9, 1944, for the express purpose of importing water from the Colorado River. President Franklin Roosevelt, cognizant

Signboard urged electric refrigeration in 1941.

Gertrude Ohlran, National City office, works under a watchful Reddy Kilowatt war poster in 1942.

San Diegans rejoiced when banner headlines announced the end of the war. The Company's efforts to aid the war industry were quickly switched to fulfilling new civilian demands.

of San Diego's key military role, approved the recommendations of a local committee that an aqueduct connecting the San Diego city water system to the Metropolitan Water District Colorado River aqueduct be constructed at government expense. Although construction began on September 1, 1945, under supervision of the U.S. Navy, the aqueduct did not begin operating until December 11, 1947.

Gas sales also increased with the construction both of governmental and private housing projects in 1944. The main reason for higher gas sales, however, was the colder weather that prevailed throughout much of the year. This boosted gas use for house-heating purposes, and the cooler temperatures were also favorable to the increased steam sales for commercial heating.

Germany surrendered to the Allies in April 1945, ending the European phase of the war. Finally, the event everyone had prayed for took place on August 8, 1945, with the surrender of Japan to Allied forces. The most devastating war in the history of the world was over, opening an inevitable period of restless adjustment to peacetime conditions. The ending of the war brought concerns about how San Diego would weather the change from a high-gear, wartime economy to a reduced-pace, peacetime economy. Al-

R.E. FARWELL

Among the many employees who have served in military conflicts dating back to the Civil War, R.E. Farwell, who worked in the Company's commercial section, holds the distinction of having been aboard the U.S.S. Ward when it fired the first shot of World War II on December 7, 1941. The ship sunk a submarine attempting to enter Pearl Harbor. Three years later, Farwell was commanding officer of the U.S.S. Ward when it was sunk in action off the Philippine coast on December 7, 1944, without losing any of its crew.

With the war over, Company workers faced a mountain of backlogged maintenance and expansion work, like the laying of this new 12,000-volt underwater power cable to serve Coronado. This was the fifth cable to serve the harbor community when it was installed in March 1946.

though most community leaders were confident that the economy would right itself eventually, a decline in sales and revenue was expected in all quarters.

Local leaders anticipated that a sizable portion of the population employed in the military and the war industries would leave the community at the end of the war. A considerable number of these people from other parts of the country did leave the area at the close of the conflict. After having experienced life in sunny San Diego and enjoying the beautiful surroundings, many wartime workers and servicemen from other parts of the country later returned with their families to make San Diego their permanent home.

Trading in his uniform for mufti (civilian clothes) is Lee Lambert of the personnel department. He spent 21 months in the Navy during the war before rejoining the Company in late 1945. This photo was taken by Les Kobler, Company photographer at the time.

To take advantage of the anticipated postwar lull, and to keep its returning servicemen busy in the short term, the Company planned to catch up on maintenance projects that had accumulated during the war and to make a number of desired changes in the electric transmission and distribution system. The local experts were wrong in their estimations, and the economy recovered in a matter of months. The return to a strong civilian economy forced postponement of most of SDG&E's maintenance projects. The upsurge also delayed construction of planned changes in the electric system and kept the entire roster of employees working at top speed to meet the huge demand for gas and electric service. During the war, applications for service numbered in the thousands because of the influx of workers, and many times it was impossible to connect service to these new customers. Many of the requests came from the outlying areas where new line construction had to take place before service could be connected. The Company anticipated a $40 million expansion program between August

With the end of the war, the manufacture and sale of appliances was restarted. Displays like this one in the window of Umbargers Radio Store in East San Diego were soon replaced with the real thing.

1945 and the end of 1948 to accommodate the demands for service.

Revenue from wartime industries declined sharply in 1946 as large numbers of government contracts were canceled, but the decline was more than offset by increased business from old and new customers, including a large number of commercial concerns established immediately after the war.

The Company's customer gains surged, and during the first four postwar years, services were extended to 37,126 new electric and 21,269 new gas customers. Not all customers had immediate service because a shortage of trained linemen and construction materials slowed the pace of installations. To augment the numbers of available linemen, the Company organized and conducted its own apprentice lineman training program. The Company also returned to a 40-hour workweek after two years of working on a 48-hour workweek basis.

On July 1, 1945, the War Production Board allowed appliance manufacturers to begin making a limited number of appliances. The board authorized the production of 700,000 washing machines, 265,000 refrigerators and 500,000 irons. Gas ranges (which had been manufactured on a small scale throughout the war but were available only on priority) continued to be manufactured on a limited basis. The production of electric ranges and electric water heaters was still very limited because those items used critical materials. San Diego, along with other coastal cities, was in a particularly difficult situation to receive new appliances. All available warehouse space was utilized by the military, and freight transportation to the West was slow and unreliable.

Because of steel and copper shortages caused by the war, the Company experimented with plastic gas pipe. George Day holds pipe at the Pacific Beach residence where it was first tried in December 1946. Plastic pipe is widely used today.

An announcement by Company officials in December 1945 indicated that the phenomenal war growth was a permanent feature of life in San Diego. SDG&E planned an $8 million expansion program to add new generating and distribution facilities to the system. Funds totaling $5.75 million were earmarked for the purchase and installation of a 50,000-kw steam-operated generator, the largest on the system for Silver Gate Unit 2. An additional several million dollars were allocated for improvement of existing distribution facilities and extensions of service into rural areas, such as Borrego Springs. A new substation to adjoin Silver Gate was built, in addition to a new 66-kv substation at Station B power plant.

The new Unit No. 2 generator was housed in an addition to the Silver Gate station. Purchased from General Electric, the equipment was shipped in the spring of 1947 and required construction of a special spur track. This line was necessary to move the heavy generator section directly from the railway cars to the foundation where the generator would sit. Six railway cars were required to carry the main generator sections, while more than 100 cars were needed to transport the allied parts, boilers, condensers, switches, pumps, gears and the crane, which was built within the power plant.

Silver Gate Units 3 and 4, scheduled for operation in 1950 and 1952, were already in the planning stages. Land for the entire Silver Gate station of four units had been purchased at the time of construction for Unit No. 1, and due to the size of the parcel, further expansion at Silver Gate beyond the four units was not possible. Further expansion of SDG&E's capacity would take place at its third generating station, Encina. Plans for Encina were begun during 1946–1947, and land was purchased south of Carlsbad in 1947.

The land for the Encina Station was located on the oceanfront just south of the Hedionda Creek outlet, bounded on the east by the railroad right-of-way. This site was selected because of the large quantities of water needed for cooling at a steam-electric generating plant and because long-term, large-scale growth was anticipated in the North County area.

Construction at Encina did not start until 1954 because efforts to increase generating capacity were focused on the Silver Gate station for several years. Completion of Silver Gate was the first priority, then construction would begin on Encina. The 110-acre site in Carlsbad was suitable for a sizable facility, and plans were made to make Encina the Company's largest generating station.

Other changes took place in the postwar years, reflecting the Company's desire to meet the new challenges ahead. In a move to redistribute executive responsibilities, the board of directors created the office of chairman of the board at the December 1946 meeting. SDG&E President Hance H. Cleland was named to this new full-time position, and Laurence M. Klauber was

LAURENCE MONROE KLAUBER

Laurence Klauber, born in San Diego on December 21, 1883, was the son of Bohemian-born Abraham Klauber who emigrated to the United States in 1849 and traveled to California in 1852 by way of Nicaragua. Laurence attended Sherman Elementary School and was graduated from San Diego's Russ High School in 1903. He worked for Klauber Wangenheim in Los Angeles before attending Stanford University, where he received a B.A. in electrical engineering in 1908. Laurence began work as a salesman for San Diego Consolidated Gas & Electric Company in January 1911, the same year in which he married his high-school classmate, Grace Gould. They had two children, Alice and Philip.

In 1912, Klauber became engineer in charge of the Record Department. He moved steadily upward in the Company, becoming general superintendent in 1920, vice president in charge of operations in 1932, vice president and general manager in 1941, president in 1946, and chairman of the board and chief executive officer from April 1949 until retirement in January 1954. Well organized and hardworking, Klauber always answered his own telephone and was known for his good sense of humor. He wrote humorous poems for many Company occasions.

Klauber's deep interest in San Diego and in his profession led him to join many organizations. He was a member of the San Diego Electric Club, the major professional engineering societies, a fellow of the American Institute of Electrical Engineers, and chairman of the city's Library Commission from 1940 until his death in 1968. Klauber's interest in the study of reptiles encouraged him to become the San Diego Zoological Society's first curator of reptiles.

Son Phil Klauber, also an engineering graduate of Stanford University, joined the Company in 1963 and served as vice president, customer services from 1965 to his retirement in 1980. Phil served as president of the San Diego Historical Society from 1984 to 1986. Grandson David Miller, son of daughter Alice and her husband David Miller, began working for SDG&E in 1980, continuing the Klauber family tradition since 1911.

A gas pipeline, bringing gas from Texas, was rushed to completion after the cold weather of 1949. In this photo the pipe is ready for laying into the trench in the hills north of Mission Valley.

elected president. Klauber would remain in this post until April 26, 1949, when he became chairman of the board.

Succeeding Klauber as president was Asher E. Holloway, an SDG&E employee since 1910. One of Holloway's first positions had been connected with the Company's initial extension of service to the rural areas in 1911 when 10 miles of line were installed from La Mesa through El Cajon to Santee. He was appointed manager of new business in 1911, commercial superintendent in 1921 and vice president in charge of sales in 1932.

Natural-gas supply development had reached new highs during the postwar years under Klauber's direction. The Company was concerned during this time about the narrow margins between peak-load demands and the capacity to serve rapidly increasing consumer needs. The Company's principal supply of natural gas was a 90-mile pipeline tapping Southern Counties Gas Company's transmission system at Huntington Beach with a daily delivery capacity of 33 million cubic feet.

Another major construction project, a second pipeline from the north, got under way in early 1946. Preliminary engineering plans were begun for a 50-mile, 16-inch pipeline to be built from the San Diego County line near Rainbow to Mission Valley, connecting San Diego to the famed 30-inch, "Biggest Inch" pipeline that brought natural gas from Texas to the Los Angeles area. The "Biggest Inch" project was a cooperative effort between Southern California Gas Company and Southern Counties Gas Company. The transmission pipeline was capable of delivering 40 million cubic feet of gas per day to San Diego.

SDG&E negotiated with its supplier, Southern Counties Gas Company, for an allotment of the new supply. The latter agreed to construct a 16-inch, 35-mile transmission pipeline north from the Rainbow area of San Diego County to the tap near Moreno in Riverside County. SDG&E would then

Workers hastily built this gas holder in El Cajon to supplement the winter gas demands that were taxing the existing system of pipes and gas plant.

complete the section from Rainbow to Mission Valley. Steel pipe was not readily available due to a nationwide shortage, and the project was temporarily shelved. Construction plans were resumed two years later when an allotment of steel was allocated to the Company, and the first deliveries of fabricated pipe arrived in the spring of 1949.

San Diegans experienced one of the coldest winters in San Diego history, starting early in 1949. A wave of freezing temperatures arrived unexpectedly during the first week of January and remained for about four weeks. During the night of January 4, when the temperature dropped to 29 degrees (only the third time in San Diego's history of weather records), the gas sendout soared to 54 million cubic feet, a peak from which the company could not recover until the following day. San Diegans tried to cope with the weather by turning up the heat, causing a maximum demand on the system. The gas manufacturing plant, though old and obsolete, functioned at maximum capacity for a prolonged period, averting a major crisis during the emergency created by the freeze.

With every source of gas strained to its limit, including the gas manufacturing plant, fuel reserves were nearly depleted. A gas emergency was declared, and various measures went into effect to protect San Diegans from the cold spell. Customers were asked to economize in their use of gas for heating. On the stormy night of January 10, 1949, an area shutdown was

This steam locomotive from the San Diego & Arizona Eastern Railway was hooked into the gas manufacturing plant at Station A to help meet the unexpected cold-weather demands of January 1949. The locomotive's steam was needed to manufacture gas from oil.

A worker cleans ice and snow from the steps of City Hall in January 1949. It was only the third time in recorded history that snow had fallen on San Diego.

narrowly avoided when the peak gas load climbed to 56.3 million cubic feet.

This same rain-soaked night, customers consumed more electric power than in any other 24-hour period of the Company's history. Despite the fact that the system was overloaded by the use of more than 250,000 kilowatts, there were no major power failures. In the city of San Diego, only 16 small transformers burned out. Distribution lines to Lake Henshaw and Lake Cuyamaca were out for brief periods, and a freak lightning strike in Oceanside caused a short disruption in service during the early morning hours.

Heavy rainfall during the freezing days added an extra dimension to the cold snap, and on January 12, the streets of San Diego were covered with snow! Many schools were closed because of the snow, and students from outlying areas faced transportation problems. Libraries were forced to take a "holiday" and closed due to an emergency gas curtailment. La Jolla librarians wore gloves to serve patrons as they struggled to keep the library open. Small oil burners were used to maintain services in as many libraries as possible.

While the "big freeze" was still prominent in everyone's memory, the materials necessary for the Rainbow to Mission Valley pipeline were delivered in the spring of 1949. Construction on the $5 million second pipeline began in July 1949 and was completed in November 1949. The new line's daily capacity—40 million cubic feet—more than doubled the supply of natural gas previously available to the county. At the San Diego terminus of the new 16-inch line, the company built a propane-air mixing plant to replace the old manufacturing plant as a stand-by reserve source of gas. The propane-air plant was capable of producing about 87 million cubic feet of gas from the one-million gallons of propane liquid stored nearby at the "tank farm."

The $1.3 million auxiliary propane "tank farm" was built in Mission Valley near Murphy Canyon in order to assure an adequate supply of gas. The 36 steel tanks contained more than a million gallons of propane when filled to their full 90-foot height. This provided a reserve of 70 million cubic feet of gas, to be drawn on in case of an emergency arising from failure of one or both of the natural-gas pipelines that served the local community. The tanks were arranged in two rows standing above ground, and a conversion plant was built a short distance away.

With the new pipeline in operation and the tank farm ready for backup supply, the gas manufacturing plant was dismantled in 1950. The plant had served the Company well during the freeze of '49, but now the technology had progressed to the point that the facility was no longer viable.

The Company had weathered the tumultuous World War II era because of the solid base created during the previous 60 years of operation. Nevertheless, the postwar years taxed its resources heavily. New, increased demands for electrical power were met by additions to the existing substations and construction of transmission gas lines to provide ample supplies from sources outside the county. During the second half of the decade, 1,741 miles of new pole line were added to the electric distribution system, mainly in the

ASHER E. HOLLOWAY

Asher E. "Doc" Holloway began his 41-year career with San Diego Gas & Electric Company as a salesman in 1910. Born on a farm near Colfax, Indiana, Holloway graduated from Purdue University in 1908 with a degree in electrical engineering. After college, he entered the Westinghouse apprenticeship course and came to San Diego upon completion of this training.

Holloway joined San Diego Consolidated Gas & Electric Company as manager of new business in 1911, and was commercial superintendent from 1921 until his election as vice president in charge of sales in 1932. From 1949 to 1951 he served as president of the Company.

Holloway was a long-time member of the Pacific Coast Electric and Gas Associations, serving as president of the Gas Association. In addition, he was elected president of the San Diego Chamber of Commerce and sat on its board of directors for 14 years. He founded both the Bureau of Home Appliances of San Diego County and the Electric Club of San Diego.

A trench was dug across the San Diego River in Mission Valley to install pipe.

After meeting the winter demand of 1949, the veteran Station A gas manufacturing plant was torn down in the summer of 1950. Both the new gas pipeline from Riverside County and gas storage facilities made the plant unnecessary after more than 60 years of use.

rural areas. Service was extended to far corners of the county to assist agriculture that was responding to the need for expanded food supplies.

The agricultural crops produced in the county totaled more than $55 million annually by 1949. During the year, more than 3,400 new homes were started in the San Diego vicinity, and approximately 1,000 new businesses began or moved into this region. More than 160 public, private and parochial schools served the educational needs of the rapidly growing community as the postwar "baby boom" began its upward climb.

During 1949, San Diego began the development of Mission Bay, a $23 million project, giving the city a prime tourist attraction. Expansions were planned for all parts of the county as the postwar prosperity took hold, leading the region into the decade of the 1950s. San Diego, whose climate had always attracted large numbers of visitors, continued as a prime destination for travelers. The convention and visitor industry took its place as a major business alongside the fishing and agricultural industries in the county.

The area's growth and that of San Diego Gas & Electric Company were inextricably linked. Each contributed significantly to the progress and development of the other. The changes and demands both faced in the 1940s would be far surpassed by the challenges to come in the 1950s. To keep up with new demands for service, SDG&E would soon explore alternative sources of power to meet future customer needs.

The Reddy Kiloettes of 1945 upheld the Company's winning traditions in its first season of play. Team members (from left) Cleo Heathon (captain), Miriam Hurst, "Skip" Hansen, Bessie Parchen, Pat DeBurn, Gloria Stewart, Wilma Kregear, Irma Iszler and Grace Bingham.

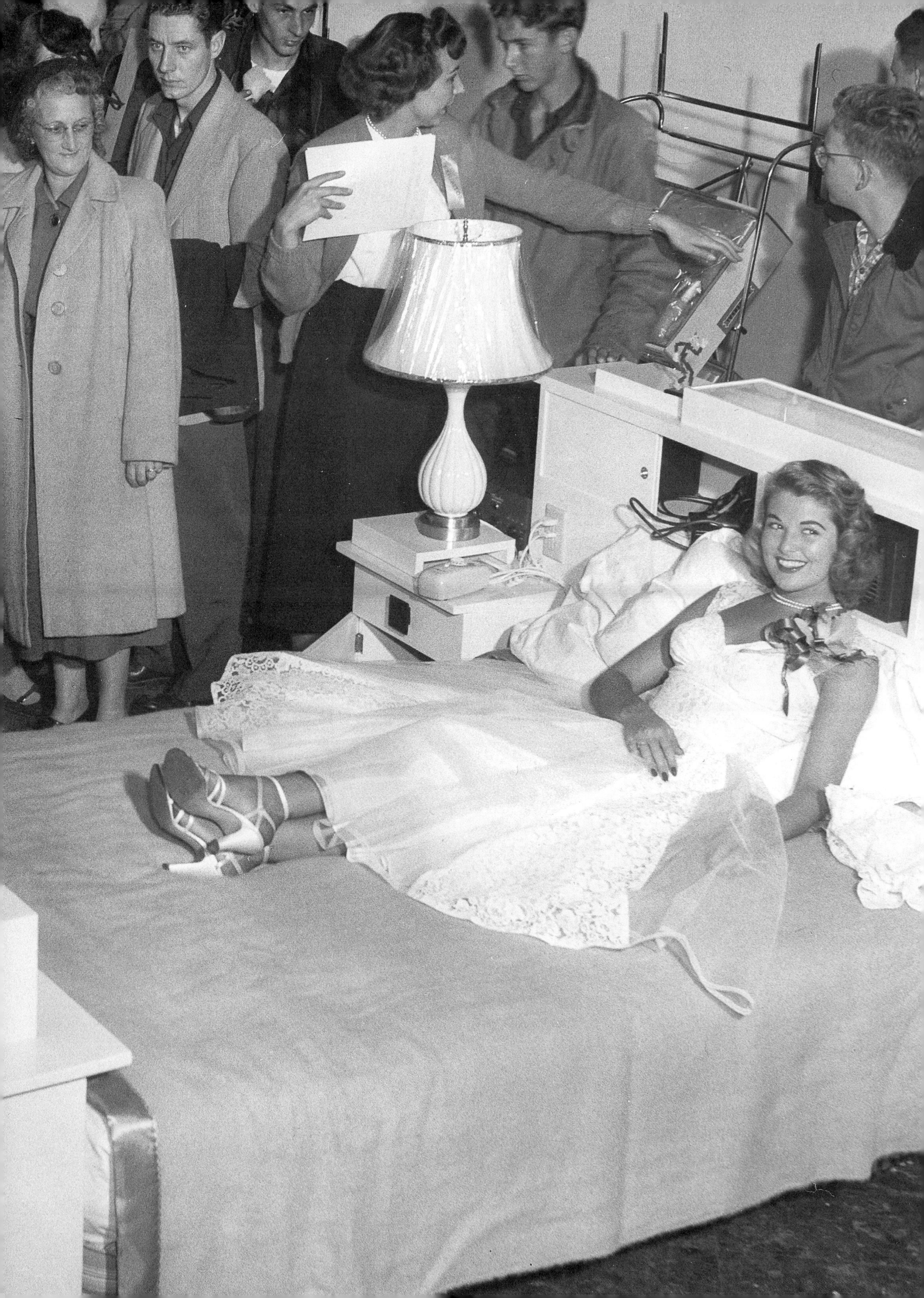

Chapter 8

1951-1960
Lighting the Way

San Diego's population maintained its pattern of growth even after the frenzy of wartime development lessened. During the 1950s, the increasing popularity of the automobile offered greater mobility to residents and contributed to the geographical expansion of the area. As retail shopping centers developed in the suburbs, SDG&E's energy services kept pace without interruption. A public utility such as SDG&E, when compared to other types of companies, has more than the usual interest in the growth of the community it serves. Not only is that community the home of its workers, each resident and business is also a customer of this unique industry. As the community grows, slow at times, faster at others, the local utility has an obligation to meet energy needs. Planning, therefore, is the key to continued success.

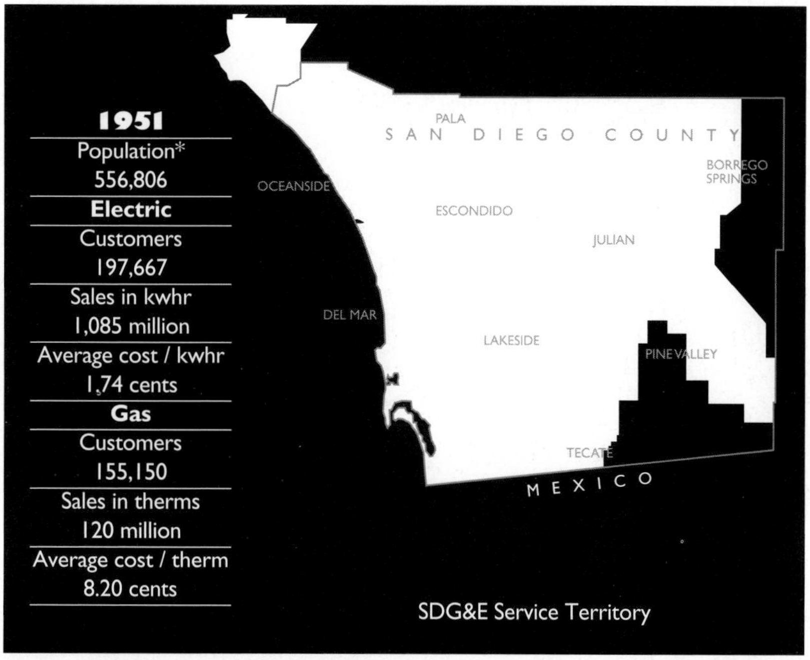

1951
Population*
556,806
Electric
Customers
197,667
Sales in kwhr
1,085 million
Average cost / kwhr
1,74 cents
Gas
Customers
155,150
Sales in therms
120 million
Average cost / therm
8.20 cents

SDG&E Service Territory

*County population based on census 10-year estimates

Growth is usually considered an indication of community stability and strength, and by 1951 San Diego ranked 31st in population in the entire nation. This growth had been stimulated by the presence of the various military installations and defense and shipbuilding industries, which provided a solid employment base and a major boost to the local economy.

In addition, San Diego's industrial expansion program was designed to create additional employment opportunities for an expanding populace. Major aircraft industries—Convair, Rohr, Ryan and Solar—employed thousands of people in fulfilling defense contracts. During the 1950s, the Kearny Mesa Industrial Tract began attracting diversified light industry to the county. Eighteen electronics firms were based in the county, and it was expected that the area would become a major national electronics center.

< Miss California, Joanne Durant, tries out the Company's $1,000 Magic Bed at the November 1950 Electric Show. The bed, a showpiece for consumer appliances, included an electric blanket, coffee maker, clock, two reading lamps, night lights, telephone plug, heating pad, electric razor, radio, vibrator, sun lamps and a television with remote control.

San Diego on December 30, 1953, was dominated by the open space of Balboa Park. In less than 10 years, freeways would crisscross the city, and homes would fill many of the vacant spaces visible here.

The presence of the military and defense-oriented companies alone did not make the region prosper. The county was also an important agricultural area, growing various fruits such as lemons, oranges and avocados in short supply elsewhere, as well as products that were considered off-season in other regions. San Diego was 20th in agricultural production among more than 3,000 counties in the United States. The temperate climate of the county was a major boon to farmers and ranchers, allowing them to produce crops year-round.

San Diego's scenic bay and harbor areas provided a safe anchorage and home port for its large tuna fleet and shipping industry. The bay also attracted boating enthusiasts, pleasure and commercial, and was a draw for tourists and conventions. San Diego's mild winters and pleasant summers attracted visitors throughout the year and made it a popular retirement area.

Development of the area led to an increased net income for SDG&E, a larger physical plant, and more employees and customers than at any point in the Company's history. Reductions in operating expenses occurred because of the natural-gas transmission pipeline completed in the fall of 1949. The new line allowed the Company to use a greater proportion of gas, as compared with fuel oil, as a power-plant fuel. Gas was a significantly more economical fuel. In addition, the need to generate artificial gas during a crisis, such as in the disastrously cold winter of 1949, was averted. The Company had been forced to sell the expensive gas at a loss during 1949.

By the end of 1951, SDG&E was serving a total of 155,150 gas and 197,667 electric customers, representing a 78 percent increase since 1940. During the same period, the population of San Diego County increased more than 85 percent with rural areas showing the greatest overall gain.

The South Bay area was one of the fastest-growing sections of the county. New communities, such as Palm City, rose in short order to meet the needs of families in search of a suburban home and a pleasant place to raise their children. A population boom began during the postwar period, and record-breaking new-housing starts continued the trend that had begun in 1941 as newcomers flooded into San Diego County. In La Mesa alone, more than 3,000 homes were completed in 1951. This type of growth was taking place all over the county. Accompanying this rapid residential development was a corresponding increase in churches, schools, libraries, shopping centers and medical facilities, all with their individual energy requirements.

To meet the energy needs of an expanding population and to improve its service, SDG&E enlarged its facilities. A new 50,000-kilowatt, turbo-electric generating unit had been placed into operation in September 1950, and work continued on Unit 4 at the Silver Gate power station. New electric transmission and gas distribution lines and substations were constructed throughout SDG&E's territory, particularly in the rural areas. As gas distribution lines were extended to Bostonia, Palm City and Imperial Beach, an innovative technique—aerial photography—aided the effort.

Normally the routing of distribution mains through areas is influenced by the number and grouping of homes, the patterns of streets and topographical features. The footwork involved routinely took months. Aerial photography allowed planners to have a bird's-eye view of the affected area. The photographs provided enough information for a tentative mapping of the proposed route. The final routing of gas lines

Rapid expansion of the electric transmission system was needed to distribute the electricity coming from the new power plant at Encina. This August 1954 photo shows work in the area between Mission Valley and Carlsbad.

Fueling the rising demand for energy was a new range of postwar appliances. Gas stoves were popular and attracted celebrity endorsements, such as this 1951 display poster.

depended on how residents wanted service, a question answered by commercial department employees, who took the applications for service.

A vigorous postwar program of advertising and sales promotion by the Company was designed to aid the Bureau of Home Appliances and appliance dealers and distributors in SDG&E territory. This effort contributed to an all-time high volume of $37 million in appliance sales by local dealers, a jump from $16 million in sales in 1949. These sales created an increase in gas and electricity demands in homes, and the trend continued throughout the next three decades. New homeowners in the mushrooming suburbs were steady customers of appliance dealers. The dream of the 1950s was to have a home in the suburbs with a sparkling kitchen filled with time-saving appliances.

During the 1950s, a 25-ton, $40,000 mobile-unit substation, with a capacity of 6,000 kilowatts, quickly became one of the most useful and valuable pieces of equipment owned by the electric transmission and distribution department. The mobile unit was built especially for SDG&E by General Electric and could literally do the work of any one of the 21 substations on the Company's 69,000-volt transmission system. The huge substation on wheels was used to facilitate substation maintenance. It transformed high voltage for local distribution to customers when the permanent transformer was de-energized for routine maintenance. The mobile unit was also capable of substituting for regular substation equipment in an emergency or when repairs were needed.

Helping with the planning for new power lines was this 1954 DC calculating board, operated by Bill Davis (left) and Ray Ganzer. The board could be made to simulate current flow in the electric system.

Innovative ideas of all types were put into practice during the decade. Automobile drivers in San Diego were treated to the largest single installation of mercury-vapor traffic-safety lighting in California during this period through a cooperative effort between SDG&E and the State Division of Highways. The 138 lights went up along the Cabrillo Freeway and were placed at points where traffic merged, separated or crossed. The lamps were twice as efficient as the incandescent lamps commonly used at this time for street lighting. A 485-watt incandescent lamp, the largest size available, delivered 10,000 lumens or 1,000 candlepower. A 400-watt mercury-vapor lamp delivered twice as much candlepower but used less energy. In 1955, the new lamps were in use on Broadway, the first San Diego street to be lighted by the mercury-vapor system. A special pageant depicting the three phases of lighting was staged by SDG&E on August 2 for the crowds that gathered to witness the lighting of the new lamps.

As the decade of the 1950s opened, another international crisis, the Korean War, brought renewed conflict to a nation weary of war and turmoil. The military and defense needs generated by the Korean War created new

The Company installed new mercury vapor lighting on Broadway in 1954. This view looks west from Seventh Avenue.

demands on SDG&E as once again a vital defense industry relied on the Company for its energy requirements. San Diego's firms had gained a national reputation in the production of stainless-steel engine components for aircraft. The power needs of these aircraft plants and military installations during the Korean conflict exceeded the requirements generated during World War II. Public utilities often found it difficult to make long-range plans in time of great national crises, but due to SDG&E's careful planning and anticipation of shortages, equipment for both the Silver Gate and Encina power plants had been ordered long before it was actually needed.

The heavy dependence on SDG&E's energy services became abundantly clear at 12:55 p.m., September 27, 1951. Lights and power in the county failed, and service was not restored until 5:14 p.m. the same day. Virtually all industry and most businesses in the vast area from Tijuana to the Orange County line, and from the ocean to the desert, were abruptly halted or seriously impaired when trouble developed at the Silver Gate Power Plant.

SILVER GATE POWER PLANT

Silver Gate's history of electric production began on January 27, 1943, when Unit 1 was placed in operation. Unit 2 went on line in May 1948, and by September 1950, Unit 3 was fully operational. The completion of the Silver Gate station took place when Unit 4 was officially placed into operation on September 22, 1952. The name-plate ratings of the four generating units totaled 185,000 kw, but under full-load conditions, the four units could generate about 242,000 kw. The operation of Unit 4 brought the Company's total generating capability to 404,000 kw.

Silver Gate's Unit 2 was the largest of the Company's eight turbo-generators. It alone could supply the normal electrical needs of a city with a population of 140,000. Weighing 400 tons, the turbine-driven generator was "tailor-made" to the conditions under which it served. Operated at a constant speed of 3,600 revolutions per minute (rpm), the blade tip speed was 830 miles per hour (mph). Turbines 1 and 2 operated at a steam pressure of 850 pounds per square inch (psi) and a temperature of 900 degrees Fahrenheit.

Unit 3 generated steam with boilers that contained a combination of gas-fuel and oil-fuel burners. When the boilers operated on fuel oil at full capacity, they consumed in excess of 105,000 gallons of fuel per day. Boiler feed pumps were driven by 1,250-horsepower motors that operated under full load at a speed of 3,580 rpm. Taking suction at 46 psi, the pump discharged water to the boiler at a pressure of 1,750 psi.

To place Unit 3's turbo-generator in proper dynamic balance, the operators were called on to start and stop the unit time and time again as vibration readings were taken and balance weights installed. Achieving perfect balance was absolutely necessary. The rotating portion of the machine weighed in excess of 86,000 pounds and rotated at a speed of 3,600 rpm. At this speed, the longest blade on the turbine was rotating at the rate of 1,218 feet per second.

The construction of Silver Gate's four units gave the Company increased capacity to address the needs of the expanding community. New technological improvements allowed SDG&E to employ the most up-to-date equipment.

Workers carefully lower the turbine spindle of Silver Gate Unit No. 4 in January 1952. Unit 4 was the last generator to be constructed at Silver Gate.

Many firms, including the telephone company, one of the aircraft factories, all hospitals except one, and other establishments of various kinds were able to continue operations by switching to their own emergency power systems, but thousands of others, including every home and farm, were automatically shut down.

The problem started at noon when one of the three 50,000-kilowatt steam-driven turbo-generators at the Silver Gate plant went out, throwing too big a load on the remaining electric system, which cascaded down through both power plants and tripped all the turbines. Station B also lost power and, since the entire system was out, dispatchers had to disconnect all customers to clear the system before power from the Southern California Edison Company and the Imperial Valley Irrigation District could be supplied to the local system to restart the turbines.

People all over the county were trapped in elevators and workers were sent home due to lack of power to operate machinery, resulting in an estimated $500,000 loss in time and production. Fish at the canneries remained unprocessed and were lost to spoilage, patients were "caught" in dentist's chairs, and Lindbergh Field resorted to emergency equipment to bring planes in for safe landings. At the Hotel San Diego, SDG&E President Asher E. Holloway was addressing the Rotary Club when the lights began to flicker. Candlelight was furnished so he could finish his talk.

Shortly after this incident, Holloway's term as president came to an end. On October 22, 1951, Emery D. Sherwin, a long-time employee, followed him as president of the Company. Sherwin would remain in the position of president until April 25, 1961. When he was first employed by the Company in 1916, Sherwin was an engineering student at Stanford University, one year away from his degree. Over the years, he held various positions as chainman, surveyor, inspector, and estimator and then moved into the position of superintendent of electric transmission and distribution. He moved through various administrative positions and in 1944 was elected vice president in charge of operations.

By 1952, the Company's investment in physical property—plants, substations, and transmission and distribution lines—was more than twice what it had been at the end of World War II, including a $15 million investment in one year alone. The gas division installed more than 350,000 feet of distribution main in Company territory in 1952, bringing natural gas to more than 11,000 new customers. In December, a $500,000 natural-gas compressor station was completed at Rainbow, just south of the San Diego County line. This new facility increased the Company's ability to store and deliver many additional millions of cubic feet of natural gas.

< The new power line to the Palomar Observatory on Palomar Mountain was soon testing line-crew repair techniques, as this winter storm in March 1953 shows.

EMERY D. SHERWIN

Emery D. Sherwin drew his first Company paycheck in 1916, when on summer vacation from his studies at Stanford University, he was employed in the engineering department to work with a survey crew. One year later he received a civil engineering degree from Stanford and returned to the Company as a full-time employee. His employment was interrupted by World War I when he joined the Army Engineers.

In 1920, following a period of employment in the U.S. Reclamation Service, Sherwin returned to remain as a permanent employee. He was appointed assistant superintendent of electric production in 1924, assistant to the general superintendent in 1930, assistant general superintendent in 1932, and general superintendent in 1941.

In 1944, he was elected to the office of vice president in charge of operations, and in the same year took a seat on the Company's board of directors. Sherwin was elected president in 1951, taking office on October 22, the date of A.E. Holloway's retirement.

Over his 40-year career at SDG&E, Sherwin was known for his exceptional executive abilities, his readiness to delegate responsibility and authority, and his interest in the training and development of personnel to fill positions of management. He also was widely respected within the community for his participation in civic affairs and within the electrical and gas industries. He served as president of several utility organizations and as a director of the Edison Electric Institute.

Completed in 1954, the compressor station at Rainbow was an important addition to the Company's gas distribution system. It was followed shortly by the compressor station at Moreno, in Riverside County.

A 66,000-kilowatt turbo-generator, Unit 4, was installed at the Silver Gate station in 1952 at a cost of $8 million. The following year, more than $7 million was budgeted for further expansion of similar facilities. Groundbreaking ceremonies for the Encina steam-electric generating station took place on January 14, 1952, and work progressed steadily on the first unit of the Encina station, scheduled for opening in 1954.

A major component of the Encina station was completed in 1953. A 20-

Laurence Klauber (left) and Emery Sherwin break ground on January 14, 1952, for the Encina Power Plant, which would become the Company's largest single generating station on its system.

The company's new El Cajon office, opened in December 1954, represented another move to service an expanding territory. Previously, customers had to travel to La Mesa for Company business.

inch-diameter marine pipeline, one of the many unique features of the station, was 4,200 feet long and extended into the ocean floor for more than 3,000 feet. Oceangoing tankers used this pipe to transfer fuel oil to storage tanks near the plant.

Installing the underwater section of the pipe was a major effort. First, 30-foot lengths of concrete-encased pipe were welded into 270-foot sections, then three such sections were placed end-to-end and welded into one 810-foot length. The huge, 810-foot sections were then rolled onto trucks along a specially built railroad track to the mouth of an 8-foot-diameter tunnel beneath Highway 101. From that point, the pipe was pulled through the tunnel until its forward end rested on the beach. A metal sled with three buoys was then welded to the front of the pipe so it would not dig into the ocean floor as it was dragged out to sea. The pipeline was pulled through the water by means of steel cables extending from the seaward end of the pipe out to a floating derrick powered by steam engines. This process was repeated until the entire pipeline was in place. During fueling operations at Encina, the seaward end of the 20-inch-diamter marine pipeline was connected with a 125-foot length of 12-inch rubber hose from the oil tanker.

New energy-related facilities were not the only SDG&E construction projects at this time. A new automotive-repair shop in San Diego, buildings for the new Eastern Division, preliminary construction of a new customer-service building and extensive exterior remodeling of the Electric Building were undertaken during 1953. The expansion of the suburban communities necessitated a change in the Company structure early in 1953. The Eastern Division was formed in late 1953 to accommodate East County needs and consisted of operating, commercial, and accounting department personnel. Located at the corner of Main and Johnson streets in El Cajon, the new division consisted of three buildings—a large warehouse, an operating garage with offices and an office building.

Workers connect pipe on the beach at Carlsbad to form an underwater pipeline. Once in place, the pipe allowed tankers to deliver oil, which was burned in the Encina generators.

THOMAS ALVA EDISON

In 1879, Thomas Alva Edison stood poised on the brink of an entirely new technology with unlimited possibilities. His invention of the electric light began the progress of the electrical industry. Many of the problems he grappled with in his quest for electrical illumination were considered by the brightest minds in his field to be insoluble. It seems incredible today to realize that when Edison first created the light bulb he was considered by some to be a scoundrel and a fraud. An individual named C. Tessie du Motay openly derided Edison in the *New York World* by saying that "one must look upon Edison's new electric playthings as the experiments of a semi-practical prestidigitator." Fortunately, time has proven the validity of Edison's creations.

Thomas Edison changed the way we illuminate our world, but his other inventions added to modern life in a myriad of wonderful ways. Edison created a number of fascinating items his family used at their home in Florida, Seminole Lodge. He completely wired the home for electricity in 1887 and ran all the wiring underground for storm protection. He built one of the first modern swimming pools with waterproof light switches for swimming at night.

Other household inventions included waxed paper, lead foil, and the first double-compartment sink. Electric wires were run around the baseboards in the living room at Seminole Lodge to "zap" insects for his children's amusement. Asked to create a special birthday gift for a neighborhood child, Edison made a doll and installed a tiny phonograph inside—the world's first talking toy.

Other historical "firsts" that Edison created include: the electric fan, toaster, heater, iron, hair curler, hot plate, percolator, cigar lighter, Christmas lights, and waffle iron. Over the course of his life, Edison was granted 1,093 patents for his various inventions. Family and friends complained that he worked too hard, so hard that he did not seem to have time to change his clothes. Edison's response was to say that "I made myself a stratified shirt out of 365 layers of silk, and every morning all I do is pull off one layer and I've got myself a clean shirt front."

Adapted from the August 1991 issue of *Victoria Magazine*, a Hearst Magazine publication.

Plans were also made during 1953 for the Company to join in the 1954 nationwide Lights Diamond Jubilee, the 75th anniversary of Thomas Edison's invention of the incandescent electric lamp on October 21, 1879. Prior to Edison's discoveries, many others had contributed tremendously to man's understanding of electrical phenomena. The invention in 1831 of the dynamo, which produced electricity mechanically, led to increased experimentation, ultimately resulting in arc lighting. Arc lighting was functional in large, open spaces, and Edison sought a solution to the problem of lighting smaller interior spaces. Long experimentation with more than 1,600 different types of substances of all kinds finally culminated with the carbonization of a tiny bit of thread from Mrs. Edison's sewing basket. This was the first filament used to light Edison's incandescent lamp.

Edison clearly saw the possibilities behind this modest achievement and envisioned "great cities lighted from central stations" and proceeded to develop an unprecedented generating and distribution system, complete in every detail from dynamo to fuses and sockets. With the construction of the first central station on Pearl Street in New York City on September 4, 1882, 59 customers received electricity for their lamps and the modern electric era had begun.

One of the events scheduled by SDG&E for the celebration was the public showing of the world's largest light bulb. The bulb, a 75,000-watt incandescent lamp developed by the General Electric Company especially for the observance of the 75th anniversary, produced as much light as 2,874 60-watt household bulbs burning simultaneously. It contained enough tungsten to make the coiled filaments for about 67,500 60-watt lamps.

The year 1954 also recorded other events important to SDG&E. On January 1, 1954, President Emery D. Sherwin assumed the duties of chief executive officer of the Company, in accordance with action taken by the board of directors on December 14, 1953. At that meeting, and upon their acceptance of Laurence Klauber's resignation as chairman of the board and chief executive officer, the board voted to abolish the office of chairman of the board and amended the bylaws of the Company so as to designate the president as chief executive officer. In

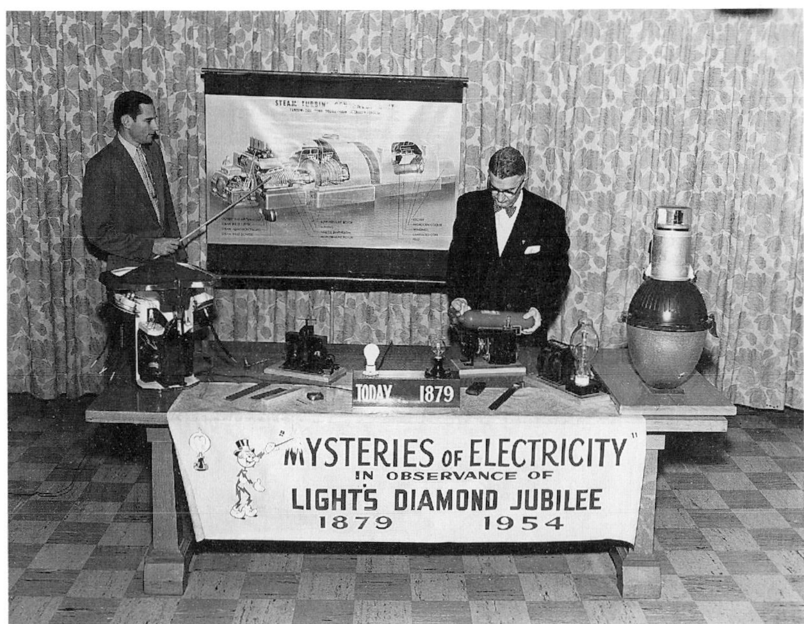

Carl Barker (left) and Dan Turner with the equipment they used in the "Mysteries of Electricity" program, a part of the Company's Visual Education Department.

addition, the bylaws were changed to provide for the new office of executive vice president.

Action taken by the board of directors in 1954 had long-range impacts on service. The Company's negotiations to purchase the Escondido Mutual Water Company utility's electric distribution system for $915,000 were concluded on April 30, 1954. Effective in May, SDG&E assumed ownership and operation of the 139-mile distribution system, which then served approximately 2,200 customers in the Escondido area. The operation of Mutual's electric system began in 1914, when the utility erected two small hydroelectric generating plants—one in Rincon and one in Bear Valley—to serve only 60 customers.

SDG&E spent more than $25 million on electric department facilities in 1954, with the bulk of the expense directed toward the construction of the Encina station in Carlsbad. Encina Unit 1 began commercial operation in November 1954; the total construction cost was $45 million. The completion of Encina Unit 1 expanded the Company's total electric generating capacity by 30 percent. When operated under full load conditions, Unit 1 could generate up to 106,000 kilowatts, slightly under the 112,000-kilowatt capacity of the combined six units at Station B. Just 15 years earlier in 1941, the Company's total generating capacity was 112,000 kilowatts. In 1954, SDG&E's total capacity was 460,000 kilowatts, more than four times greater than the 1941 total capability.

Burnet C. Wohlford (left), president of the Escondido Mutual Water Company, accepts a check from E.D. Sherwin for the purchase of Mutual's electric distribution system.

The new plant was built on a portion of the 689 acres allotted for the station, including about 190 acres in

The Encina Power Plant during construction of generation Unit No. 3 in 1957.

Agua Hedionda Lagoon. A marsh and about 80 acres in a man-made lagoon were dredged to provide cooling for the power plant. Agua Hedionda, once part of a Mexican rancho, was used as a hideout for rumrunners during Prohibition. An oceanfront area was set aside at Encina for employees and their families. A lifeguard tower and covered picnic tables were located at the north end of the beach. The power plant was seven stories high in the front and 15 stories high in the rear, including the stacks. Auxiliary buildings contained shops, offices and control houses. Behind the power plant stood the substation where power was distributed across three transmission lines linked to the San Luis Rey, Mission and Old Town substations. Power from Encina, Station B and Silver Gate served about 285,000 electric customers within SDG&E territory in 1954.

Construction of Encina Unit 2 was begun during 1954, with completion scheduled for 1956. Other capital expenditures for the year included the installation of a microwave system that provided the Company with a communications network connecting its headquarters in San Diego with key locations throughout the service area.

The cost of natural gas was higher in 1955 due to an increase in the Company's wholesale rate for purchasing natural gas. In March 1954, SDG&E negotiated a new contract with its supplier of natural gas, Southern Counties Gas Company of California. The maximum daily delivery of gas was increased to 95 million cubic feet as a result of the contract. A new gas-compressor station was constructed in 1955 at Moreno, Riverside County, on the Moreno-to-San Diego natural-gas transmission pipeline. As a result, capacity of the line increased from 83 million cubic feet to 112 million cubic feet per day. The combined capacity of the pipeline and the Huntington Beach–to–San Diego line was 137 million cubic feet per day. The Company obtained all its supplies from Southern Counties Gas Company and shipped the gas through these two transmission pipelines.

A new electrical system operation headquarters, Mission Control Center located on the grounds of San Diego's Mission substation, was also placed in operation. The building housed the load supervisor's office and the switching center, as well as a busy communications center to relay all information about the electric system to the supervisor. Forty-six telephone lines, 30 microwave channels and 80 radio-equipped vehicles continually relayed vital information regarding daily operations, allowing the supervisor to determine suitable operating conditions for the electric transmission system so that no overloads would occur.

During the 1950s, service was extended to Imperial Beach (1951), lines climbed to the top of Palomar Mountain (1953), and new lines reached Vista (1953). In 1957, a fifth submarine cable was laid across San Diego Bay to

The Mission Control Center was the operational heart of the Company's electric grid. Load supervisor Jack Morse (left) takes readings from a panel of telemeters while George Clark operates the radio. Mission Control operators coordinated electric generation and transmission, and maintained adequate system voltages.

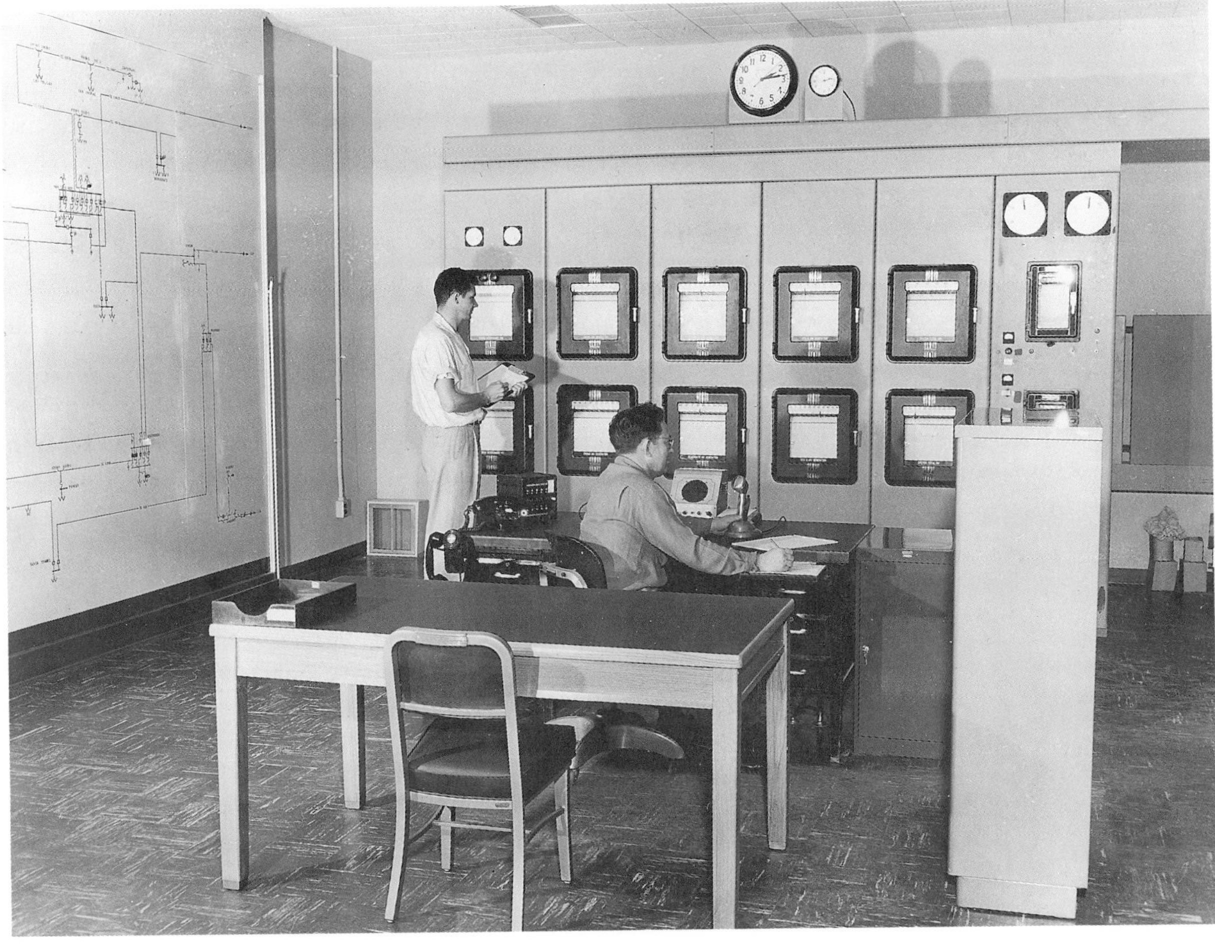

boost Coronado's electric power supply to 30,000 kilowatts. As a 3-conductor, 12,000-volt cable, it carried a load of approximately 7,000 kilowatts. The cable was first secured at the Coronado side of the bay and unreeled from a barge as it was towed across to the San Diego shore.

These expansion projects required large amounts of additional capital. Beginning in 1950, the Company marketed six issues of bonds in various amounts totaling more than $100 million; two issues of preferred stock, totaling 700,000 shares; and four issues of common stock, totaling more than 2.5 million shares. Ownership of the Company's preferred and common stock became even more diversified as the number of individual holders increased from 17,400 in 1949 to 27,500 in 1959. A considerable percentage of each successive issue of stock was purchased by existing shareholders.

The Company was operating on a schedule decided upon many years earlier. Every two years, another major source of power was geared to go on line. In 1958, Encina Unit 3, with a generating capacity of 106,000 kilowatts, was put into operation, and ground was also broken for the South Bay Power Plant project. The first unit of the South Bay plant was constructed on 144 acres of Company property fronting San Diego Bay. The property was bisected by L Street, the southern boundary of Chula Vista. South Bay Unit 1, with an open type of construction exposing most of the equipment, was slated to have a generating capacity of 130,000 kilowatts, the largest steam-electric generating unit ever installed by the Company. The $25 million cost of bringing Unit 1 on line included land purchase, dredging and excavation. As scheduled, Unit 1 was completed in 1960.

In addition to major construction projects such as South Bay and Encina, the Company constructed smaller buildings for a variety of purposes. In 1957, a new, 50,000-square-foot Accounting Building was constructed at the corner of Arizona and Howard streets to relieve crowded conditions in the Electric Building downtown.

From left: Robert C. Dent, San Diego County Board of Supervisors; Chula Vista Mayor Peter De Graaf, Company President Emery Sherwin and San Diego Assistant City Manager Tom Fletcher handle the official groundbreaking shovels for the South Bay Power Plant on October 9, 1957.

Efficient power-plant operation depended on a steady demand for the kilowatts generated. With ample quantities of electrical power available, the Company embarked on innovative programs to build residential consumption. These ideas included the "Housepower" program and the Electri-Living Home in Del Cerro. The promotion of the home was co-sponsored by SDG&E and the magazine *Living for Young Homemakers.* The award-winning home, designed by the architectural firm of Paderewski, Mitchell & Dean and built by Jackson & Scott, Inc., was constructed to show the public what the term "Live Better Electrically" meant in the modern, technological era of the late 1950s and also to encourage the use of electricity in the home.

This Gold Medallion home in the Severin Hills area featured all-electric appliances and advanced electric-design features.

"Live better electrically" was promoted through model homes like this one in Del Cerro in December 1957.

The model home received the Gold Medallion award that was created by the electrical industry in the nationwide Live Better Electrically campaign during the 1950s. The medallion was a symbol of electrical excellence in a home and encouraged extensive use of electrical appliances. This award was also given to another all-electric model home constructed by SDG&E in Escondido at the same time, and both structures helped to educate the public as to the positive aspects of electricity, a continuation of SDG&E's desire to bring new information to its customers.

The wiring and lighting systems in the homes were designed by SDG&E's residential wiring section, and the Sales Department assisted the builder, Rorex Homes, Inc., in publicizing the home. Other features included all-

STATION B WHISTLE

The Station B whistle, famous all over the county, was known as the "Gas Company whistle," although it was located on an electric generating station and was a manually operated steam whistle. When the whistle was installed, it was used at first to call out the police and fire departments, give signals for general mobilization and to sound riot calls. The Station B whistle replaced an earlier whistle at Station A, was fully two tones lower than the earlier whistle and could be heard for 10 miles. The Station A whistle, originally blown 10 times a day and used to call various Company officials and employees, sounded the 9 p.m. curfew by order of the city council. Over the years the whistle tempted college students, interrupted symphony concerts, and alerted citizens during the World War II years to air-raid emergencies.

By 1934, Station B had taken over the duties of the earlier whistle and reduced its number of daily blasts from 10 to five. By 1938, the 8 a.m. blast was silenced by special request of the Hotel Managers' Association. The whistle blew four times daily—noon, 1, 5 and 9 p.m. All special signals, except for three-alarm fires, blackouts and air-raid precaution signals, were canceled. The 9 p.m. signal caused more comment than all the other blasts.

The ordinance creating a 9 p.m. curfew was originally adopted by the city council in 1892. In 1904, the council "ordered" the Company to blow its whistle to aid in enforcing the ordinance. For 30 years, Station A sounded the 9 p.m. whistle. On Memorial Day 1934, Station B took over the curfew warning from Station A and continued the duty until the late 1970s when city noise-abatement ordinances deemed it offensive and retired the whistle.

An amusing story is still told concerning the whistle and its role in San Diego's history. The famed maestro Otto Klemperer was directing the Los Angeles Philharmonic Orchestra in a premier rendition of Daniel Gregory Mason's "Abraham Lincoln Symphony" at the Savoy Theatre. The second movement ended on a soft B-flat and, lowering his baton to signify a completed passage, Klemperer found his pleasure in the ending of the note abruptly interrupted by a perfectly pitched, but with an upswinging crescendo, B-flat note. The note sounded for 30 seconds (it seemed like 10 years to the quavering woodwind section under the scrutiny of Klemperer's stony gaze), and GASCO employees in the audience knew exactly where the uninvited note came from—the Station B whistle sounding the 9 o'clock curfew. It was never known whether the maestro was informed as to what had really occurred with split-second timing during his appearance in San Diego. Maybe it was better left unsaid.

News-Meter cartoonist Wilson Cutler's 1934 impression of the Station B whistle.

electric appliances in the compact, ultra-efficient kitchen that was equipped with overall lighting or "sunshine ceiling." Built-in appliances included a blender and clock set into the wall, an electrically heated rack for drying towels; recessed lighting and remote-control switches in the living areas of the home; an all-electric heat pump that operated automatically to warm the house in winter, and to purify the air and control humidity; a two-way intercom system and a radio-controlled garage door, all reflecting the most up-to-date equipment and technology of the times. Tours of the model homes drew more than 60,000 visitors in 60 days.

By constructing model homes to show consumers the benefits of electricity, the Company attempted to acquaint the public with the operations of SDG&E. Many other educational activities took place during these years. Groups of high school students, businessmen, educators, community leaders and members of other adult organizations were routinely invited to tour facilities. The purpose of the tours was not just to familiarize the community with their power company but to encourage young people to think of engineering as a viable career choice. Company executives wanted to promote the energy industry as a potential occupation for the next generation of customers.

In this same vein, one of the lesser known, yet still important, departments in the Company was the Visual Education Department. One of its primary functions was the training of adult leaders for the county's 4-H electric project. The project began in 1950 and was located in California, Nevada and the Hawaiian Islands. Sponsored by the Pacific Coast Electrical Association and operated by the University of California Agricultural Extension Service through local farm advisors, the project began each fall and continued until July. Representatives from each electric utility company attended a statewide meeting with 4-H specialists and planned the year's program, including the "gadgets" the boys and girls would be taught to make. Small electric motors, buzzers, hotbeds, lamps and alarm systems were just a few of the things that were made by the children. This project was one phase of the Company's public-relations activities devoted to rural electric customers. It had the dual purpose of assisting young people in worthwhile activities and introducing them to the many practical uses of electricity on their farms and ranches.

Home economist Mary Means dishes up some holiday fare at a Company display. The home economists demonstrated appliances and provided cooking tips as part of the Company's education program for homemakers.

SDG&E reached out to the community in other ways as well. The Company felt that in most homes, the extent to which gas and electricity were used was determined by the woman of the house. Therefore, the sales division, led by the Home Economics department, directed many of its activities toward the homemaker. A four-woman home economist staff—Mary Means, supervisor, Thelma Walters, Marie Bull and Shirlee Smith—worked exclusively with women in the Company's service area. The department had two principal aims—to assist women in the most efficient and productive use of their modern appliances, and to encourage them to own and use the new equipment as a means of obtaining greater comfort and convenience for themselves and their families.

In order to attain these goals, the home economists conducted a program of activities to reach not only homemakers, but the wives and mothers of the next generation, the school-age girls. Cooking classes conducted for the daughters of SDG&E employees proved to be a great success in teaching the young girls skills in the kitchen. Group meetings at Company facilities and local appliance dealers' showrooms presented information about nutrition, food preparation and preservation, and proper care and use of appliances.

Two daily radio shows broadcast over KFSD, "Home on the Ranch" and "Listen to Lorraine," and the very popular SDG&E "Homemaker of the Week" television show offered an opportunity to address a larger audience. The cooking program brought new menu ideas and creative culinary techniques to local viewers as well as acquainting the viewer with new equipment available.

The Public Relations Department also publicized the 75th anniversary of SDG&E in April 1956. A well-planned program of activities highlighted the

Exterior sign lighting, popular since the early 1920s, remained a popular business-advertising trend in the 1950s.

The 75th anniversary of the Company on April 18, 1956, was marked by costumed employees serving cake to customers. From left are Peggy Bush, Olive Bostrom, Georgia Georggin, Betty Kellerstrass, Mary Means and Kathleen Bowen.

celebration. On the day itself, April 18, customers who visited both the main office and the district offices were greeted by employees dressed in fashions from the 1880s. A 20-page booklet describing the Company's history was given to all comers. The first public showing of a sound-color motion picture depicting the Company's development was a featured attraction. Newspaper, radio and television ads rounded out the promotional celebration.

All these programs helped to educate the public about the Company, its operations and the energy needs of the future. A request for a rate hike had received a great deal of attention in the local press, and consumers sought to understand the reasons for the rate changes. Rate increases in electric, gas and steam services provided by SDG&E were approved by the California Public Utilities Commission on October 22, 1958. The increases were the first since 1920 for steam power, first since 1950 for gas, and the first since 1955 for electricity. The average utility bill became approximately $1 a month higher in the city, less than what the Company had asked. The Commission also ordered a change in the firm's zoning system, which had the effect of lowering utility rates in some cities—La Mesa, El Cajon, Chula Vista and Imperial Beach.

Reddy Kilowatt was frequently seen as a parade-float rider in the 1950s, here appearing in the 1958 Mother Goose Parade as Genie of Aladdin's lamp.

Future changes proposed for the industry received the full attention of the executives at SDG&E during the late 1950s. With the development of the atomic bomb during World War II, more experimentation and exploration of this form of energy was inevitable. As early as 1957, the Company began participating with the General Atomic Division of General Dynamics Corporation in research programs that sought to develop a nuclear reactor system to produce electrical energy at unit costs lower than those realized by conventional fuels. Again, anticipation of future needs and possible restrictions on energy sources spurred top executives to investigate as many options as possible. Industry leaders felt that at some point in the future, conventional fuels would become scarce or exceedingly expensive, and they wanted to develop new energy sources.

In November 1958, the Company became a member of High Temperature Reactor Development Associates that consisted of 51 investor-owned utility companies in the United States. The group submitted a proposal to the Atomic Energy Commission for the development and construction of a high-temperature gas-cooled nuclear power plant of 40,000-kilowatt capacity on the property of the Philadelphia Electric Company. The proposed reactor was a form of experimental research and development work that arose out of the association between SDG&E and General Atomic. The experiment promised to provide a major shortcut to the nation's goal of economic nuclear power.

Gordon Belt operates a card sorter of the Company's first computer system in March 1959. The computer was used to produce customer bills, a far quicker way than the foot-operated Remington Rand tabulator operated by Nellie Back in 1946.

During 1958, General Dynamics Corporation's General Atomic Division moved into new facilities in San Diego—the $10 million John Jay Hopkins Laboratory for Pure and Applied Research. This new facility ranked as one of the world's largest and most diversified centers of general-purpose nuclear research and development. Theoretical and experimental work carried on by General Atomic resulted in the development of a reactor for training, research, and isotope production; contracts for development of a marine-propulsion nuclear reactor; a novel concept for nuclear space propulsion; a program of research in controlled thermonuclear reactions; and the development of a high-temperature nuclear power system. Thermoelectricity, the direct conversion of heat to electrical energy, was a topic of extensive research since data indicated a possibility of eventual success in this field.

While SDG&E explored other power alternatives, daily operations continued with new hookups proceeding at a rapid pace. Extending from a tap into the Moreno transmission line at a point where it paralleled former Highway 395 (now Interstate 15), the new 17,300 feet of 6-inch gas-pipeline installation marked the extension of service into the Poway area in September 1958. More than 1,600 new homes were under construction at that time in the former farming and ranching community, and access to the main line was accomplished by laying 3,000 feet of 2-inch pipe within the first unit of the

The turbine of Encina Unit No. 3 is examined before installation in March 1958. In operation, the impact of high-pressure steam against the fan-like turbine blades caused the turbine to rotate and thus spin the generator, producing 106,000 kilowatts.

tract. The line's construction was the culmination of a one-year negotiation between the contractor, developer, the California Public Utilities Commission and SDG&E. Increased water facilities and the construction of a new sewage-disposal plant in the valley were responsible for the sudden upturn in construction scheduled for the area. The Company felt that this section of the county was slated for large-scale growth, and arrangements were made to continue to add to the service as required.

The nationwide recession in 1958 ultimately had less effect on San Diego business conditions than on other major population centers around the United States. A slight dip was experienced by local businesses, particularly the aircraft industry, but it was more than offset by gains in other areas of the economy due to high levels of population growth and capital investment. In each month of 1958, the index of business activity exceeded year-earlier levels. By the end of the year, following a gradual but steady increase in employment to a record total, almost all segments of the economy were at all-time highs, and overall business activity reached a new record peak.

Groundbreaking at the Kearny Mesa Industrial Park was an explosive occasion in January 1959.

In 1959, Harold A. Noble, vice president of operations, announced plans to establish four new operating headquarters. The largest of the four was to be located on 15 acres of Company-owned property near 33rd and F streets in San Diego (formerly the Dells Housing Project) and named the Dells Operating Headquarters. Other locations chosen for new projects were two six-acre tracts, one near the mouth of Rose Canyon and one east of Otay on Main Street, near the Otay substation. The fourth location had not been chosen yet. The planning of new headquarters buildings began, and organization was similar to that of Eastern Operating Headquarters in El Cajon. Each center was to have gas and electric construction crews, troubleshooters, servicemen, a storeroom and garage. When completed, the new stations relieved Station A of all crew activity. Station A had experienced severe overcrowding due to the rapid expansion of the Company's service area.

The decade ended on a high note. Business conditions during the year were good, with a 25 percent gain in gas and electric customers. Construction activity in San Diego was exceeded nationally only by New York, Los Angeles, Chicago and Houston—all with populations much greater. Earnings improved because 1959 was the first full year with the rate hike in effect. A counteracting effect was the unusually warm fall and winter months. Planning for the next decade was complicated for Company executives since large-scale cuts were anticipated in the defense industry. The shift from aircraft to missiles had been made, reflecting the new military priorities. Housing needs had stabilized so plans were not made for large numbers of new customers to begin service.

In population, San Diego ranked 31st nationally in 1951; by 1959 the city had reached the position of 20th largest in the United States and fourth largest in the 11 Western states. At the close of 1959, the Company was

Lights illuminate the South Bay Power Plant's first generating unit in November 1960, shortly after it became operational. The plant was designed as an outdoor plant, meaning no external building was constructed around the generator and boiler.

serving a total of 315,847 electric customers and 254,740 gas customers. Total sales reached 2.3 billion kilowatt-hours in electricity, accompanied by a new gas-sales record of 20.1 billion cubic feet.

Construction of new power plants—Encina and South Bay—dominated the building program during the decade. Other steps were taken to increase the gas supply line capacity and to provide for the projected growth generated by the new customers during the next decade. At SDG&E's request, the Southern Counties Gas Company added 14.4 miles of pipeline to loop a section of the Moreno–to–San Diego line, one of the two pipelines serving the Company. Upon completion of the line in November 1959, the aggregate capacity of the two pipelines was increased from 154 million to 175.7 million cubic feet per day. Provisions were made for delivery of added quantities under certain specified conditions.

The decade of the 1960s brought significant progress to San Diego Gas & Electric and a continuation of the growth trends of the previous decades. During 1960, the Company gained more than 25,000 new customers, a satisfactory number even though it was lower than the two previous record-breaking years. Electric and gas sales increased substantially during 1960 as more customers needed service, and existing customers used more energy to power many of the new appliances and machinery available.

An unusual transmission tower was designed to carry electric lines from the South Bay Power Plant to other areas of the service territory.

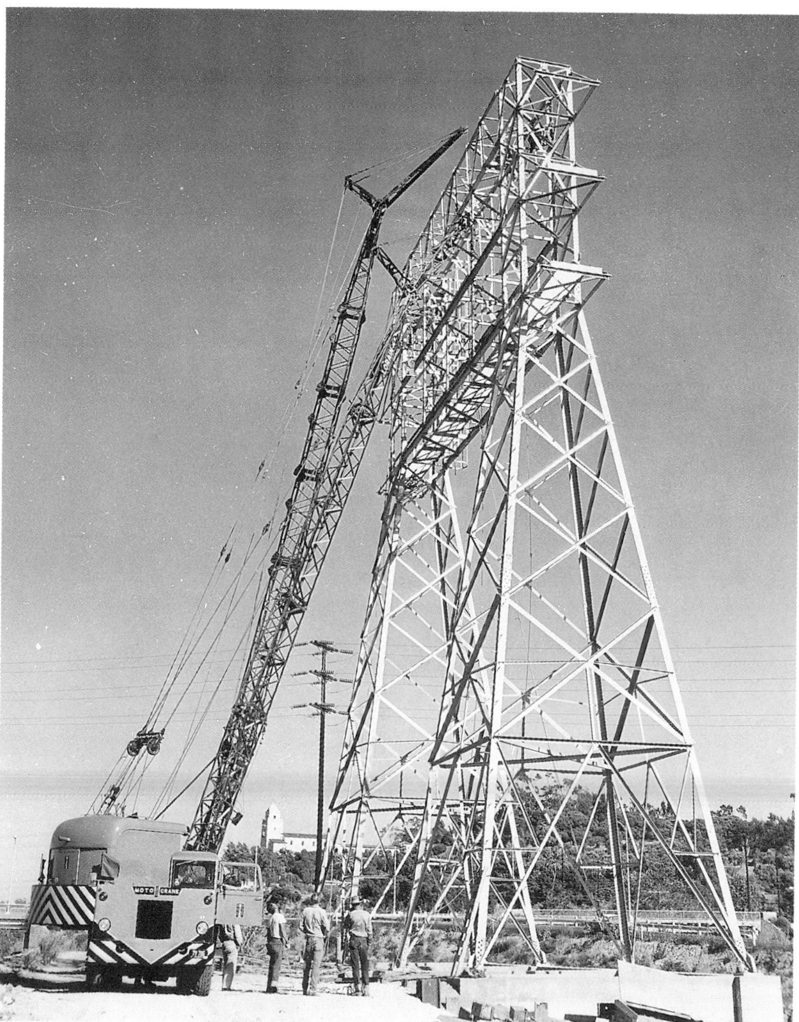

NEWTON YARD

As a section of the stores department and the Company's main depot for delivery and disbursement of hardware and equipment used in extending the gas and electric services, Newton Yard stocked items ranging in size from the nuts and bolts that held braces to crossarms, to huge transformers standing 15 feet high. Some of the larger items kept on hand were the structural steel, poles, reels of wire, gas pipe, and transformers. Small articles were all stocked in quantities of 5- or 6-digit figures, and the yard foreman was expected to know what was available at all times.

Located on Newton Avenue west of Sigsbee Street, the yard stored supplies that were delivered by both truck and rail. Removed by crane from the delivery vehicles, the items were stored on racks until loaded on Company trucks for delivery to the job site.

Another operation of a different nature took place in the pipe wrapping shop. Treating the various sizes and lengths of pipe used by the gas department was a smooth and simple, yet thorough procedure, and the "tar babies" in the shop could wrap more than 750 feet of pipe in an hour. On the average, they wrapped 80,000 to 90,000 feet of ¾-inch pipe per month.

First, the pipe was fed through a roto-blast machine that removed residue from the pipe by a blizzard of small steel pellets. Then the pipe was guided to the wrapping center where it received a coating of hot tar; then a wide strip of fiberglass was wound around the pipe, followed by a final wrapping of heavy paper. As each length of pipe was wrapped, it was removed from the assembly line to a cooling rack by means of hooks at the end of ropes.

Capital expenditures to keep up with the demands for services amounted to more than $30 million for the second consecutive year. The completion of South Bay Power Plant Unit 1 and the beginning of construction of Unit 2 accounted for more than $7 million in expenses for the electric division. Further extensions of service lines to new customers and new subdivisions accounted for another $6 million.

The major project for the gas department was the construction of a 30-inch gas-transmission pipeline, 52 miles in length, from Rainbow to San Diego costing $7 million. Before the new line was completed in 1960, the Company took delivery of natural gas through two pipelines that were capable of delivering a total of 176 million cubic feet of gas per day. With the new pipeline in place, the capacity was boosted to 354 million cubic feet per day. This doubled the former total and was expected to be sufficient to meet gas demands well into the decade.

The three new operating headquarters planned in 1959 for the San Diego metropolitan area were opened in 1960 to house construction, maintenance and service crews. The Dells Operating Headquarters, located between Mar-

UTILITYMEN'S ABRIDGED DICTIONARY

ALLIGATOR—high-voltage line tool

BANJO—shovel

BEAN BAG—connectite bag

BEAR CLAW—guy hook

BELL—insulator

BROWNEY—4-kv insulator

CANDY GRABBER—lineman's pliers

COMEALONG—wire grips used to pull slack from wires

DIVING BOARD—lineman's platform

FIREWATER—gasoline

FORT KNOX—tool room

FUNNY PAPERS—blueprints

GAFFER (or "ramrod")—foreman

GOLD BRICK—copper-wire connector

GOURD COVER—hard hat

GRUNT BAG—canvas bucket used to hoist tools up pole

HALF SOLE—half diameter of metal pipe patch

HARDHEAD—log bolt

HOG EYE—3/4" or 5/8" bolt eye

HOT STICK—tool used for handling live wires

JOHNNY BALL—insulator used on guy wires

PIG—(or "pot") transformer; also a device to clean pipelines

REPTILE BAG—line hose container

SNAKE—rubber line hose that slips over wires to protect linemen

SNIFFER—gas detector

SOAPED SUDS—gas-meter fittings checked for leaks with soap and water

THREE-PHASE SET—shovel, spade and digging spoon for pole setting

WALTZING MATILDA—pneumatic tamper

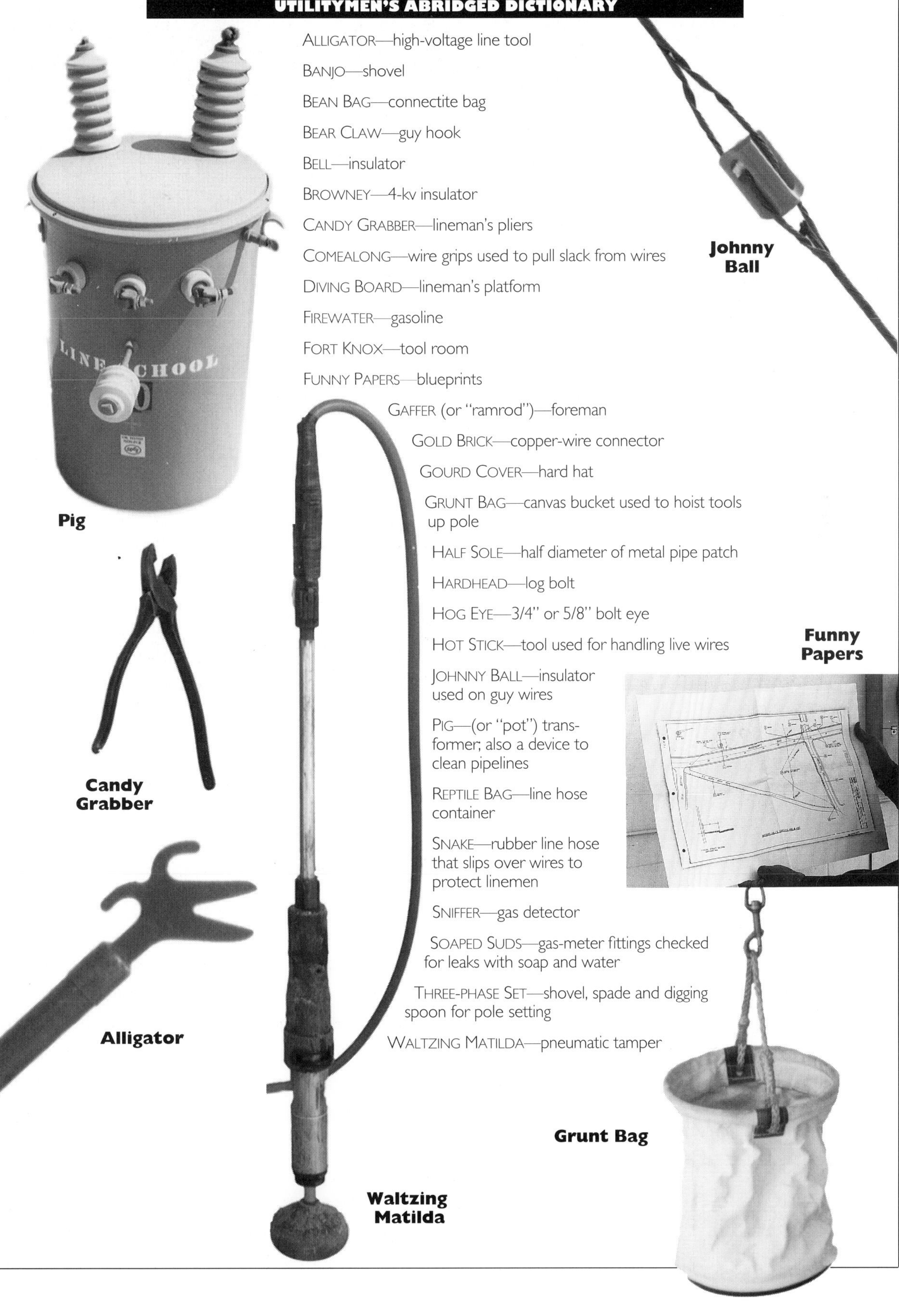

Pig

Candy Grabber

Alligator

Johnny Ball

Funny Papers

Waltzing Matilda

Grunt Bag

Electric linemen and ground crew are issued yellow hard hats in July 1959. This was the first time all field crews wore hard hats as part of the Company's safety program. Previously, only ground crews had worn the hats.

ket and F streets, east of 33rd Street, was the largest of the new facilities. The other two were the Southern Operating Headquarters, located in Chula Vista, and the Rose Canyon facility. All three were similar in size and design and provided for the decentralization of personnel in the service area. Decentralization located personnel and equipment closer to the service areas and provided greater efficiency due to decreased travel time and distance to job locations.

The Company experienced no difficulty in meeting the increased demands on the system. The peak demand on electric facilities in 1960 reached 690,500 kilowatts, occurring on December 8. This peak was no problem for SDG&E because with Unit 1 of South Bay in operation on July 23, the electric system generating capability had been increased from 667,000 kilowatts to 809,000 kilowatts.

The new unit was the largest of the Company's steam-electric generating units with a capacity of 142,000 kilowatts. Unit 2, already under construction by the end of 1960, was built to have a matching capability. These two units were expected to handle the energy needs of the rapidly expanding community for several years to come. One of the largest pieces of equipment at the South Bay plant was the gantry crane. It would ride on tracks having a span of 106 feet set at operating floor level (32 feet above the ground) and with a lifting capacity of 50 tons.

Despite the rise in customers and sales in 1960, the Company's net operating revenues were slightly lower than the previous year, and the earnings on net capital investment declined markedly. This condition was attributable to increases in various expenses of operation incurred in the gas department after the gas rates were established. The expenses accumulated more rapidly than the revenue, and it became evident to Company executives that unless gas rates were adjusted upward, this trend would continue. On November 23, 1960, SDG&E filed an application for authority to increase its rates for natural-gas service with the California Public Utilities Commission. Public hearings were held in February and March of the following year by the PUC. The hearings resulted in a new tariff effective on September 16, 1961, which increased gas revenues for the year.

As the county's population topped the million mark at 1,038,011 and SDG&E's service area expanded, the number of new employees grew to meet the needs of new consumers. By 1960, regular employees totaled 2,964, working in all areas of the Company. Supervisory and management development programs, begun many years before, were broadened to increase benefits to the employees and management. A management newsletter, geared to supervisory employees, was introduced as an aid to more effective communication in a time of rapidly expanding operations.

As the tumultuous decade of the 1960s got under way, San Diego Gas & Electric Company was poised on the edge of momentous changes and challenges. The Company had come a long way from the World War II years when it was a utility company meeting the small-town needs of San Diego. New forms of energy, including nuclear power, and environmental concerns would dominate the years to come, prompting major shifts in energy use and production. The old patterns of business would no longer suffice, and new types of leadership would become necessary as long-range decisions encompassed new factors.

Construction of the Company's Rose Canyon Operating Center in June 1960. The Center was one of three built to serve customers in the growing suburbs.

HIGH
AGE

Chapter 9

1961-1970
Dawning of a New Era

1961

Population*	1,033,011
Electric	
Customers	342,446
Sales in kwhr	2,881 million
Average cost / kwhr	2.08 cents
Gas	
Customers	278,692
Sales in therms	285 million
Average cost / therm	9.12 cents

PALA
SAN DIEGO COUNTY
BORREGO SPRINGS
OCEANSIDE
ESCONDIDO
JULIAN
DEL MAR
LAKESIDE
PINE VALLEY
TECATE
MEXICO

SDG&E Service Territory

*County population based on census 10-year estimates

San Diego took its place as one of the nation's major centers of population, business activity and tourism during the decade of the 1960s. A wide spectrum of new projects changed the city's skyline and gave new impetus to growth and development in the downtown area. The City of San Diego joined forces with a group of prominent local businessmen during the late 1950s to conduct an extensive series of studies regarding San Diego County. From the information gathered during this documentation of all facets of county life, the city adopted a formula for development known as the Centre City Plan. This plan provided for the construction of public buildings occupying seven city blocks in the downtown area of the city.

Activation of the plan began in 1962 with the groundbreaking for the Community Concourse, a multimillion-dollar, three-block project consisting of a 5,000-seat convention center, an 11-story exhibit hall–parking garage and a 3,000-seat civic theater. Other buildings included in the plan were a new 14-story city administration building, headquarters for the police and fire departments, and four skyscrapers ranging from 17 to 25 stories. Construction of new highways, such as the Crosstown Freeway (Highway 395) that was routed around the perimeter of the downtown area, took precedence as outlying suburban areas were developed and residents needed quick, easy access to the city.

New residential communities opened up for development during the decade as more people flooded into San Diego, drawn by job prospects and

Construction continues on the Community Concourse, October 1963. (Photo courtesy of San Diego Historical Society–Ticor Collection)

< Perched on a pole at the Dells Operating Center in January 1965, apprentice linemen and electricians pose with instructors S.E. "Dutch" Osembaugh (lower left) and P.J. "Phil" Seiter (lower right). On top crossarm are (from left) Jerry Slack, Darrell Lockett, Al Martinez, Dave Moore, Chuck Pollock, Don Snyder and Jack Minto. On lower crossarm are (from left) Jim Ford, Larry Ayres, Fred Larsen, Robert Lytton, Chris Poppoff, Robert Brown, Fred Canady, Joe Blanco and Steve Baker.

Workers weld pipe for the 30-inch-diameter gas line, the Company's second major link to the gas supply lines in Riverside County. The 52-mile-long pipe added 178 million cubic feet per day of gas supply to the Company's system when it opened in 1960.

excellent educational opportunities. Large numbers of tract homes were scattered across the suburban areas as housing needs outpaced the available units. Schools, churches, shopping centers and medical facilities increased in number to meet the demands of new residents.

Large-scale recreational areas designed for the enjoyment of permanent residents and as a draw for tourists proved to be a major addition to the attractions offered by the county. During the late 1950s, Harbor Island was created by dredging in San Diego Bay and slated for business and recreational development, similar to the way that Shelter Island had been developed a few years earlier. Mission Bay Park, destined to be a major aquatic park, was under construction and designed to rival any similar recreation area in the world.

During the decade of the 1960s, changes in personnel and management policies dominated Company organizational methods, and new ways of meeting the rapidly changing utility-industry needs were explored. Three men would guide the Company through these times of rapid growth, increased energy demands and programs investigating alternative sources of energy.

Emery Sherwin retired as president effective April 25, 1961, having served the Company since 1920 in various capacities and as president since 1951. Sherwin was succeeded by Hiram G. Dillin, who served as president from April 25, 1961, to September 1, 1963. Dillin joined SDG&E on May 14, 1924, as a draftsman and rose through the ranks in the positions of salesman, contract clerk, rate engineer, vice president in charge of sales, and executive vice president. Outside activities included serving as president of both the Pacific Coast Electrical Association and the Pacific Coast Gas Association.

A view of Harbor Island taken in June 1961. (Photo courtesy of San Diego Historical Society)

The election of Joseph F. Sinnott as president and chief executive officer of SDG&E took effect on September 1, 1963, upon Dillin's retirement. This reflected a major management realignment as Dillin moved into a newly created position—chairman of the executive committee—upon reaching the 65-

year retirement age. Sinnott, a native of Philadelphia and grandson of Judge Moses A. Luce, scion of the pioneering Luce family, started with the Company in 1929 as an electric-meter tester shortly after graduating from Harvard University with an electrical engineering degree. He served in a variety of positions—relay and instrument inspector, protection engineer system planning engineer, chief design engineer, manager of engineering, and vice president of engineering.

All three men faced complex legal situations, wide-ranging energy commitments and intense demands on services and personnel during their periods of tenure as president. As utility companies around the United States emerged from their small-town bases to become major industries meeting the demands of a rapidly industrializing nation, serious questions arose regarding monopolies, nuclear power and energy costs. Many of these questions were ultimately settled at the state and federal levels, as only the state and federal utility commissions and the higher courts could effectively rule on these critical issues.

One such situation that SDG&E followed very closely was the federal government's antitrust prosecutions of a number of large suppliers of electrical and other equipment, beginning in 1960. After much investigation, it was determined that the Company had been damaged by these firms. SDG&E retained special counsel, in addition to the Company's own legal staff, to represent the Company in litigation against these businesses. Early in 1962, SDG&E filed suits claiming damages against several manufacturers of electrical equipment. Agreements were finally reached in 1964, and SDG&E received price adjustments totaling almost $1.5 million plus minor amounts for reimbursement of legal expenses.

San Diego experienced a minor downturn in its economy in late 1960, but by early 1961 it was evident to Company officials that the local service area was emerging from that general decline. Construction of new residences, houses and apartment buildings, which had dropped from an all-time high in 1959 to a low early in 1961, rose substantially and resulted in a net gain in customers for the year. Electric sales continued to increase at a substantial rate, but abnormally warm weather resulted in a drop in gas sales during 1961. Gas revenues still showed a respectable gain during the year due to the increase in rates authorized by the Public Utilities Commission, which took effect during the last quarter of the year.

The rate increase for service to gas customers averaged about 19 percent and was estimated to yield an additional $4.8 million in gross revenues. In addition, the Commission ordered an increase in charges for gas used as fuel in the Company's electric generating plants, estimating that the increased charge would raise gas department revenues by $1.3 million. Company officials recognized that this would result in a corresponding increase in expenses of the electric department. A conclusion was reached that the

HIRAM G. DILLIN

Hiram G. Dillin served in the U.S. Navy during World War I; shortly after the end of the war, he entered college to study engineering. He began his association with SDG&E in 1922 after completion of two years of study at San Diego State University. He continued his studies in electrical engineering at University of California at Berkeley in 1923.

In 1924 he returned to the Company's engineering department as a draftsman. He transferred to the commercial division in 1926, where he held positions in sales and contracts until 1932. At that time he was appointed engineer in charge of rates, rules and regulations. Dillin became commercial manager in 1948, and in April 1949 he was promoted to vice president in charge of sales.

In December 1953, Dillin was elected executive vice president and a member of the board of directors, becoming president on April 25, 1961. He served as president of SDG&E until September 1, 1963.

Dillin was an active member of many civic organizations, including the San Diego Chamber of Commerce, Convention and Tourist Bureau, Downtown Association, United Fund and San Diegans, Incorporated. He was past master of Blackmer Masonic Lodge, past commander of American Legion Post 492, past president of the San Diego–California Club and the Electric Club, and a member of the San Diego Rotary Club.

The construction of South Bay Unit No. 2 was almost completed by February 1962. The plant was rapidly extended to four generating units by the early 1970s.

increase in rates and charges for plant fuel would provide a 6.3 percent rate of return for the gas department.

The electric division also experienced changes during this period. Major expenditures in 1961 were directed toward completion of Unit 2 of the South Bay Power Plant, built at a total cost of $17.6 million. When this unit was completed in July 1962, the plant's capacity was doubled. Another project undertaken by the electric division was the installation of a 150,000-kva transformer to provide an increase in the capacity of the Company's interchange facilities with Southern California Edison Company from 60,000 kilowatts to 100,000 kilowatts. Existing lines in both the gas and electric divisions were extended to provide service to new customers in outlying areas.

To facilitate service to suburban customers, the Company completed Kearny, the fourth facility in the metropolitan area, in 1961. This marked the culmination of a planned decentralization of construction, maintenance and service crews in order to decrease travel time. Crews working from the new facilities would also provide more efficient and timely service to customers in these areas. A facility to provide the same speedy service was constructed in Escondido during the same year.

Nuclear power became a vital area of concern for SDG&E during the 1960s. In 1961, the Company agreed to participate in the financing, construction and operation of a nuclear-fueled steam-electric generating plant that Southern California Edison proposed to build at San Onofre, on the

General Atomic's headquarters on Torrey Pines Mesa in 1963 was the center of early research into commercial nuclear reactors. Today, Sorrento Valley, Interstate 5 and North City West occupy the vacant land beyond GA's building.

coast between Los Angeles and San Diego. It was scheduled to be the largest nuclear-powered plant in the country, with a capacity of 450,000 kilowatts, and was projected to cost $78 million.

At the same time, SDG&E continued its participation in two programs of nuclear research and development originated by the General Atomic Division of General Dynamics Corporation. Projects in the field of thermoelectricity and the development of a high-temperature, gas-cooled reactor comprising the nuclear portion of a 40,000-kilowatt power plant were brought to fruition. Construction of the power plant at Peach Bottom, Pennsylvania, was begun in March 1962 and completed in 1968 by High Temperature Reactor Development Associates, an organization formed in 1958 by 53 investor-owned utilities, including SDG&E.

In the late 1950s, in anticipation of growing trends within the utility industry, accompanied by increasing demands on management, a number of changes were instituted by Company executives. SDG&E officials felt that certain innovations were necessary within the internal organization of the Company to meet the challenges of the future. By the beginning of 1962, the new organizational structure was firmly in place, having accomplished a smooth transition.

Two basic changes consisted of reorganizing the former operating division into three new divisions and regrouping various existing departments into a newly created management services division. The Management Council, formed many years earlier, was comprised of the executive officers of the

In January 1960, this was the longest span of conductors on the Company's electric system—3,554 feet between towers, with a 215-foot sag. It was part of the Fanita Junction to the Los Coches transmission line in east Lakeside. Today, Interstate 8 passes through the valley below the wires.

Company and the heads of major departments and continued to function as an effective policy-making committee.

The beginning of 1962 saw the completion of arrangements to establish pool operations of the electric generating resources of four California utilities. The power pool, created by SDG&E and the three other major investor-owned utilities in California—Pacific Gas and Electric Company, Southern California Edison Company and California Electric Power Company—was designed to provide for mutual aid during emergencies and to permit various economies in operation. The power pool joined practically all the electrical resources and facilities in California into one interconnected system. In case of disaster, the power pool would be invaluable and would also permit each individual company the opportunity to operate with smaller reserves on its own system. This in turn would save fuel and reduce expenditures for additional generating facilities. Formal application was made to the California Public Utilities Commission in 1962 for regulatory approval, which was anticipated to take until 1963.

The new construction program created for 1962 resulted in expenditures of $25.1 million to meet anticipated needs. A large share of these funds were for completion of South Bay Unit 2, with an additional gross capacity of 210,000 kilowatts, scheduled to be on line by 1964. Another addition to the electric system was construction of a 25-mile, 138,000-volt transmission line from the South Bay Power Plant to Los Coches substation.

The rate of growth in local population slowed somewhat during 1962, but it continued at a steady pace. A dip in the aircraft-industry employment picture slowed housing starts with a corresponding effect on new service hookups. This slight slowdown of the economy did not have a long-term negative effect on the Company, as the territory served by SDG&E in the early 1960s reached from the Pacific Ocean over the mountains to the Anza-Borrego Desert. There was no shortage of customers.

Clarence Lindsay operates a tensioner unit that keeps aluminum conductors from touching the ground as they are reeled onto a wire-stringing unit called a "Hootnanny."

During this same period of time, the North County area was experiencing growth, although not nearly at the rapid pace of the more southern areas of the county. This locale would retain its strong agricultural base well into the decade of the 1980s, but the trend toward suburban living reached northward during the 1960s. This expansion required construction of a distribution pipeline for natural-gas service to the community of Fallbrook. A branch from the transmission line and the installation of a distribution system initially served about 300 customers but was expanded as necessary to meet the community's needs.

Hector Hecock, assistant manager of Child Brothers Avocado Company, sorting avocados on an electric conveyor belt in Fallbrook. (Photo courtesy of San Diego Historical Society)

Plans for additional projects continued to be made by the four investor-owned utilities of the power pool. One of the most important projects undertaken by the members was the construction of a 500,000-volt transmission line extending from Los Angeles County northward through California to the Oregon border, a distance of more than 650 miles. Cost for this undertaking was estimated to be more than $100 million. The line would not only link the companies' existing systems but also would serve as a "backbone" for high-voltage ties with power sources in other states. Considerable

Gas servicemen trainees R.B. Dixon (left) and J.T. Neil Jr. make broiler ignition and top burner adjustments on a gas range.

surplus hydroelectric power was available from Oregon's Bonneville Dam. This hookup would allow the area to market its surplus power and substantially reduce its operating deficits.

Nuclear power continued to play an ever-increasing role in energy developments as the decade progressed. Contracts were signed by SDG&E and Southern California Edison Company in January 1963 for the construction of a nuclear power plant in San Diego County. The contracts were signed with Westinghouse Electric Corporation to provide the pressurized water reactor and other major electrical equipment, and with Bechtel Corporation to construct the plant. Approval had been gained from the Navy Department to use a 90-acre portion of the U.S. Marine Corps Base, Camp Pendleton, as the location for the plant.

This approval by the military cleared the way for the companies to make formal applications for the permits and approvals that had to be obtained from the Atomic Energy Commission and the California Public Utilities Commission. Construction of the nuclear power plant at San Onofre was scheduled to begin in October 1963 with a target completion date of July 1966, at an approximate cost of $82 million. SDG&E's share was 20 percent of the cost and power output of the plant.

The diversity of San Diego's economy was sufficient to support continued growth, and Company officials proceeded with long-range plans with complete confidence in the future development of the area. No single industry dominated the economy of the region, as military, recreational and agricultural activities augmented the stable local industrial and business sectors. Those factors helped cushion the effects of reduced employment in the aerospace industry. During the decade of the 1960s, all indicators of continued growth—department-store sales, bank debits, power sales—remained strong and showed an upward trend.

Highlights of local development in the 1960s included expansion of the University of California at San Diego, built to accommodate 27,500 students and attract 100,000 new residents to the area over the next decade; development of the Atlas by General Dynamics as both a space-launch vehicle and a missile; and construction of the Centaur, a vehicle scheduled for use in future space programs by General Dynamics Astronautics Division. During 1961, 608 commercial ships docked at the Tenth Avenue Marine Terminal to pick up or discharge 470,000 tons of commodities, and in 1962 San Diego voters approved the formation of a Port District for the entire bay area to develop the harbor to its fullest potential. With completion of new docking

FEDERAL REGULATORY AGENCIES

The Atomic Energy Commission was established by an act of Congress on August 1, 1946, by President Harry S. Truman to control the development and production of nuclear weapons and direct the research and development of peaceful uses of nuclear energy. The Nuclear Regulatory Commission, an independent agency of the U.S. government, is responsible for licensing and regulating the civilian uses of nuclear energy. The NRC was established by President Gerald Ford on October 11, 1974, to assume the licensing and regulatory functions of the Atomic Energy Commission, which was abolished on the same day.

The NRC is charged with ensuring nuclear safety and the protection of public health and the environment. It regulates the possession, use, handling and disposal of nuclear materials, and most of its efforts deal with the use of nuclear power to generate electricity. The commission licenses the building and operating of nuclear facilities according to its own rules and standards. Inspectors check for violations of safety standards and conduct investigations of nuclear accidents.

facilities at North Island, San Diego became the home port of two aircraft carriers—the *Kitty Hawk* and the *Constellation*—which resulted in 21,000 new residents, 6,000 new households and an addition of $25 million annually to local income.

During the 1960s, a total of 180 active and 350 reserve ships of the U.S. Navy were based in San Diego, creating an annual Navy payroll for the city of $287 million. Local purchases by the Navy reached $200 million each year. Shipbuilding continued to represent substantial additions to the local economy, thanks to the presence of National Steel and Shipbuilding. Tourists also found San Diego's water facilities appealing for sportfishing, sailing and water sports, contributing more than $225 million to the local economy annually through the use of the 4,600-acre aquatic playground, Mission Bay. Many of these visitors also attended conventions, sporting events and other forms of outdoor recreation, adding substantially to the strong economic development of the region.

Even as the decade of the 1960s brought increased prosperity to many sectors of the local economy, these years were also filled with turbulence on a national level. The assassinations of John and Robert Kennedy and Martin Luther King Jr., the Vietnam War and protests against the war dominated world headlines. The acceleration of the modern civil-rights movement created turmoil and dissension as the nation attempted to integrate its schools and work forces.

Shortly after its construction in the early 1960s, Mission Bay proved to be a popular attraction for tourists and residents.

Demonstrators protest outside the Company's headquarters on 6th Avenue. They also staged a sit-in at the building's lobby.

The Congress of Racial Equality (CORE) held a series of sit-ins and picketing demonstrations against SDG&E in November 1962, complaining that the hiring policies of the Company were discriminatory against blacks. CORE demanded that the Company hire more blacks, upgrade current positions held by blacks, and submit a minority breakdown of the Company's employees to CORE officials.

As a result of litigation, the courts ordered the demonstrators to cease their activities against the Company. Nevertheless, SDG&E began, at that time, to reassess its hiring policy in an effort to employ more persons of minority backgrounds. The move toward racial equality reflected the type of activity seen all over the country during the decade.

Other pending matters were settled during 1963 as a number of gas rate cases dating back to April 1955, including one with El Paso Natural Gas Company, were concluded by the Federal Power Commission. These decisions resulted in partial refunds to the Company based on purchases of gas made during the eight-year period. Two cost reductions made during 1963 allowed the Company to pass on savings of $1.5 million to SDG&E customers in lowered residential rates over a 12-month period in 1964 and 1965.

Rates and supply were affected by a discontinuation of services to one of SDG&E's customers, the government of Mexico. For years, by way of connections at Tijuana and Tecate, the Company had supplied electrical energy at the international border for distribution in Baja California. In 1960, the government of Mexico extended its nationalization of the power industry to include this region and began conversion of power to a new power plant built near Tijuana. SDG&E's wholesale deliveries of energy were discontinued on January 31, 1964, resulting in a loss of 2 percent in revenues. An offsetting factor was the generating capacity then available to serve other customers.

Recognizing the new demands for services that would accompany the continued expansion of the local region, the Company explored other sources of power as the decade progressed. Forecasts of future growth and projections of probable requirements indicated that San Diego's development would continue at the same pace, and Company officials spent long hours making decisions as to how and when to best provide increased generating capacity.

Two major studies occupied the attention of senior advisors during the mid-1960s. The Southwest Power Study, a joint effort in partnership with 11 other utilities, assessed the power resources of the area, including southwestern California, Nevada, Utah, Arizona, New Mexico, Colorado and a portion of Texas. Possible establishment of a southwestern power pool, similar to the California Power Pool, and the installation of large generating plants at selected locations were the potential goals of the study.

Another study, which explored prospecting operations in southern Utah in the Kaiparowits Plateau, was done to determine the extent of coal deposits in the area. This research garnered serious attention by Company officials during 1963. SDG&E, Southern California Edison Company and Arizona Public Service Company, all investor-owned utilities, were jointly engaged in the venture, and the trio had high hopes that the coal would provide the fuel for a large on-site generating plant scheduled to have a 5-million-kilowatt capacity. The low sulfur deposits were of sufficient quality for use as boiler fuel, and it was anticipated that the Kaiparowits Development could be an important link in the southwestern power network under study at this time. The project was canceled after nine years of site changes, environmental opposition and regulatory uncertainties.

Participation in these research programs enabled the Company to reap the benefits of technological improvements in power generation and transmission and to acquire the potential for increased generating capacity under favorable cost conditions. A new chapter would open in the Company's history as important links were forged with other utilities around the nation. These new associations paved the way for the amazing technological changes of the decades of the 1980s and 1990s.

SDG&E operations, which had formerly been confined to the Southern California region, were poised on the edge of important new advances and necessitated an approach different from the traditional responses that had

Additional transmission lines laced across both San Diego and the entire western United States as utilities integrated their systems. This view shows transmission lines crossing Murphy Canyon during the construction of the Friars Road bridge in January 1967.

Dan Stokke, computer operator, prepares cards for a card read-punch machine. Information on the cards was transferred to magnetic tape as part of the 1963 changeover from "post card bills" to envelope billing. SDG&E mailed 360,000 bills per month.

Ironworkers guide installation of the steam drum for South Bay Unit 3 in 1963. Boiler tubes were later welded to the drum's protruding stubs.

served the Company well for more than 75 years. Company officials predicted that the energy requirements of SDG&E's service territory would increase at a rate that required the doubling of the Company's electric generating capacity in each of the ensuing 10-year periods. This meant that future planning could leave no gaps in energy production.

Several milestones were reached in 1964, serving both as a measure of how far the Company had come since 1881 and as a portent of the future for SDG&E. Gross revenues surpassed $100 million, and electric generating capacity was pushed beyond 1 million kilowatts with the addition of South Bay Unit 3. When this facility went on line, the system was capable of generating a total of 1,166,000 kilowatts.

Two major construction goals moved nearer to completion in 1964—the first liquefied natural gas (LNG) plant and the San Onofre Nuclear Generating Station. Completed in 1965, the LNG plant was the first installation of its kind in the West, and the nuclear power station marked the Company's first entry into generation by this important source of energy. These two installations comprised half of a four-part plan to meet increasing energy demands. The other half consisted of the Pacific Northwest Intertie and the Kaiparowits Plateau project in Utah.

Power development plans played a more important role than ever before as the Company accelerated its operations to meet changing technological needs. As a member of the California Power Pool, the Company participated in the Pacific Northwest Intertie, a planned combination of publicly and privately built transmission lines that linked the low-cost surplus hydroelectric resources of the Pacific Northwest to the power systems of Oregon and the Southwest, including Nevada, Arizona and California. The $700 million intertie consisted of four extra-high-voltage transmission lines bringing energy to member utilities.

Marvin Musgrave was looking for a hobby when he took up pencil collecting. In 1940 he posed (top) with some of the 1,500 pencils he had collected in the first year. In 1950 he added a room to his house just to display his collection. By March 1967, Musgrave's collection of pencils numbered more than 40,000 and was the third largest in the nation.

In conjunction with its partners—Southern California Edison Company and Arizona Public Service Company—SDG&E began the project to build the Kaiparowits Plateau mine-mouth generating plant. The new plant, which would use water from nearby Lake Powell for cooling purposes, would consist of four 750,000-kilowatt units and two 1-million-kilowatt units. Company officials estimated that the first two units would be completed by 1970 or 1972, with the full plant operating by 1980. The underground mining operation to produce fuel for the operation would be the largest in the country and would more than triple Utah's current coal production. Because of public pressure brought about by environmental concerns, however, the Kaiparowits Plateau project was abandoned.

The plant had been expected to be one of the many resources available to members of Western Energy Supply and Transmission Associates (WEST), a program of regional power development announced in 1964. Fifteen charter members—leading utilities from nine western states—created WEST, the largest regional electric-power development program ever planned. WEST's territory of operations covered almost 20 percent of the total area of the United States and called for long-range joint planning of 36 million kilowatts of new generating capacity and an extra-high-voltage transmission network interconnecting the members' systems of operation. As a joint approach to new developments, WEST expected to save several billion dollars in construction and operating costs over the next 20-year period and allow member companies to benefit from efficient generating plants located close to available fuel sources. WEST also made long-range plans for future water needs.

Availability of water has always been a concern for San Diegans. All early settlements were located close to freshwater supplies, and the initial occupation of the area was closely linked to water sources. The continued growth and development of the area was still extremely dependent on increased availability of fresh water. Attempts to convert seawater over the decades had not been successful, but promising new desalination techniques indicated that a more economical solution was close to realization. SDG&E took the lead in local efforts to obtain fresh water economically from the extensive ocean supply. The Company devoted two years to studies connected with this goal and the application of desalination in conjunction with the operation of electric generating plants.

EMPLOYEES' ASSOCIATION

The Employees' Association was founded on May 24, 1915, and celebrated its 50th anniversary in 1965. In January 1915, a group of about 30 male Company employees met and appointed a committee of five to approach management with the idea of forming a "benefit society." After receiving management's blessing, the committee spent the next five months investigating various employee-benefit plans of other gas, electric, telephone and transportation utilities.

After thorough study, a constitution and bylaws were drawn up, and the association became a reality with 55 "charter" members. The objectives of the organization were threefold: socially, to promote good fellowship and harmony among its members; educationally, to endeavor to create a higher degree of efficiency in all departments and, beneficially, to provide for its members in case of sickness or injury.

Membership was voluntary, and by December 1915, the membership totaled 148 men. It was not until June 1918 that the constitution was revised to allow female employees to join the group. Soon after its inception, committees were formed for entertainment, relief, investigation, auditing, publicity and athletics. Card parties, dances and picnics kept the group busy.

In 1925, the association installed handball courts at Station A and furnished uniforms and equipment for baseball and basketball teams.

During the Depression years of the 1930s, membership waned and social activities were curtailed. In 1933, a "Grocery Dance" was held, and the price of admission was a can or jar of food. December 1937 marked the first Children's Christmas party. Classes in mathematics, slide-rule fundamentals, and the fine art of bridge playing were begun in 1938. Entertainment committee reports indicate that events took place at the Old Globe Theatre and Starlight Opera. The Fishing Derby and boat rides were in the harbor.

In 1940, the group adopted a health insurance plan. The bylaws were amended in 1952 to provide sick benefits, and in 1955, amendments were added to give payments to beneficiaries upon the death of an employee. The organization has continued to provide employees with a wide variety of benefits for more than 75 years.

Beatles fans crowd into an air-conditioned theater.

Desalting water was an experiment in the mid-1960s at this test facility, which was supplied with steam by the Company's South Bay Power Plant.

Engineers Jack Thomas (left) and Ash Barnes watch pure water drip from a demonstration water desalting system in a Company experiment.

The Department of the Interior had teams of experts working on a solution to this dilemma on a national level and began to accelerate its efforts during the mid-1960s. SDG&E, in a letter to Interior, suggested that the proposed West Coast module test center be located at the South Bay Power Plant, which had both seawater and low-cost steam readily available. In September 1965, Interior announced that it would build and operate a seawater-conversion test facility at South Bay.

The first unit built in the water-conversion installation was a flash distillation plant capable of producing about one million gallons of fresh water a day. The unit was a replacement for the Point Loma desalination plant, which was dismantled and shipped to the U.S. Navy Base at Guantanamo Bay in Cuba. The test facility was an extension of several years of research and experimental projects by the Company in conjunction with the General Atomic Division of General Dynamics Corporation. The experiments were aimed at achieving economical seawater conversion by using reverse-osmosis techniques.

Just a few months prior to Interior's announcement in 1965 of plans to build a desalination plant in San Diego, SDG&E entered into an agreement with the Southern California Edison Company, the Los Angeles Department of Water and Power, and the Metropolitan Water District of Southern California to develop a large, combination nuclear power–seawater conversion plant. The electric utilities would own the nuclear power plants that would furnish steam for the desalting installation.

The plant was to be built on a 40-acre man-made island off the coast of Huntington Beach in Orange County. In 1968, after four years of study and planning, during which the project's cost estimate escalated from $444 million to $765 million, SDG&E decided to withdraw as a participant. The main causes of the escalation were project-design changes and a more rapid rise than expected in the costs of labor and materials. Another factor taken into account by SDG&E executives was the fact that the cost of the power obtained from the plant would be too high to justify participation. Shortly after SDG&E withdrew from the project, Southern California Edison and the Los Angeles Department of Water and Power chose to end their participation as well.

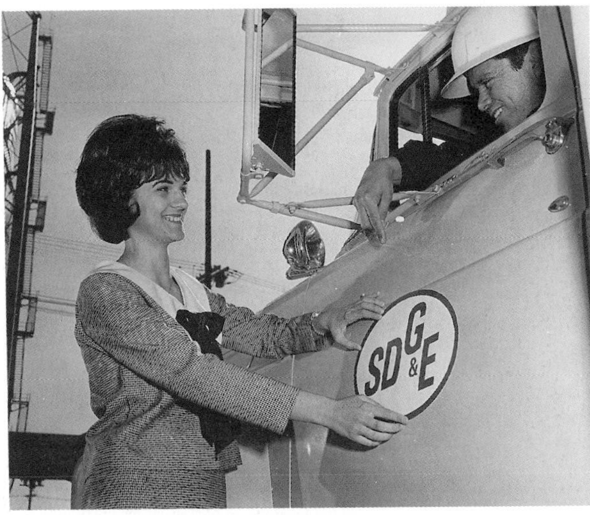

Prudy Milazzo attaches the Company's new logo to a truck driven by E. Tucker in February 1965.

The technological changes taking place in the utility industry called for skilled, highly trained workers. As part of the long-range planning needed to successfully meet the challenges of the coming decades, SDG&E instituted new programs to assist its employees in their efforts to continue the high level of service so long a part of the Company's policies. The Company created a program to reimburse employees for educational expenses that were related to acquiring new skills and upgrading one's educational background to improve job performance. This financial encouragement allowed many employees to complete an unfinished education, or start new training programs designed to add to their stock of skills and talents.

Line crews from the Escondido Operating District head toward snow-bound Palomar Mountain areas to repair extensive damage to electric lines caused by snow, ice, and gale force winds during February 1962. Deepening drifts caused men to hike another two miles with pack equipment on their backs.

In 1964, the Company inaugurated a scholarship program for the children of employees, again with an eye to the future. Up to $1,000 a year was available for college costs for qualified applicants for a period of four years. Increasing emphasis was placed on training employees to assist them in developing increased efficiency and to prepare them for higher levels of responsibility. The Company developed its own programs to upgrade skills and services on all levels of the operation.

Plans were begun in 1964 for construction of a new headquarters building in the downtown area to centralize operations and consolidate employees in one large building. Construction of the new Company headquarters marked a significant change in the development of SDG&E, a signal that the Company was moving into the future, and expanding its role as a key element in the region's development. The team of Richard George Wheeler, AIA, and his partner, W. Gayne Wimer; project designer Roger Matthews, and project architect Delbert Cole created a building for SDG&E that was "elegant with a timeless quality." SDG&E President Joseph F. Sinnott worked closely with the architects to design a building that would reflect the future goals of the Company but not be outdated in a few years.

The Electric Building under construction in 1967. This photo was taken only a block east of where the photo on page 119 was taken in the late 1930s.

The original concept was to build twin towers 20 years apart, but a decision was made to coalesce the design into one single-tower building. The architects felt it might be impossible to duplicate the first tower with the same materials two decades later and that it was better to focus all the design effort on one outstanding structure. More than 900 employees from six locations would move into the all-electric, air-conditioned, ultra-efficient building located at 101 Ash Street in 1968. The new structure would contain a number of conveniences for customers, including drive-through cashier service and a 400-seat auditorium.

Other major construction projects occupied the attention of Company officials during 1964. Construction was begun on the $3 million Liquefied Natural Gas Plant on Company property adjacent to the South Bay Power Plant. The plant was put into operation in the fall of 1965 as the first of its kind in the West and the fifth in the world. The plant embodied many unique features that were considered to be important contributions to the emerging technology of natural-gas liquefication. The plant earned the prestigious GAS Magazine's Four Flame Award, which is presented to the company in the United States considered to have made the most outstanding contribution to the progress of the gas industry for the year.

The LNG plant was designed to liquefy natural gas during off-peak periods and store it for use during peak periods or emergencies. When liquefied, 600 cubic feet of natural gas could be stored in just one cubic foot of space. Large-capacity storage was then economically feasible. The storage tank for the facility was 127 feet tall, 117 feet in diameter and held 175,000 barrels of liquefied gas, equivalent to 620 million cubic feet of natural gas. The liquefied gas could be regasified at the rate of 60 million cubic feet per day.

All these improvements proved timely as employment in the San Diego area increased to an all-time record high by 1965. San Diego County was the second largest in the state by that time, and new customers continued to swell the ranks of SDG&E's service area. At the close of the year, the electric system was serving 381,211 customers, and the gas system, 308,874, including residential and commercial customers.

101 ASH STREET

The Electric Building dedication ceremonies took place on April 20, 1968, and the building was officially opened by President Sinnott pressing a button that caused a spark of electricity to cut the ribbon. The all-electric building was described by architect Wheeler as "a basic two-story building running around a tower, with a promenade around all that. The exterior of the pedestal for the whole complex is precast concrete panels with a heavy aggregate transfer. The aggregate transfer gives a feeling of strength. We created a two-story base element in travertine marble, with doors and windows formed by precast concrete with the glass set into them. The whole skin of the high-rise building is a combination of precast concrete sun fins—10 miles of these fins, in all—and a solar bronze glass to screen out the sun's rays. The fins are two floors high; where they are joined, a scallop is formed. These scallops are staggered. By day, they behave like tiny shadows, giving character to the sleek tower. At night, they are like peerlessly matched little jewels as a light glitters behind each scallop."

Some statistics about the building include: 54,000 cubic yards of dirt were removed for the foundation; 16,000 cubic yards of concrete were poured; 4,800 tons of steel were used for the frame; the tower contains 6,860 windows; 842 electric motors of various sizes, 754 transformers, 9 elevators and associated machinery, 30 water heaters and 44 refrigerated drinking fountains were put into place. Two underground 12,000-volt feeder cables bring current to the building, and 128 light and power panels in the 24 electrical rooms transform the current into lower, secondary voltages.

Joseph Sinnott and a model of the Company's new office building.

THE LONG HAUL

Worker models special firefighting suit at the Company's LNG facility.

The 175,000-barrel Liquefied Natural Gas tank under construction in February 1965 at the South Bay Power Plant.

Experimentation with Liquefied Natural Gas (LNG) took many different forms during the 1960s. Touting its versatility, SDG&E continued efforts to find new applications for the product. A successful demonstration was set up to use a portable supply of LNG at Poway to maintain service to the community while isolating it from its normal pipeline supply to permit maintenance work on the line.

An even more impressive demonstration of LNG capabilities came unexpectedly in February 1967. An emergency situation in British Columbia, 1,500 miles from San Diego, created a demand for LNG in a hurry. The Cryogenic Enterprises Corporation (CEC) in Vancouver had fallen behind schedule in completion of their new LNG plant, but were scheduled to begin serving the Squamish area within 10 days. The deadline was not going to be met unless a temporary supply of LNG could be obtained from somewhere.

SDG&E was contacted by CEC and agreed to supply them with reserves providing the company could obtain all necessary permits and clearances from the various regulatory agencies, a task some considered to be almost insurmountable. In no time, CEC had acquired the required documents and two tanker-trucks, complete with drivers. Four days after the initial telephone call, the tankers arrived at the LNG plant in Chula Vista to receive the first of two loads and begin the long haul back to Canada. Driving day and night, each of the two-man crews reached home in 40 hours, then returned to San Diego for a second load.

Within 10 days following the call for help, LNG from SDG&E's plant was already piped into customers' homes. In what was certainly one of the longest hauls of LNG ever made (and certainly one of the swiftest), the tankers had delivered a total of 25,600 gallons of LNG, the equivalent of about 2,150,000 cubic feet of gas in vapor form.

The nationwide interest in the construction of SDG&E's LNG plant had resulted in CEC knowing exactly where to turn for help when its completion date moved out of reach. This alliance of services was one of the many examples of SDG&E's commitments to not only its own community but other regions, a practice that continues to be an important part of Company policy.

This new LNG installation at Camp Horno, a 2,600-man tent camp in an isolated sector of Camp Pendleton, was the first of its kind in the country when it began operating in October 1967. The LNG was trucked to the facility from the Company's main storage tank in Chula Vista.

A significant change in Company procedure occurred during the 1960s. An increasing number of electric lines, providing electric service to new customers, were placed underground. By mid-decade they represented an important phase of the electric division. Underground distribution lines had first been installed in 1911 as new electric power lines were placed underground in congested downtown areas. There simply was not enough room for the poles and lines necessary to provide the enormous amount of power to the new business buildings. Underground systems were the most efficient and least expensive way to serve the downtown area.

Beginning in the 1920s, some of the more expensive new residential areas received underground utilities. High installation costs restricted this service to just a few areas, since the cost was 10 to 12 times higher than overhead service. Not until the late 1950s did underground installation become more common. New technology brought about cost reductions in the service, and by 1965, 70 percent of all service extensions were put underground, except where soil conditions and terrain made it impractical. In conjunction with the move to underground as many utilities as possible, efforts were under way to improve the appearance of overhead facilities in areas where it was not cost-effective to go underground.

"Beautility" was the word chosen by the editors of *Electrical World* magazine to describe the activities of utility companies to harmonize the appearance of overhead power and communication systems installations with their surroundings. New types of equipment, such as a blue-gray fiberglass insulator bracket that eliminated crossarms, were chosen by SDG&E's three-man Overhead Electric Appearance Committee. These new ideas were just two of the ways that SDG&E implemented its "Beautility"

Gibson Girl outfits were everyday apparel for Nancy Barter at the Company's Old Town office in Squibob Square, seen here with a turn-of-the century room heater. The office and its employees were part of the Company's celebration of San Diego's 200th anniversary in 1969.

program. Alternate sites were chosen for proposed high-voltage transmission towers to help beautify the original areas, such as in Old Town, a historic section of the city.

The committee's job was to develop ways and means of making newly designed and existing lines, including poles and allied equipment, more attractive to the public, all with due regard for economy. Some of the more innovative ideas were poles painted in harmonious colors with pole-top equipment painted blue-gray to blend with the sky. A Utilities Appearance Committee, composed of representatives from 24 other utilities in the Southwest and West, was available to member companies for advice in all areas of design and materials.

To improve service to the ever-increasing number of customers and to meet the highly technological demands of the coming years, SDG&E began an internal reorganization in 1965. Company officials, in conjunction with the management consultant firm of Booz, Allen & Hamilton, Inc., made a decision to create a distinction between operation activities and corporate activities. The changes were prompted by a general reevaluation of services and personnel and were aimed at achieving better coordination and efficiency of all operations.

The operations organization performed tasks related to the day-to-day business activities and included five major divisions—Customer Services, Electric Supply and Engineering, Gas Supply and Engineering, Operations Services and Sales and Promotion. The corporate organization activities were related to the growth of the Company and provided specialized counseling for the top executives, particularly President Sinnott. The corporate

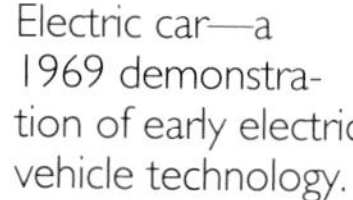

Electric car—a 1969 demonstration of early electric vehicle technology.

section was also divided into five divisions—Corporate Planning, Rates and Valuation, Finance and Control, Legal, and Secretarial.

One of the reorganization's effects was the formation of a new Marketing Division. The division was given the responsibility of broadening the Company's sales promotion activities and formulating effective load-building programs. The marketing "umbrella" also included a newly formed Area Development Department to attract new business and industry to the San Diego area and work in conjunction with local governmental agencies and civic groups.

The total number of employees at the close of 1965 was 2,999, and they reflected some new attitudes. The actual number of employees had not changed significantly since 1960, but the skills of the workforce had altered. The Company needed to have staff who were highly trained in new technologies. An increasing number of employees had specialized professional and technical training. In response to the high demand for professionals at all levels, SDG&E continued to emphasize educational programs and financial assistance to help employees acquire new job skills. The use of computers expanded during these years, creating a whole new level of technological expertise.

The new divisions immediately began to function during the transition period. SDG&E signed a contract in 1966 with the California State Department of Water Resources to assist three other utilities—Southern California Edison Company, Pacific Gas and Electric, and the Los Angeles Department of Water and Power—to supply power for the $2 billion State Water Project, designed to bring surplus water from Northern to Southern California. The power requirements to pump water over the Tehachapi Mountains were expected to reach nine billion kilowatt-hours per year. The project was scheduled to be in operation by 1972 and would be the largest single load carried by the four combined systems.

Other construction projects for 1966 included the installation of a 22,000-kilowatt gas-turbine generator at the South Bay facility. A compact, quick-response unit that reached full load within three minutes of start-up, it was the first unit of its kind to be installed by the Company and would be used to meet system peak loads.

WOMEN AT WORK

Women workers have been essential to the functioning of SDG&E from the beginning. In the past, they traditionally held positions such as secretary, switchboard operator and support staff. During the Great Depression of the 1930s, married women were expected to give up any jobs that could possibly be held by a man with a family to support. This national attitude changed during World War II when the lack of manpower encouraged most companies to hire women to work in nontraditional jobs in order to keep the nation functioning in a time of severe crisis.

After the war, many women found they liked working in a variety of jobs and slowly began to pursue different careers. By the 1970s, women could be found in a wide range of jobs at SDG&E, both white-collar and blue-collar.

The first two women meter readers—Peggy Waltner and Esta Hill—went on duty in January 1943 during World War II. Alyne LeGrand started with the Company in 1942 as a messenger and received a promotion to draftsman in April 1943.

The first two women to achieve journeyman status were Nancy Brackman, journeyman electrician, and Claire Gee, journeyman meter tester. Pat Kuhl became the first buyer in the Purchasing and Material Control Department. Mickey Reed was the first woman to become a right-of-way agent at SDG&E.

The Company's policy of placing the most qualified person in available job positions has enabled several women to pursue career goals. The first female district manager was Mildred Reading, who was appointed to the position in the Coronado office in 1974 after working for SDG&E for 35 years. Margaret (Toby) Dixon became an engineer in 1973.

Kathleen McDaniels, helper, fleet maintenance

JOSEPH F. SINNOTT

Joseph F. Sinnott was a native of Pennsylvania and a graduate of Harvard University, receiving a bachelor's degree in electrical engineering in 1929. He joined SDG&E in August 1929 and was assigned to electric meter testing. He became relay and instrument inspector in 1932, and a protection engineer in 1938. He moved on to relay and system planning engineer in 1951, chief design engineer in 1956, and in 1961 was elected vice president–engineering. In December 1962, he was elected executive vice president and a member of the board of directors. On May 21, 1963, Sinnott was elected president and chief executive officer of SDG&E. He officially began his duties on September 1, 1963.

Sinnott served in many civic capacities, including two terms as president of the San Diego Chamber of Commerce.

Continuing the family tradition at SDG&E is Joe's son, Terry. He currently holds the position of Director–Northern Regional Operations and remembers his father's warm sense of humor and ability to lead the Company through challenging times. He feels that his father's style of leadership was right for the era—a mix of humor combined with solid knowledge of the Company and its needs. A strong president, Sinnott was instrumental in many key programs of the decade. The Sinnott family has had a long and productive association with SDG&E for more than 60 years.

Norman P. Livermore, administrator of the State Resources Agency, with Joseph Sinnott at the dedication of the Electric Building on April 20, 1968.

Also in the same year, SDG&E began a program to improve residential street lighting by converting all existing incandescent street lights—about 15,000—to more efficient mercury-vapor lights. Rates were reduced for the lights to encourage more communities to install them. "Dusk-to-dawn" lighting fixtures were made available by SDG&E with the approval of the PUC and were operated by a photoelectric cell that turned the lights off and on according to the amount of available daylight.

The overall economic growth of the city proved exemplary as residential and commercial construction in 1968 reached record levels. Major industries such as Burroughs Corporation, Ratner Manufacturing Company, the National Cash Register Company and the new Naval Undersea Warfare Center moved to the region, attracting thousands of employees and additional utility customers. A new category of industrial activity—oceanics—became a viable industry during the decade, with interest centered on San Diego. One of the most highly regarded ocean-research centers, Scripps Institution of Oceanography, was joined by more than 90 other agencies, firms and industries engaged in ocean-related research, product development and manufacturing.

Other major achievements of the late 1960s were the surpassing of the half-billion-dollar mark in total capital investment in utility plants in 1968, the dedication of the nuclear power plant at San Onofre and the completion of the new 21-story office building in downtown San Diego. The establishment of LNG service to an isolated sector of Camp Pendleton made it necessary for supplies to be hauled by tanker from the plant in Chula Vista. The gas was then transferred to a tank in a storage-vaporization facility that had been installed to provide gas service to a tent camp for combat trainees. The LNG was vaporized for transmission to the camp and used for heating water, and was believed to the first service of its kind in the United States.

A second satellite LNG facility was established in a 300-acre mobile home community in Borrego Springs, 90 miles northeast of San Diego. This unit provided beyond-the-main service and was the first to be located in a residential community. The LNG storage facility, supplied with fuel tankered in from Chula Vista, was installed at the park, and gas was drawn from storage, vaporized and distributed to homesites and a clubhouse recreation center.

During 1967–1968, the Company conducted extensive testing with SDG&E fleet cars to determine the viability of using LNG as an automotive fuel. The preliminary test results indicated that LNG use would drastically reduce smog-producing emissions from automobile exhausts. Plans went forward to produce an economical fuel that was easily adaptable to internal combustion engines and suitable for all types of vehicles, especially fleet cars and trucks.

In 1968, an SDG&E four-man driving team, and an auxiliary fuel truck with two driver-mechanics, completed a 50,000-mile road test of cars operating on LNG. The extensive road test and follow-up studies concluded that exhaust emissions from an LNG car contained less than half as much smog-producing pollutants as gasoline-fueled cars. The cars were driven to the annual meeting of the Institute of Gas Technology in Chicago and visited 18 other cities where large demonstrations showed the car to federal officials, automotive representatives and gas-industry executives. Television coverage brought the experiment to the attention of large numbers of people who did not have an opportunity to personally witness the cars' performance.

Construction of the San Onofre Nuclear Generating Station began in 1964, and the facility was declared ready for commercial operation on November 15, 1967, an event of major importance to the Company, the Southern California area and the nation. The station officially began operations on January 5, 1968. Other utilities around the nation were completing similar plants, ushering in the age of nuclear power. Utility officials felt that much of the nuclear power was destined for California where the demand for electric energy was expected to continue at record-setting rates. More nuclear facilities were expected to be built to accommodate demands, and the completion of San Onofre was seen as an important opportunity to gain valuable operating experience.

As the county's first nuclear power facility and 72nd in the world, the $87 million plant was hailed as a "symbol of the future" and as a "major step forward in the peaceful use of atomic energy" at its dedication

On December 19, 1969, the LNG "smog cutter" car returned from a cross-country tour that went all the way to Washington, D.C. From left: Jim Nugent, W.P. White, A.L. White, R.V. Martin, Rich Swanson and F.N. Anderson.

ceremony. Twenty percent of the 450,000-kilowatt capacity was allotted to SDG&E, and the remaining 80 percent went to Southern California Edison.

As new technology took over from the functional but inadequate machinery still in operation from earlier eras, certain equipment began to fade from the scene and was replaced by the more modern high-tech installations. Demolition started in March 1969 on two San Diego landmarks—the huge natural-gas storage tanks on L Street between 10th and 12th avenues—marking the end of an era and heralding the start of a new one. Because the gas storage was now located at Chula Vista in the form of LNG, the tanks were retired from service in August 1968 and slated for removal. The old tanks held a total of 8 million cubic feet of gas and had telescoping roofs that could be lowered or raised according to users' demands. The new liquefied natural-gas tank at South Bay held the equivalent of 620 million cubic feet. In addition, a second LNG facility under construction at the South Bay facility was designed to store 1.2 billion cubic feet of gas.

When it arrived in June 1965 at the San Onofre site, the Unit 1 reactor vessel was the largest in the world at that time.

When completed, the San Onofre Unit I reactor was housed inside the dome structure. The turbine and generator are located outside the dome, just to the left.

The two old tanks had been placed in service in 1912 and 1923 and at one time comprised nearly 95 percent of the Company's total storage capacity. When they were constructed, the Company was manufacturing its gas from crude oil in a plant at Station A. Natural-gas service began in 1932. Gas stored in the holders was used for peak shaving. As they telescoped up and down, depending on usage, they served as barometers that indicated the weather of the day, cold or warm.

Workmen balance atop a section of gas holder being dismantled in June 1969. This is the smaller holder built in 1912; the larger 1923 holder is in the background. Holders were removed after introduction of LNG plant.

Another element from the past also changed in 1968. A 50-year franchise held by SDG&E with the City of San Diego to provide utility service to the area was replaced by a new franchise. In June 1968, SDG&E was granted the franchise by the Board of Supervisors of San Diego County to supply electricity to all of the unincorporated area for San Diego County. An agreement between the City of San Diego and SDG&E was reached at this same time to install and operate a 1,600-watt gas-turbine generator at the city's sewage-treatment plant, and to use the plant's ventilating air as turbine combustion fuel. Operation of the generator effectively disposed of the sewage treatment plant's two undesirable waste products that had been piped to an incinerator and burned, an environmentally unacceptable solution in the decade of the 1960s.

Other major projects at the end of the decade included construction of the Peñasquitos substation, a new major transmission system substation, the completion of the 138-kv transmission line from the Encina Power Plant to

NEWS-METER TO UPDATE

In July 1925, the first *News-Meter* was published by SDG&E, replacing the earlier publication, *Glow*, started in 1921. Producing *News-Meter* was a function of the Company library for many years, but with the retirement of librarian Kay Gates Frazer in September 1945, the magazine was transferred to the advertising & public relations department.

The first *News-Meter* editor was William A. Cyr, who joined the Company in 1922 as the editor of *Glow*. Other editors included Forrest M. Raymond, Ruth E. Creveling (the Company librarian as well), Kay Gates Frazer, Lauran Clapp, Delavan J. Dickson, William B. Dyke, Fred Jeffries, Pat Munster, Roy Oakes, Tom Larimore, Fred Vaughn, Laura Farmer, Karen Hamilton and John Britton. *News-Meter* was discontinued with the October 1985 issue, and *UpDate* was created between then and its first issue in January 1986.

News-Meter could never have become the special publication it was without the help of Pauline McKnight, assistant editor. Since 1946, she has been the indispensable "right arm" of editors, offering her comprehensive knowledge of the Company, its facilities and employees to ensure a quality product. Pauline commented that "having an inborn sense of curiosity adds a lot to the pleasure of this kind of occupational pursuit, and a working knowledge of the English language comes in handy."

Writing for the Company's publications has kept Pauline McKnight busy for 45 years.

Peñasquitos, and the addition of the Mountain Empire Electric Cooperative. These projects strengthened the transmission system ties with other California utilities and provided for load growth within the service territory.

The 337-square-mile area of the Mountain Empire Electric Cooperative in southeast San Diego County was acquired in December 1970 for $1,691,000. The Company had been selling the co-op about $100,000 worth of electric power a year, and its purchase allowed the Mountain Empire to serve as a base for expanded service in eastern San Diego County. The 10 employees of the co-op became SDG&E staff members, and the Company gained 1,547 customers. Sixteen of the new customers actually resided in Imperial County, allowing the Company to claim service to three counties—San Diego, Orange and Imperial. One of the first changes was a 25 percent reduction in rates for the newest customers.

The Mountain Empire Co-op, incorporated on November 10, 1938, encompassed such back-country communities as Campo, Pine Valley, Jacumba, Mount Laguna, Potrero and Mountain Springs—territory ranging from brush country to arid desert to mountain meadows and forests. First energized on March 30, 1940, the early system included 139 customers who received their electricity from the SDG&E pole-top substation at Potrero. At the time of inclusion in the Company's system, the Glencliff Substation provided additional power to the Mountain Empire area. In 1940, the Co-op employed one jack-of-all-trades, Leroy N. Miller. He performed the duties of manager, lineman, groundman, troubleshooter, repairman, meterman and bookkeeper—all from his home near Campo.

The year 1970 marked the time for SDG&E to renew its franchise fees with the City of San Diego. The previous rates had been 1.1 percent of gross electric receipts and 2 percent of gross gas receipts, both on an annual basis. After months of debate and controversy, the San Diego City Council settled the current issues with SDG&E in December 1970 and approved a final adoption of a franchise to provide gas and electric service for the next 50 years. The terms of the agreement called for the Company to pay a straight 2 percent of gross annual receipts for the right to use the city streets. The California Public Utilities Commission authorized the Company to collect a surcharge from its city customers to defray the added costs to

SDG&E. Under terms of the revised franchise, SDG&E increased its allocation for undergrounding of utility lines. This was one of many environmental concerns with which the Company would deal in the future.

With these diverse changes, SDG&E entered the decade of the 1970s. The many projects undertaken in the 1960s would pave the way for the new directions chosen during the tumultuous years of the 1970s. San Diego Gas & Electric Company faced enormous challenges brought about by new technology coupled with large-scale population growth and important environmental concerns.

The San Diego skyline at the end of the 1960s shows the brilliant lighting effects of the new Electric Building at Christmas. The building's unique lighting system allowed it to be seen from many miles away.

Chapter 10

1971-1980
Transitional Years

Environmental and conservation issues dominated the decade of the 1970s with a new awareness of man's impact on the planet. A major shift in the direction taken by the Company would emerge from the challenges posed by these issues. SDG&E, seeking to increase conservation measures while still meeting the energy needs of consumers, would lead the way with a wide variety of plans to encourage customers to use energy resources with maximum efficiency.

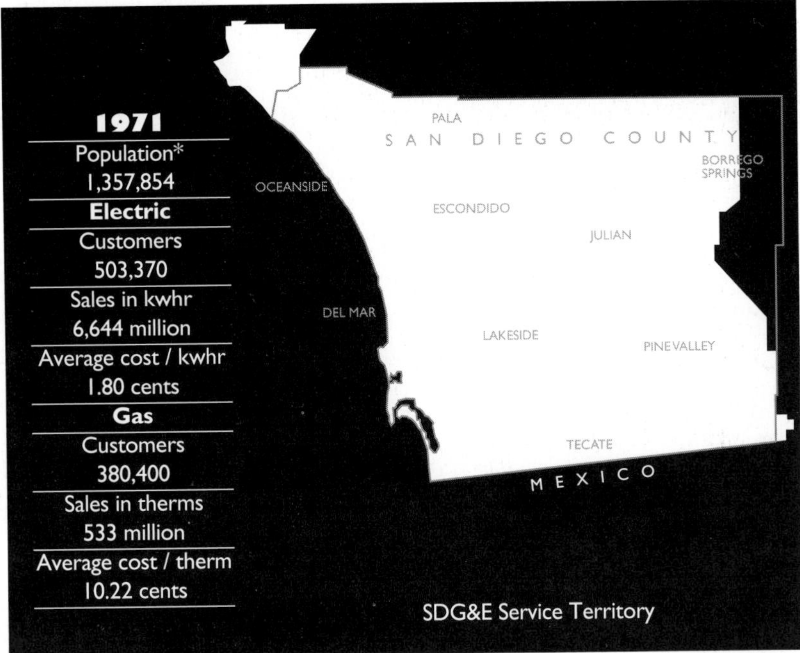

*County population based on census 10-year estimates

The utility industry changed dramatically over the 1970s. The golden age of gas and electricity bargains and customers purchasing great quantities of energy had ended. During the 1950s and 1960s, the Company had been able to produce a product with a declining unit price. Utilities focused on the technological aspects of the business and construction of new facilities. Those halcyon days were over as energy became an essential commodity, locking companies and consumers into a mutually dependent relationship where many choices, long taken for granted, were no longer options.

One of the first events to signal a change in direction took place when Joseph F. Sinnott, originally a meter tester and later president of the Company during the greatest growth era in its 89-year history, announced his retirement, effective January 1, 1971. During his 41 years of service with SDG&E, Sinnott saw the electric peak load increase by a factor of 20 and the payroll increase from 1,300 employees in 1929 to more than 3,330 in 1971. Some of the most significant developments in the Company's nine decades took place under Sinnott's guiding hand.

A few highlights of Sinnott's career included: bringing operating revenues from $98 million in 1963 to $142 million in 1969; activation of the San

< The impact of the country's first energy crisis in the mid-1970s caused the Company to darken its once-shining corporate headquarters, a dramatic symbol of the times. (Photo by Kenneth Robert Shearer.)

WALTER A. ZITLAU

Walter A. Zitlau was born in 1912 in Douglas, Arizona, and attended school in the nearby mining center of Ajo, Arizona. His father was the superintendent of the first power plant at Ajo, and his example and encouragement convinced Walter to choose mechanical engineering as his major in college. Zitlau obtained a degree in this field from the University of Arizona's College of Engineering and continued his education in the fields of engineering and utility management at the University of California and the University of Michigan.

Walter Zitlau began his career with SDG&E in 1941, when he joined the Company as an engineering assistant. He progressed through various engineering posts and was elected vice president of production in 1961. In 1963, he was elected executive vice president, and in January 1971, he became president and chief executive officer.

He also served on a wide variety of community boards, including the San Diego Chamber of Commerce, Junior Achievement Advisory Board, California Chamber of Commerce, the Economic Development Corporation and the California Council for Environmental and Economic Balance.

Onofre Nuclear Generating Station, jointly owned by SDG&E and Southern California Edison; introduction of liquefied natural gas as both a cold-weather reserve fuel and a motor vehicle fuel; and construction of the 21-story headquarters building. Among the research projects were development of a generating station in a southern Utah coal field and sponsoring studies in diverse areas such as fish breeding, lightweight batteries for powering cars, and new types of nuclear generating systems.

Sinnott was succeeded by Walter A. Zitlau, executive vice president and a 29-year employee of SDG&E. Zitlau began his career with the Company as an engineering assistant, later serving as assistant master mechanic, Silver Gate station chief, assistant superintendent–electric production, manager of production and transmission and vice president–production and transmission. Zitlau headed the Company until his resignation on November 17, 1975.

One of the first issues confronting Zitlau was the transition from conventional fossil-fuel generating plants as the chief source of power to nuclear power plants and the effort to minimize air emissions at existing stations. Each type of electric generating plant had some effect on the environment, and ways to cut down on harmful by-products of the conventional plants took a variety of forms. One method was to burn cleaner fuels such as the low-viscosity, low-sulfur diesel oil introduced by SDG&E during the winter of 1971. The decision to use this new oil was made after a successful evaluation was obtained at Silver Gate, where 4,500 barrels were utilized in a test program during January 1971.

Fuel oil produced from Alaskan low-sulfur crude oil, had a sulfur content of .5 percent or less and was burned effectively at the Encina and South Bay power plants. The positive aspect of this fuel was the emission of fewer pollutants than the California residual fuel oil containing a higher sulfur content. The Company was actively involved in research to cut the emission of nitrogen oxides at the various plants. Supplying the energy needs of the rapidly growing region, with a minimum of adverse impacts on the environment, was a challenge faced continually by the Company during the decades of the 1970s and 1980s.

In 1971, the second LNG storage tank became fully operational on the grounds of the South Bay Power Plant. Pronounced "world's largest above-ground metal LNG [Liquid Natural Gas] storage tank," the new tank had a capacity of 1.2 billion cubic feet of natural gas, twice the size of the first, and was adorned with a smiling polar bear. The polar bear represented the increasing use of LNG as a fuel for a "polar bear fleet" of sedans and trucks and referred to the temperature of LNG—a minus 258 degrees Fahrenheit. LNG was a product of cryogenics, the science of the super-cold.

Nearly 80 vehicles had been converted in the preceding 18 months to operate on the clean-burning LNG. Most of the vehicles belonged to SDG&E, but company cars owned by the State of California and the County of San

Painters complete a giant logo for the Company's newest LNG tank in the early 1970s. The specially constructed tanks held super-cold liquefied natural gas that was to be used to meet high winter demands.

Diego, and tour buses at the San Diego Zoo were changed over to the new fuel. Three new service stations, believed to be the first of their kind in the world, fueled the cars. The service stations were located at the state's Division of Highways facility in Old Town, the Dells, and the zoo.

Rocketing fuel-oil costs, which soared from $2 a barrel to $5.02 a barrel during the early 1970s, combined with inflationary pressures, resulted in a decision by the Company in August 1971 to ask the PUC for a rate increase. SDG&E was the last major private or publicly owned utility in California to seek general rate relief in more than a decade. New revenue generated by the increase was expected to be $35.5 million in electric revenues, $9.98 million in gas and $233,800 in steam revenues. Application for a rate increase is a long, involved process, requiring production of reports, applications and other exhibits for filing and the hearings. A total of 13 different reports were produced for exhibit and, since multiple copies of each report were necessary for various purposes, more than 2,000 copies were eventually produced! The rate increase, totaling $17.1 million a year, was granted in August 1972.

Rich Swanson shows a container of LNG to a San Diego Zoo official in the early 1970s. The zoo arranged for several of its tour buses to use LNG as a clean-fuel alternative. The test program was successful.

Construction progressed during 1971 on a 4,200-foot dual pipeline for a new chilled-water service for air conditioning in office and commercial buildings in downtown San Diego. Applied Energy, Inc., a subsidiary of SDG&E, obtained a franchise from the city to use city streets for construction of the system. A successful cooling system was already in place at the Rancho Bernardo Industrial Park, and plans proceeded with a second system in downtown San Diego.

President Walter Zitlau and electric troubleman Ken Cobbs show Mr. and Mrs. David Ross, of Paradise Hills, the Company's 500,000th active electric meter, set at their home January 7, 1972.

A central cooling plant, located at Kettner Boulevard and E Street near Station B, contained two electric-driven centrifugal chiller units, each with a capacity of 1,250 tons of refrigeration. The plant cooled fresh water to 42 degrees Fahrenheit and then pumped it through a closed circulatory pipeline system to customers' buildings. The water circulated through a building's system, picked up the heat and returned to the plant for chilling. The first customer for the service was scheduled to be the 18-story Security Pacific National Bank building, under construction at the time. Advantages to the customer included greater cooling efficiency and no costs to the consumer for installation of an expensive system.

An SDG&E milestone was reached on January 7, 1972, when the Company hooked up its 500,000th electric customer, Mr. and Mrs. David Ross of Paradise Hills. SDG&E President Walter Zitlau said that the installation of this particular electric meter symbolized a major accomplishment for the Company in fulfilling its responsibility to provide electric service for the rapidly developing San Diego County and southern Orange County areas. It took the Company 68 years, from 1887 to 1955, to reach 250,000 electric customers, but only 16 years to double that mark! The electric customer mark hit 100,000 in December 1940; 200,000 in March 1952; 300,00 in April 1959; and 400,000 in April 1967.

While all the usual Company operations were taking place, SDG&E continued to explore alternative sources of energy. In 1972 the Company joined with Magma Power Company and Magma Energy, Inc. in drilling exploratory geothermal wells in Imperial Valley. This area was considered to contain one of the largest reservoirs of geothermal energy in the world. Electric production fueled by geothermal energy was already in existence at four other facilities in the world. The original one, with a capacity of 400,000 kilowatts, was constructed in Italy in 1904. The other facilities are located in New Zealand with a capacity of 25,000 kilowatts; the Geysers in Santa Rosa, California, operated generating plants using dry steam from the wells, and Cerro Prieto, Mexico, provided 75,000 kilowatts of capacity.

Applied Energy, Inc. (AEI) chilled-water plant at Kettner Boulevard and E Street. The chilled water was supplied to several downtown buildings for air-conditioning use.

The environmental concerns of the 1970s embraced a number of interconnecting issues. Open space—a rapidly decreasing commodity in the Company service territory—was a key environmental issue. By necessity, SDG&E had acquired certain quantities of open space in the form of transmission rights of way, mainly to provide transmission routes for gas and electric lines. The Company had control over the property in the rights of way, and once the gas or electric lines were installed, then the land containing the lines could be used for other noncompetitive purposes.

Recreational and commercial uses, as long as they were compatible, were acceptable. A number of golf courses in the county were built on these areas, including La Costa and Lomas Santa Fe. Little League facilities, hiking and riding trails, and small parks with picnic and children's play areas occupy SDG&E property. The policy of the Company is to restore the rights of way to a natural condition after the transmission lines are completed. Commercial developments, such as citrus and avocado groves, tomato and flower production areas, tree farms, nurseries and parking or storage areas, have all been viable uses. These areas were ideal for community recreational development and helped foster another positive link between SDG&E and the local communities.

The Company conducted ongoing projects in the early 1970s to improve service to customers. In 1972, renewal of gas service lines in low-pressure areas was begun. Polyethylene pipe was inserted into the deteriorating cast-iron system. The pipe was pushed through the existing system, resulting in a huge savings because little digging was necessary and labor costs could be cut accordingly. The pipe was also protected by the iron "shell," and pressure was increased from ¼ pound per square inch to 60 pounds per square inch.

Geothermal steam roars from deep under the Imperial Valley during exploration for alternative energy resources in 1972. High-pressure steam is emitted from the cone-shaped silencer, low-pressure steam from the vertical flash tank.

Agricultural work is only one type of business that is under the Company's power lines in many parts of the service territory.

Easy-to-use plastic pipe, first tried in 1946, was inserted into old cast-iron pipe that served downtown San Diego, allowing the Company to rejuvenate its gas system without extensive street excavation.

Another project undertaken in 1971 and 1972 was the construction of seven fuel-oil tanks with a combined storage capacity of more than two million barrels. Fuel oil stored in the tanks was destined to fire boilers in the largest fossil-fuel electric generating units. The largest unit was Tank 6 at Encina with a 445,000-barrel capacity. With a diameter of 315 feet and a height of 32 feet, the structure surpassed all units on the West Coast. Mindful of ocean views for passing travelers, SDG&E engineers designed an excavated area for the tanks behind a landscaped bank alongside southbound Interstate 5 in Carlsbad.

Demonstrating its continuing concern for national issues related to the utilities industry, SDG&E joined with more than 100 other utility companies around the country to form the Electric Power Research Institute (EPRI) to coordinate and expand energy research and development. Original goals of the institute included improving present methods of power generation; developing new technologies in transmission and distribution, environmental protection and energy conservation; and improving plant efficiency.

SDG&E's research partnership with EPRI included mariculture and aquaculture research at two of the Company's power plants. This work concerned utilization of thermal plumes—warm water discharged from power-plant condensers—for sea life experiments. One aspect of this type of research was to create a favorable environment for rapid production of edible fish. Investigation into potential beneficial uses of warmed water discharged from power plants occupied SDG&E research scientists, and all results were shared with EPRI and its member utilities.

KEN ARNONE

Engineer Robert Meinzer surveys a newly completed 450,000-barrel-capacity oil-storage tank on the grounds of the Encina Power Plant in 1977. The oil tanker *Chevron Hawaii* lies offshore unloading residual fuel oil for storage in the new tank.

Dr. Richard Northcraft (right) and an assistant examine a basket of oysters in the Agua Hedionda Lagoon, next to the Company's Encina Power Plant in July 1973. Researchers have long used the water around the plant for studying marine growth.

The Company's largest generating unit, Encina 4, was completed in May 1973. Its capacity of 300,000 kilowatts nearly equaled the output of the first three units at Encina, each of which had a capacity of just more than 100,000 kw. The new unit was fossil-fueled, like units 1, 2 and 3. All could burn either natural gas or low-sulfur fuel oil, allowing fuel diversity. Housed in an extension of a building that contained units 1, 2 and 3, Unit 4 was a versatile plant and designed for either daily start-up and shut-down, or for continuous operation.

SDG&E came to the conclusion that it would have to either build an environmentally acceptable refinery or face possible shortages of cleaner-burning fuels that were essential to protect San Diego's air quality. In 1973, plans to study the feasibility of building a refinery to produce low-sulfur fuel oil and synthetic natural gas (SNG) were announced by SDG&E officials and Pacific Resources, Inc. of Hawaii. The Macario Independent Refinery was to be situated on 310 acres three miles east of the Encina Power Plant. The

Steelwork frames construction of the No. 4 unit at Encina.

proposal was to create a plant capable of producing about 40,000 barrels of low-sulfur fuel oil for use in the electric generating plants. The refinery was expected to produce 100 million cubic feet of SNG per day and 30,000 barrels per day of extremely low sulfur-distillate fuels (diesel and kerosene) to be used in gas turbine generators. Due to environmental concerns and local opposition, plans for the project were scrapped in 1976.

Conservation measures became a fact of life for most Americans during the 1970s. The outbreak of the Yom Kippur War aligning Egypt and Syria against Israel in October 1973 began a complex series of events that ultimately led to an oil embargo by the Arab nations and disruption of supply lines. On October 17 the Arab members of the Organization of Petroleum Exporting Countries (OPEC) announced a 5 percent cut in oil production.

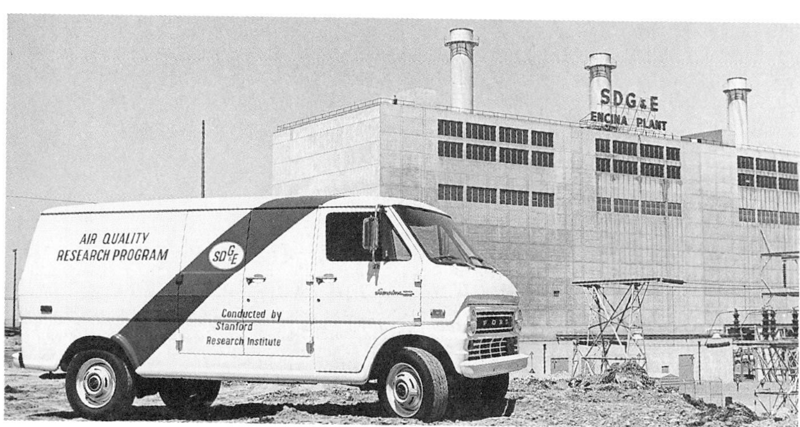

This air-quality research vehicle was used to conduct early testing that led the Company to begin using low-pollution fuel in its power plants.

More cuts each month would continue until Israel gave up territory taken in 1967. The Nixon administration promptly offered $2.2 billion in aid to Israel, prompting the OPEC nations to cut off oil shipments to the United States and its ally in Europe, the Netherlands.

A crisis of great proportions ensued from this decision. The United States was currently importing 2 million barrels of oil a day, and this severely hampered a nation wasteful of oil and energy. Increased imports from Libya, Iran and Nigeria helped to offset the embargo, but Americans began to panic as supplies fell. A dramatic increase in oil prices accompanied the curtailment of supplies. What Americans did not anticipate at the time was that the days of cheap and plentiful oil were over.

Efforts to deal with the crisis took many forms. On November 13, 1973, the California Public Utilities Commission ordered all utilities under its jurisdiction to cut electric energy usage each month by 10 percent below the corresponding amount from the previous year. SDG&E was directed to comply, even though it had enough fuel under contract to meet its energy requirements until 1976. Other utilities found themselves facing severe shortages, as much as 70 percent in some cases in the state. The PUC was committed to keeping all electric systems in California in operational condition and was prepared to take drastic measures to keep service open to the state.

At this time, utilities across the country began exploring alternative sources of energy. The industry realized that never again would the United States be able to meet all its energy needs from conventional sources, such as natural gas or oil. Supplies of natural gas in readily accessible areas were largely tapped, and federal government price controls discouraged new, more costly exploration. The lack of adequate supplies was already hamper-

ENERGY TERMS

Blackout—a complete interruption of service.
Brownout—a lesser use of power in a number of different applications. Certain operations requiring the use of electrical power would have to be curtailed, if not stopped altogether.
California Power Pool—an emergency supply agreement between SDG&E, Southern California Edison Company and Pacific Gas & Electric Company.
Load shedding—selected circuits would be disconnected while maintaining service to critical loads involving public health and safety.
Voltage reduction—a step taken to spread available power over an entire utility system in an attempt to reduce the load on the system during emergencies while minimizing effects on customer service.
Western Systems Coordinating Council—a cooperative effort of 41 member utility companies voluntarily coordinating the planning, operation and related activities of bulk power and electric systems in 14 states and western Canada.

KENNETH ROBERT SHEARER

Energy conservation became a way of life in the 1970s. Modeling these promotional T-shirts for the 1977 Del Mar Fair are summer students Bill Becktel (left), Jan Huey and Jan Moullen; and employees Rick English and Nina Hazard.

Environmental awareness became increasingly important in the company's operations during the 1970s. Susan Vergne, environmental analyst, and Joe Dietz, environmental manager, examine zoobotryon, a marine animal that clogs seawater intake screens at power plants.

Conservation auditor Lynn Trexel (right) helps a customer conduct a computer-assisted home-energy audit. The audits helped customers pinpoint energy waste and reduce bills.

ing industrial and residential development in some areas. In the 1970s, gas accounted for one-third of the nation's energy consumption.

The most accessible source of major new natural-gas discoveries were the offshore areas of the outer continental shelf bordering the United States. Many of the areas believed to have the best potential were under federal control, and in 1972 the Department of the Interior began leasing drilling rights to about one million acres off the Texas and Louisiana coasts. Industry experts estimated that two million acres a year would have to be leased on a regular basis to meet demands. Geology experts estimated that 38 trillion cubic feet of natural gas existed in the Gulf of Mexico.

Three environmental groups posed legal challenges to lease sales scheduled by the Department of the Interior, but dropped the suits after realizing that offshore drilling was the quickest way to make more natural gas available to replace other, more polluting fuels. Offshore drilling would make energy resources available to consumers with a minimal danger of environmental pollution. Opposition from environmentally concerned citizens became another fact of life during this decade, and utilities responded by developing policies and programs to help protect fragile, and finite, resources.

SDG&E marketing policies during the 1970s also changed to reflect new environmental concerns. Instead of "sell," the key word for customers was "save." Customer sales representatives offered free energy audits, efficient energy-use techniques, energy conservation tips and ways to shift loads off peak to both residential and commercial customers. Extensive efforts were made throughout the utility industry to educate consumers in the most effective energy-efficient methods and enlist their help in the nationwide conservation movement.

SDG&E officials considered it necessary to lead the way in the conservation issues in the community. During the early months of 1974, the Company cut its own usage by 54 percent. To be a guiding light in energy conservation meant that the Company had to turn off its own lights! Many lights in Company facilities were turned off permanently or their use time was rescheduled. Interior light levels were reduced by removing fluorescent lamps and encouraging employees to turn off lights when not in use. Other measures included turning off air-conditioning systems and setting thermostats at 68 degrees for heating and 78 degrees for cooling. As the lighting load dropped, so did a building's air-conditioning requirements. During cold weather, energy from the fluorescent lamps was drawn off and used as a basic heating source for the entire building.

The Electric Building, a shining example of how light could enhance architecture, became a darkened building after hours. No longer were lights left burning all night to make the structure a city landmark in the night sky. Only enough lighting remained for safety. Janitors cleaned floors in groups,

KING FREEMAN

King Freeman, an SDG&E employee assigned to the Escondido Operations Department as a helper on a polyethylene gas pipe crew, played an important role in the North County area. Freeman was tribal chairman of the Pala Indians and their official spokesman.

In his role as tribal chairman, he worked on many improvement projects on the Pala Reservation, located along Highway 76, east of Highway 395 and north of Escondido. Freeman participated in a program called Center for Awareness and Development of Resources and Education (CADRE), which received vital assistance from SDG&E, the U.S. Navy and Marine Corps and other interested groups. The military assisted with road development on the reservation in memory of the many Pala Indians who served with distinction during our nation's wars.

A baseball park, coin laundry, trading post, the Pala Education and Development Center with library, hobby shop and the Pala cable-television studio, and development of a lake and campgrounds were projects created on the reservation by community efforts. The dedication event for these projects was held on August 22, 1973, and SDG&E president Walter Zitlau was a key speaker during the full day of festivities.

Freeman was one of two Pala Indians working for the Company. The other was Mario Moro, a street repair laborer, at the Escondido Operations Department.

Car pools, which employees initiated during World War II, were popular in the conservation-minded 1970s. These 1974 commuters are (from left) Sally Oberhaus, Yole Whiting, Roberta Bernstein and Monica Hutchins.

lighting only five floors at a time instead of the whole building. Three-light fluorescent fixtures in the general offices building had the center tube removed, resulting in a monthly savings of 82,000 kilowatt hours. All decorative and exterior lighting effects in the Electric Building, including the 88 1,000-watt floodlights, the pumps and lights on the front patio fountains, eight lamp fixtures on the promenade, the first-floor-lobby high bay lights, the third-floor cove lights and the yellow crown lights ringing the top of the structure, were turned off, resulting in a savings of 81,200 kilowatt hours.

Efforts by SDG&E executives to anticipate and meet future energy needs led to the decision to expand the San Onofre Nuclear Generating Station. Final clearance for expansion plans was granted on February 20, 1974, by the California Coastal Zone Conservation Commission. Approval from 19 local, state and federal regulatory groups was required to give permission before plans could proceed for the construction of two 1,100,000-kilowatt (net) nuclear-powered steam-generating units. SDG&E and Southern California Edison Company shared the cost and generating output on the same basis as the original Unit 1—80 percent for SCE and 20 percent for SDG&E. Later, the percentage would be reduced to

Al Panton, right, Company governmental sales manager, provides conservation tips to Commander Mat Mlekush at the U.S. Naval Station, San Diego, as Lieutenant John Thom removes a fluorescent bulb from a fixture in this 1974 photo.

75 percent with 5 percent going to a group of cities. The two new units were scheduled for completion in 1980 and 1981 and would result in an increase in the station's electric generating capacity to a total output of 2,710,000 kilowatts. Total cost of the project was estimated to be $1.4 billion.

The Company's two-year program to reduce emissions of oxides of nitrogen (NO_x) from power plants was highly successful but expensive. By 1974, all SDG&E power-generating units met the San Diego County Air Pollution Control District's air-quality standards, generally acknowledged to be one of the most rigid of any in the nation. Success came with a high price tag, including a reduction of generating capacity and operating efficiency. Expenditures for instrumentation of boilers, development of different firing techniques and addition of new equipment boosted the total overall cost of compliance.

Beautification through utility-line undergrounding was dramatically demonstrated with the removal of the center-of-the-street power line along Mission Boulevard in Mission Beach in February 1975.

As the Company moved forward with complex, highly sophisticated solutions to the new set of energy concerns, the traces of past power systems slowly faded from the San Diego scene. New high-technology energy equipment replaced systems that remained from an earlier era. A prime example of this process was the installation of a new underground system and removal of utility poles and overhead electric lines along Mission Boulevard from Pacific Beach Drive to the Mission Bay Channel jetty in South Mission Beach.

The center-of-the-street pole line was constructed in 1915 by San Diego Electric Railway for its trolley lines, and purchase of the line by SDG&E was completed in 1940. The $1.4 million project to make Mission Boulevard an open-sky street was the Company's largest undergrounding prior to this decade.

Inflation, coupled with environmental concerns and rising fuel costs, created significant financial problems for SDG&E. President Zitlau and senior management officials felt service would be seriously jeopardized without rate relief. In April 1975, SDG&E asked the PUC for a $119.4 million annual rate increase. The new rates would enable SDG&E to attract capital to finance construction, comply with new regulations and meet customer energy demands. Additional nuclear facilities were considered to be the answer to lowering fuel costs. The construction budget for 1975 reached an all-time high of $193 million—a direct result of the higher cost of borrowed money and expenditures for environmental projects, which alone were projected to exceed $100 million during the next three years. The resulting rate increase, however, was much less than expected. In the summer and fall of 1975, the Company laid off about 300 employees to cut costs. Many were rehired the next year. Company morale was at an all-time low.

The mid-1970s brought another serious crisis to the Company. Inadequate earnings reflected the impacts of Arab oil embargoes, rising fuel costs, inflation, and environmental issues. Because of these problems, the Company lost its double A bond rating, and without substantial rate relief, the rating might continue to drop. Derating led to higher costs for all future security issues and severely limited the market for bonds. All these higher money costs would eventually end up on consumers' monthly utility bills, a situation the Company was hoping to avoid.

Linemen connect wire (conductor) to insulators during construction of a new power line on an existing set of transmission towers.

Until the 1970s, SDG&E was able to keep rates relatively low. In 1971 the Company asked for its first electric-rate increase in 13 years. Between 1971 and 1974, rates increased 13 times, primarily due to fuel-cost adjustments. As oil prices increased, fuel-cost increases were passed on directly to the consumer. Environmental protection regulations permitted the burning of only the more expensive low-sulfur fuel oil, which also increased customer rates. In 1950, the Company had spent 18.2 cents of every revenue dollar for fuel and purchased power costs. By 1960, the cost had risen only .3 of a cent. In 1970, the cost had risen to 24.4 cents.

A major reorganization of management in November 1975 resulted from the resignations of Walter A. Zitlau, president, and Martin R. Engler Jr., executive vice president. The board of directors elected Robert E. Morris to the positions of both president and chief executive officer on November 17, because the board felt he had the background and experience to respond to the special needs of SDG&E at that time. The Company was experiencing serious problems, and Morris' election signaled a needed change in direction.

During his first management meetings in December, Morris outlined new plans to revitalize the Company to staff members. The course he outlined for these difficult times revolved around the theme that "the reason for our being is service to the customer." The three main Company goals would be: service to customers, financial integrity and accommodation to regulation. The reorganization resulted in policies that reflected the new directions set by the PUC and the public's rapidly changing attitudes toward the production and use of energy.

Morris had joined the Company in 1965 as manager of the Marketing Division, was elected a vice president in April 1969 and became a senior vice president in January 1971. He was a registered professional engineer, with a bachelor of science degree in electrical engineering from Georgia Institute of Technology. Various positions in the management consulting firm of Glengayle Associates in St. Louis and New York, the chemical operation of the Monsanto Chemical Company, and the Allis-Chalmers Manufacturing Company in Milwaukee prepared Morris for his role at SDG&E and gave him the background to effectively face the challenges posed by new regulations and environmental concerns.

Morris took over after the Company had announced its plans to build the Sundesert Nuclear Plant in the Palo Verde Valley area near the city of Blythe, California. Construction of the 1,300-megawatt generating plant was scheduled to begin in 1977 with completion around 1985. Electricity generated at the new facility was to be transmitted westward to SDG&E's service territory. On July 1, 1974, the Company had created the Nuclear Department and the Power Plant Engineering & Construction Division to manage the licensing and engineering of Sundesert.

ROBERT E. MORRIS

Robert E. Morris graduated with a degree in electrical engineering from Georgia Institute of Technology and was a registered professional engineer. Before joining SDG&E, Morris was a managing partner of the management consulting firm of Glengayle Associates in St. Louis and New York. He had 25 years of experience in engineering, sales and industrial marketing management, which included a position as general sales manager at Allis-Chalmers Manufacturing Company. He also served for a time as director of sales for Monsanto Chemical Company.

Morris joined SDG&E in July 1965 as manager of the marketing division where his extensive background in engineering, sales and industrial management was a key factor in his success. In April 1969, he was named vice president of the division. In 1971, he became a senior vice president, responsible for the Public Relations and Engineering Land Departments and the operations of four critical divisions —Rates and Valuation, Customer Services, Marketing and Administrative Services.

Morris became president and chief executive officer and a member of the board of directors on November 17, 1975. In addition to his position as president, he also served as president and member of the board of directors of the Company's three subsidiaries— Japatul Corporation, Applied Energy, Inc. and New Albion Resources Company.

Artist's concept of what the proposed Sundesert Nuclear Plant would have looked like if it had been built.

Cheryl Valencia, Gene McElroy, Alan McCutcheon and Stephanie Hitt with some of 130,000 signatures collected by employees in support of the Sundesert Plant.

SDG&E also supported the development of alternative energy sources during the mid-1970s. In 1975, SDG&E began construction of a $7.6 million geothermal loop experimental facility at Niland in the Imperial Valley. The U.S. Energy Research and Development Administration assisted the Company by providing funding, technical support, and carrying out specific studies and programs. The facility began operations on June 4, 1976. At the opening ceremony, keynote speaker U.S. Representative Clair W. Burgener told the audience that the station was "an excellent example of how cooperation between government and industry can further the development of new and much-needed sources of energy."

Even as efforts were directed at using energy from beneath the earth, SDG&E looked skyward to explore ways to tap into solar power. A three-year program of solar research began in 1975. Solar-powered homes, solar collection systems, and mass marketing of solar energy were studied by the Company in an effort to explore all potential sources of energy.

January 30, 1975, was a day to remember in SDG&E's history. On that day the Company coincidentally established record peaks on both the gas and electric systems. The new electric-system peak-load record was 1,654,000 kilowatts, breaking the former record of 1,649,000 kilowatts established on December 11, 1972. The new gas-system maximum daily firm sendout record was 3,378,534 therms, compared to the former record of 3,096,651 therms established January 6, 1971. One month later, in February 1975, the

Dedicated in 1976, the Niland Geothermal Loop Demonstration Facility, in the Imperial Valley, was designed to demonstrate energy production.

total number of electric customers was 598,766, and the milestone of 600,000 customers was expected before the end of March 1975.

New departments were created for experimental research and to handle issues generated by the 1970s. The Governmental Affairs Department, established in November 1976, centralized all activities dealing with federal, state, regional and local levels into one division. Negotiating legislation and land-use concerns were to be major focal points of the department.

In 1976, legislation introduced by Proposition 15, the Nuclear Power Shutdown Initiative, brought SDG&E employees into high gear as the Company banded together in concerted efforts to defeat the proposition. A dedicated corps of Company speakers emerged from the ranks to educate the public on the value of nuclear power. "NO on 15" groups spoke at debates, school programs, church events, community-wide public meetings and walked door-to-door in their attempts to make the facts known to the people. The proposition was soundly defeated by the voters.

Joanne Reel demonstrates the heating of water with sunlight for students at a local school. Solar-power water heating became a popular way to use alternative energy sources in customers' homes and businesses.

During 1976, the Company completed another substation. The Urban Substation at 14th and F streets in downtown San Diego began operations in January 1976 and won a beautification award from the Central City Association of San Diego. The Spanish-style, slumpstone building, designed by SDG&E employees Don Pray and Paul Rosenberg, won the honor for "construction of an environmentally unique electric power substation facility in Central City." This style was chosen to reflect San Diego's Spanish heritage and was compatible with the architecture of nearby San Diego City College. The college had expansion plans that were anticipated to create greater electric demand, and the increase was to be supplied by the Urban Substation.

On July 22, 1976, construction began on the long-delayed Encina Unit 5. Originally scheduled to go into service in 1975, the project had been subjected to more than four years of hearings, reviews and court challenges. Finally, the need for highly efficient, base-load generation was clearly established, and the project moved forward. Community resistance to the project included opposition to the proposed Macario Refinery, just east of the station, which was ultimately dropped by the Company.

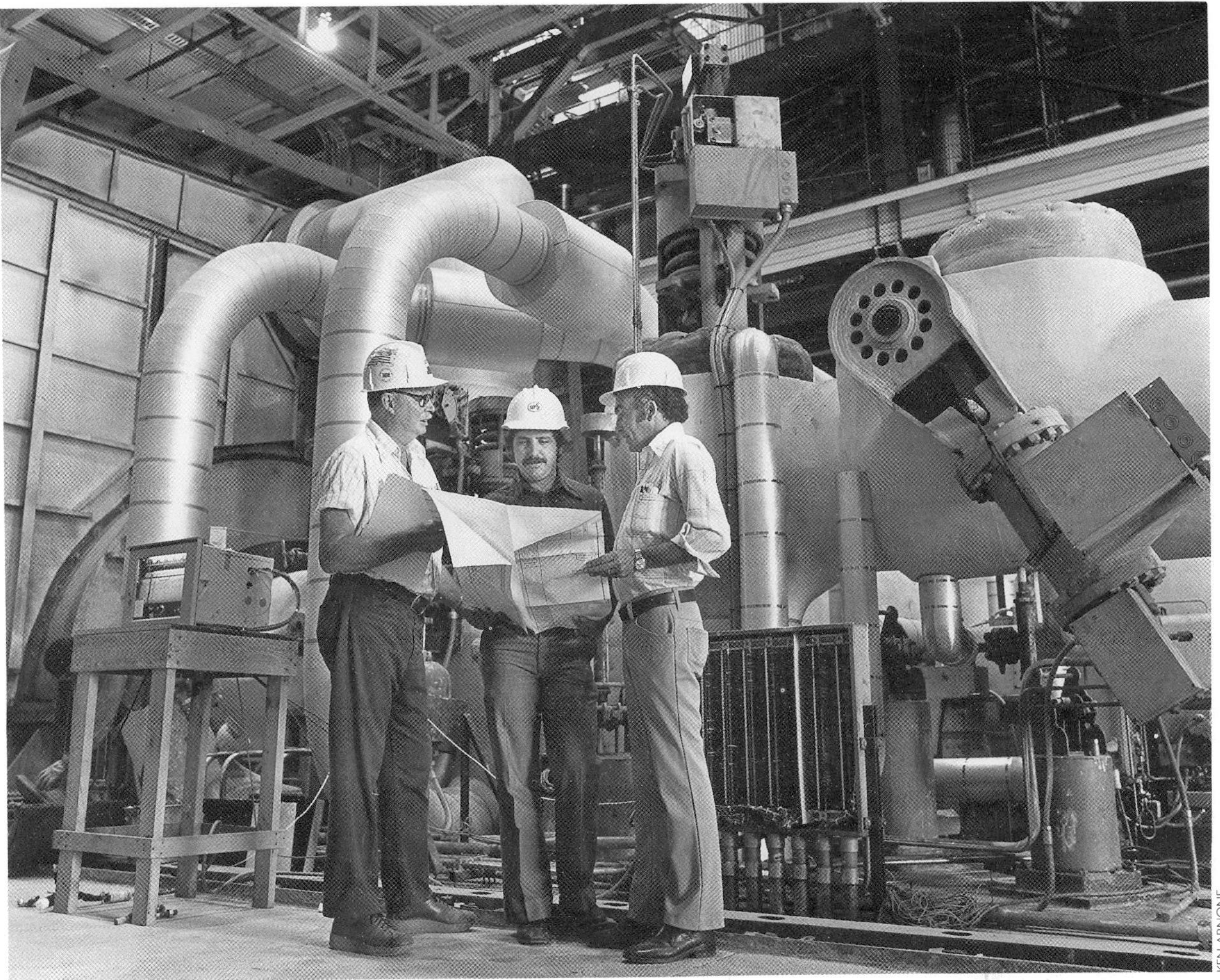
KEN ARNONE

The 1978 construction and start-up of the Encina Unit 5 generator marked the last major power-plant addition to the Company's existing generating sites. Here, J.A. (Red) Campbell, Edwin Guiles and James Sheffer review plans for a turbine generator.

Encina 5 was to be a 292-megawatt, oil-fired generator that would save 600,000 barrels of oil per year by reducing the use of other, less-efficient base-load units. On October 2, a tragic accident occurred when a 190-foot tower crane collapsed, killing six workers. After investigation and clearance by the California Division of Industrial Safety, construction was begun again.

By 1978, many of the goals outlined by President Morris in 1975 when he took office were well under way. The first satellite office was started in 1976 in La Jolla. Improvements in customer service in 1977 included new satellite customer-service offices in National City, San Diego, Vista, La Mesa, Poway and Solana Beach. Special training sessions for customer-service personnel increased productivity by 10 percent. Introduction of a new telephone system with 22 additional incoming lines allowed staff members to field 1.3 million customer calls per year.

Financial integrity, a key element in the Company's ability to meet customers' needs, showed significant positive response to new policies. But the growth of the service area and the resulting need to spend as much as $1 billion over the next five years on new plant construction was an immense challenge to Company leaders.

KENNETH ROBERT SHEARER

Elizabeth Ginn (right) customer information clerk in the Company's first satellite office in a La Jolla bank, helps a customer with service via a computer terminal connected to the Company's main system.

A positive change was the greatly improved working relations with the California Public Utilities Commission. Changes in computer technologies and streamlining of procedures resulted in faster application processing and better overall interaction between SDG&E and the PUC. However, a moratorium had been placed on nuclear-power development in California, raising concern over the fate of Sundesert.

The year 1977 brought significant progress to the Company, adding new gas and electric customers at a record rate, with revenues exceeding one-half billion dollars. More than 36,000 new electric customers and 15,000 new gas customers were connected to the Company's service lines. Total electric output for the year was 8.9 billion kilowatt hours, and natural-gas sendout for the same period was 479.9 million therms. These figures were outstanding in view of several weather crises in California and around the nation that resulted in orders to curtail gas and electricity consumption. Cold weather, extreme heat, heavy rainstorms and a violent windstorm all created problems for the service crews and meant long hours out in stormy weather. The crewmen were dedicated to restoring service to customers in affected regions as quickly as possible.

During 1977, the Company's widespread and aggressive marketing and sales program, designed to help customers save energy, showed results as energy use per customer decreased slightly. Traditional patterns of consumption were changing slowly as customers became aware of the benefits of energy-conservation measures, such as water-heater insulation blankets, flow-restricting showerheads, night setback controls for thermostats and solar heating units.

As a pioneer in the field of energy conservation, SDG&E participated in more than 40 conservation programs nationwide. These programs shared a common goal: to defer the need for new generating capacity and keep within necessary financial constraints. Residential conservation programs targeted sales of conservation products and included promoting the use of energy-efficient appliances, solar-energy use and energy-conservation education. Passive heating and cooling systems for residences featured low-cost building materials such as insulation and solar panels.

During 1978, an all-new energy education program for San Diego area schools was created. The culmination of a three-year cooperative effort between the Company and local educational leaders, the project was expected to reach more than 74,000 students a year. Making the next generation of consumers aware of energy issues had been a longstanding policy of the Company. As new issues or concerns came to the forefront, innovative approaches were necessary to keep pace with the changes in the industry.

Ernie Roberson conducts a teacher training class for the Captain Power program. The program provided teachers across the nation with facts and information on energy use and costs.

Electric Division projects in the late 1970s with Arizona included a key agreement with the Arizona Public Service Company for an interconnection of the two utilities' systems via a 500-kilovolt transmission line, enabling the Company to purchase energy from Arizona and New Mexico. Other projects involved the development of geothermal energy; an agreement to purchase electricity from the Tucson Gas & Electric Company; and a feasibility study with 10 other utilities to increase from three to five the additional units under construction at the Palo Verde Nuclear Generating Station in Arizona.

Work also proceeded on a potential interconnection and power-exchange agreement with the Comisión Federal de Electricidad of Mexico to obtain surplus electricity from Baja California by 1983. A contract was signed in

HELICOPTERS IN USE

Helicopters have been an important part of SDG&E operations since the decade of the 1940s. Air patrols with small planes were started on April 9, 1941, but were grounded by the military for a few years during World War II. By 1947, helicopters were used on a trial basis to patrol the service lines in the rugged back country. In February 1954, regular patrols by helicopter were begun. Helicopter pilots and an accompanying observer looked for damaged poles, trees crowding the lines or other problems that might disrupt service.

SDG&E strings miles of electric transmission lines across rugged mountains, steep canyons and rough, open terrain, without disturbing the fragile environment by using helicopters, eliminating the need to cut roads or crush plants and animal habitats with heavy equipment.

On two electric-transmission-tower construction projects, helicopters pulled 10,000 feet of line at a time from tower to tower, where construction department linemen inserted the rope into pulleys attached to each crossarm. Once the ropes were attached to the row of towers, they were then secured to the conductors, which were pulled in by regular ground equipment.

Helicopters cut time on the job considerably and have been used over the years for a variety of jobs. The "whirlybirds" have been used to set poles and towers and to carry concrete, construction equipment and personnel into remote areas.

October 1979 with the Mexican government to sell SDG&E energy by way of an existing 69-kv interconnection between San Ysidro and Tijuana. This arrangement marked the first time that Mexico had agreed to sell electricity on a non-exchange basis.

The Gas Division experienced a slight decrease in gas sales in 1977, but a severe cold snap increased total usage for 1978. Projects under way at the end of the decade for the Gas Division focused on the need for new sources. Southern California Gas Company (SoCal), the Company's principal gas supplier, signed contracts to supply gas obtained from more extensive drilling in Alberta, Canada. Plans were also made to purchase additional long-term supplies from Pacific Gas and Electric Company and from sources in Alaska and Mexico. Other long-term gas prospects included gas manufactured from Southwestern coal. In addition, the PUC granted conditional approval in 1978 for construction of California's first liquefied natural-gas terminal at Point Conception. This planned new supply was expected to bring gas to SDG&E's major supplier, SoCal.

Pat Fleming balances a multimillion-dollar copy of the 30-volume, government-required environmental report for the Sundesert Nuclear Plant in 1977. The Company eventually spent nearly $100 million on the plant before the project was canceled.

Plans pursued in the early 1970s, such as Sundesert, never materialized due to opposition by public groups. The Company lost a final attempt to gain approval for Sundesert in 1978 when it asked the state legislature for an exemption from California's restrictive nuclear-fuel cycle laws. The struggle continued for four months, and more than 500 SDG&E employees started grass-roots organizations to demonstrate citizen support for the project. While the bill to exempt SDG&E from the laws was in the legislature, the PUC announced on May 2 that it was prepared to order the Company to cease activity because it was not planning to grant the necessary rate relief. The board of directors dropped plans for Sundesert the next day. After months of planning and tons of paperwork, the project was canceled due to environmental concerns and pressure from citizens' groups. The realities of government action precluded forward movement on the project. The rapid customer growth of the decade, coupled with the loss of planned projects, led SDG&E to adopt an extremely flexible approach to meeting future energy needs.

Increasing instability in the Middle East produced another oil crisis in the summer of 1979. A fuel shortage created massive problems once again for homeowners, business and industry. During the crisis, the OPEC cartel opted for an additional price increase. President Jimmy Carter announced a plan to counteract the effects of the new price hike by the creation of a vast synthetic-fuels industry to replace America's dependence on OPEC oil supplies. This presidential declaration helped to promote increasing research into alternative energy sources as a long-term solution to this type of problem.

Nuclear-power production also faced a serious crisis during the same period, which led to increasing public concerns about nuclear energy. The advance of nuclear power came to a virtual standstill in 1979 with a cata-

Gail Belgum poses with animated animals and low-energy lighting of the Company's Christmas tree in December 1978.

strophic incident at Three Mile Island in Pennsylvania. The plant suffered a near meltdown of its nuclear core, and this accident resulted in a serious reexamination of nuclear power and its potential liabilities. New regulations, ordered by the Nuclear Regulatory Commission to upgrade the unit's ability to withstand earthquakes, went into effect as a result of the incident, and San Onofre Unit 1 was shut down from April 1980 to the fall of 1983 for repairs and retrofitting required by these changes in policy.

As the tumultuous decade of the 1970s ended, SDG&E executives faced the coming years with growing uncertainty. Major questions regarding availability of fuels, new energy regulations, inflation, capital costs and conflicting governmental policies were left unanswered. A "hedging" strategy was developed to enable the Company to have maximum flexibility under any circumstances. Many resource options were explored in an effort to find the most viable solution to meeting energy needs. Two principles were at the heart of the plans for the 1980s: gaining access to generation that did not require oil as a fuel so diminished accessibility would not cause a crisis, and an increase in purchasing power supplies wherever possible to minimize the need for capital investment.

Purchasing energy was seen not merely as an interim solution for the 1980s but as a solution that would buy Company planners additional time to develop creative answers to new conditions. Purchased-power contracts with New Mexico and Arizona utilities were expected to end in the late 1980s and early 1990s because those utilities would need the energy for their own customers. Replacement of this power with SDG&E's own system was the only solution seen at the time, which meant adding to and replacing less-efficient plants with new plants that used less oil. Low-cost, low-risk on-system generation plants would have to be constructed within the maze of new federal and state regulatory statutes. By taking steps to reduce the rate of growth in energy sales, and by slowing the growth in peak demand, it was thought that the Company could accommodate more customers while adding new capacity at a slower, more manageable rate.

Despite the massive problems faced by the Company during the 1970s, SDG&E executives remained optimistic toward the future. Positive changes had occurred even under the adverse conditions of the previous 10 years. New facilities were under construction, and an intensive maintenance and improvement program helped to keep existing plants in good shape, extending service lives. Having weathered the storms of the 1970s, the Company's approach to the new decade was summed up in the words of President Morris: "If we deal wisely with the challenges of these transitional times and the era of uncertainty they bring, SDG&E will emerge a stronger, more resilient company.

President Robert Morris (center) inspects some of the 12,000 fluorescent lamps removed from service in an energy-saving effort at Scripps Clinic and Research Foundation. The clinic was one of many businesses adopting new lighting standards in the 1970s to save energy and reduce its energy bill.

Chapter 11

1981-1990
A Decade of Challenges

San Diego Gas & Electric began its second century of operations on a muted note as the utility industry was challenged by a myriad of energy problems and the economic pressures of a recessionary year. The Company faced mounting criticism from the local community for rising utility rates due to its dependency on costly foreign oil. At this time, SDG&E's industrial customers were paying the nation's highest electric rates, and residential electric customers were coping with rates among the top 10 highest in the country. Nevertheless, Thomas A. Page, elected president and chief executive officer in 1981, remained optimistic. He set the tone for the decade when he told shareholders: "Our Company is in the midst of change, and the achievement of our goals will have a significant impact on SDG&E."

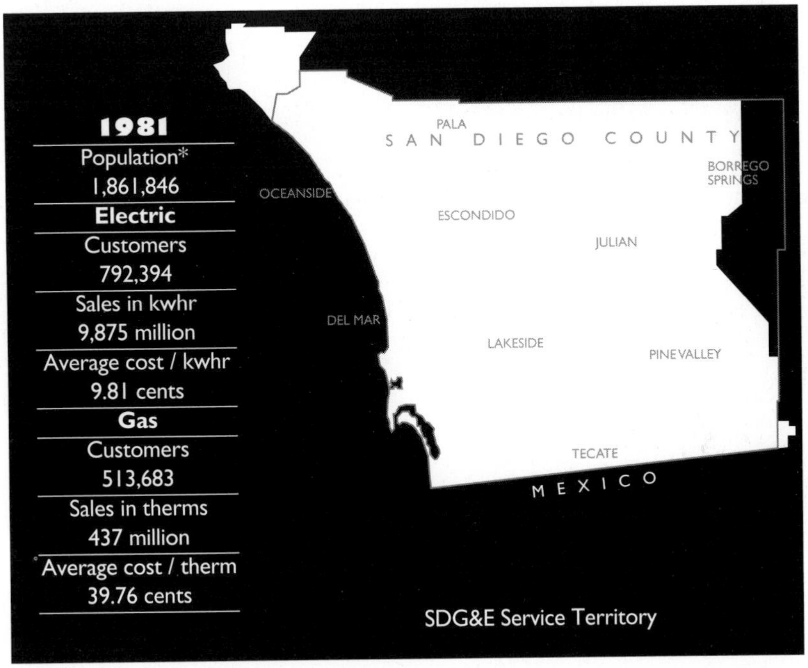

1981
Population*
1,861,846
Electric
Customers
792,394
Sales in kwhr
9,875 million
Average cost / kwhr
9.81 cents
Gas
Customers
513,683
Sales in therms
437 million
Average cost / therm
39.76 cents

PALA
SAN DIEGO COUNTY
OCEANSIDE
ESCONDIDO
BORREGO SPRINGS
JULIAN
DEL MAR
LAKESIDE
PINE VALLEY
TECATE
MEXICO

SDG&E Service Territory

*County population based on census 10-year estimates

During the 1980s, a transformation took place within SDG&E as management and employees responded to the challenges posed by economic pressures. The entire Company rose to meet the problems in a variety of ways by cutting costs, adopting innovative approaches, and when it did not seem possible to tighten the budget anymore, they tightened it anyway. At the beginning of the decade, few people predicted that the Company could achieve the gains that it did in just 10 years.

Effecting a turnaround took time, and the problems were not resolved overnight. The first half of the decade was tumultuous. Costs kept rising, oil deals were mismanaged, pressures from abroad continued to wreak havoc, and environmental activists created new issues for beleaguered Company management to resolve. By the middle of the decade, the various measures and programs begun by management, and implemented by employees, had started to pay off. As it became apparent that the steps taken to ease these

< Like a giant insect on the loose, a Sikorsky SkyCrane lifts a 15,000-pound section of a transmission tower during construction of the Southwest Powerlink in 1983.

Protesters were not an unusual occurrence during the years of high rates and construction of the San Onofre Nuclear Power Plant Units 2 and 3. President Tom Page, however, made his intentions clear at the 1983 shareholders meeting.

dilemmas were working, the Company built a solid base of workable solutions. Employees met challenges head-on, economizing at every opportunity and becoming more creative and flexible in their approaches. By the end of the decade, SDG&E would once again go on record as a financially sound company with record-high customer satisfaction and some of the lowest rates among the investor-owned utilities in California.

Before these gains could be accomplished, however, the Company had to survive the trials of the intervening years. The major issue was SDG&E's dependence on foreign oil, which also raised rates. The lack of hydroelectric power or coal reserves in the service territory meant that the Company was forced to purchase its supplies from elsewhere. Although reducing dependency on oil imports was a major problem facing many utilities around the nation, SDG&E's challenges were greater because California's tough environmental laws required pollution controls that resulted in even higher costs.

SDG&E was not alone in these times of trouble. The utility industry across the nation was facing a period of great emergency. An editorial in the *London Economist* warned early in 1981 that "America's electricity-generating industry is in such deep financial trouble that it will provide the Reagan administration with its biggest industrial problem, dwarfing the troubles of steel and cars." Industry leaders feared that some utilities around the nation might go broke. This foreboding was not entirely unwarranted, due to problems with long-term borrowing and record-high interest rates reaching as high as 17.4 percent to finance new construction. The current safety margins for meeting peak loads were so thin in these difficult years that many utilities were already facing serious brownouts.

SDG&E struggled with mounting costs as the OPEC cartel nations priced oil supplies beyond reasonable limits. The price of a barrel of oil reached

$42.50 in 1982. Since the Company depended on oil for approximately 50 percent of its energy generation at this time, fuel costs skyrocketed. Natural-gas purchases accounted for another 25 percent of energy generation, 6 percent came from nuclear power, and the remaining energy requirements came from purchased power in other portions of the Southwest. On the positive side, the Company had developed tight controls over non-fuel costs such as operations and maintenance. SDG&E's expenditure of $132 per electric customer was substantially lower than the industry average of $201 in 1981. In fact, increased maintenance programs and an ethic of Company pride began to produce results of higher productivity without additional costs.

Many of the Company's facilities held open-house activities for the public to celebrate SDG&E's 100th birthday.

To effectively meet the challenges of the 1980s, SDG&E had implemented a five-part, five-year plan in late 1979 to restore financial stability. Five key financial objectives had been set: (1) limit cash spent each year on construction to 10 percent or less of total capitalization; (2) improve earnings before income taxes and interest charges to three times interest charges; (3) increase the common stock portion of total capitalization to 40 percent or more; (4) increase the portion of capital requirements paid for by internal generation of funds to 40 percent or more; and (5) to maintain dividend growth. All of these goals were met by 1984, giving the Company a positive footing for the second half of the decade and proving that their strategies had worked.

Centennial lunch in April 1981 was held for community and civic leaders at the historic Station B Power Plant. The dining tables were set up on the turbine deck.

As part of the Southwest Powerlink project, two connections were made to northern Baja California in 1983. This allowed for the interchange of electricity between the United States and Mexico.

Tom Page's succession to the position of president and chief executive officer on October 1, 1981, resulted in changes in organization and management. The basic management functions of the Company were organized into three main groups: finance, customer service and operations. Robert E. Morris, having been instrumental in setting the stage for the Company's future success, remained as chairman of the board until his retirement in 1983.

At this same time, a decision to reduce future capital spending and to concentrate on electric purchase, transmission and distribution rather than generation reflected another basic change in the Company's long-term business approach. The strategy for the 1980s was that SDG&E would drop large-scale projects requiring a huge investment of capital—in other words, the Company would build no new power plants. This announcement shocked the utility industry. A focus on a diversified energy mix, with a major emphasis on purchased power, dominated planning sessions. In 1977, oil provided about 73 percent of the electricity fuel requirements. In 1981 it dropped to 41 percent, and the goal of Company officials was to reduce that figure to 20 percent by 1985.

Decisions by the California Public Utilities Commission during 1981 aided the Company in its endeavors to diversify its sources of power and decrease oil dependency. SDG&E's management team had foreseen that there would be opportunities for low-cost power purchases from the southwestern United States. New Mexico and Arizona had built new facilities to generate power in anticipation of expected growth, but the growth had not materialized as expected. Excess power was available for sale to other utilities that could connect to the power sources.

Approval to proceed with the Southwest Powerlink (also known as the Eastern Interconnection), a transmission line connecting SDG&E with cheaper, coal-fired power in Arizona and New Mexico, was granted by the CPUC. In addition, two rate increases, totaling $96 million and $166 million, helped recover fuel costs and major capital investments, providing a further earnings improvement. By the end of 1981, the financial picture was starting to improve and the Company came close to earning the authorized rate of return, despite lower sales, higher interest rates and climbing inflation.

The Southwest Powerlink, a 280-mile, 500-kilovolt line from San Diego to Arizona, was scheduled for completion in 1984. The line would be the

Company's first 500-kv line. This project signaled a major change in operations because it would diversify the system without building new power plants. The existing Encina and South Bay power plants, however, would continue as the mainstays for system stability. In addition, a plan to create an arrangement with Tucson Electric Power Company for its less-expensive coal-fired power as the base source of electricity was analyzed for its money-saving potential. This move was projected to save the Company more than 5.5 million barrels of oil a year.

By 1982 the $326 million project was well under way. Groundbreaking ceremonies were held on December 15 in Boulevard, California, one of the sites along the route of the new line. While this event was certainly a beginning, it was also the end result of four years of planning and examination of route choices and equipment designs, negotiations of contracts, and legal challenges. The line extended from the Palo Verde Nuclear Power Station switchyard near Phoenix to the Miguel substation of SDG&E in Bonita, southeast of San Diego, passing through desert and rugged mountain terrain. Environmental concerns necessitated the placing of equipment by helicopter to reduce road-building impacts. Single-pole towers were used for the 26-mile stretch that ran through Imperial Valley farmland in order to limit the total amount of acreage taken from farmers in the area.

CHARLES SCHNEIDER

President Tom Page and Guillermo Ortega, supervisor of dispatching, Comisión Federal de Electricidad, Mexico, at the Southwest Powerlink groundbreaking marker in December 1982. The 500,000-volt transmission line was an important element in the Company's effort to reduce rates.

The Powerlink also allowed the Company to tap into Mexico's lower-cost geothermal energy produced at Cerro Prieto, near Mexicali. This facility was being expanded by the Mexican government in order to sell energy to the United States. A 230-kilovolt line was built from the 500-kv Imperial Valley substation to the international border slightly west of Mexicali. This line was one of two 230-kv lines built by SDG&E to connect with Mexican energy sources.

The other line under construction at this time was located near the

Bill Yturralde (right), head of SDG&E's Mexico Project, shakes hands through the border fence with a Mexican lineman.

metropolitan area of Tijuana/San Diego. A 13-mile, 230-kilovolt line from the Miguel substation in Bonita was run to the substation in Tijuana owned by the Comisión Federal de Electricidad, the Mexican national utility. Completed in 1983, this system carried the first continuous flow of energy from Mexico to the United States and became an important link of economic cooperation between the neighboring countries. Previously, the two energy systems had not been operated as part of one integrated electric system.

At this same time, the start-up testing phase began on the new Unit 2 at San Onofre Nuclear Generating Station. Units 2 and 3 were both expected to be in full operation by the end of 1983. Construction plans for these additions to the original San Onofre power station had begun in the early 1970s.

Late in 1982, another groundbreaking was held. This time the project was the 45-megawatt Heber Binary Cycle Geothermal Project, located near the community of Heber in the Imperial Valley, along the Southwest Powerlink line. This was one of several areas in the region where hot brine was close to the surface of the earth. The binary cycle used hot brine from underground to heat and vaporize a separate working fluid. The high-pressure vapor produced by this process would spin a turbine to generate electricity. Because of the high cost of construction, the Company solicited federal funding through the Department of Energy. U.S. Congressman Clair Burgener, a member of the House Committee on Appropriations, persuaded his colleagues to appropriate $60 million for the project, which, if successful, would

Joe Herringer, plant engineer, surveys the Heber Binary Geothermal Demonstration Plant while it was under construction in 1984. Geothermal steam rises in the background.

provide a new technology for the utility industry throughout the country. Completion of this plant put into operation the world's first large geothermal binary-cycle power plant. It demonstrated the value of a relatively low temperature geothermal field, but as oil prices came down, it was not cost effective. SDG&E was the major owner of the research project, with additional ownership held by the State of California, the Imperial Irrigation District and the California Department of Water Resources.

BRENT BAILEY

San Onofre Nuclear Generating Station Units 2 and 3 (two dome structures) during construction in 1981. Unit 1 has been covered by a new protective "silo" structure.

SDG&E became involved in a wide range of political and legal efforts to influence proposed legislation that directly affected the utility industry. In 1982, pressure began building in Washington, D.C., to accelerate natural-gas deregulation. Company officials, while favoring deregulation, were concerned that sharp increases in prices might result without a corresponding surge in supplies.

Industry leaders met to discuss the possibility that natural gas could price itself out of the market as a fuel source for electric generation. Pressure was brought to bear on natural-gas suppliers and legislators by an aggressive letter-writing campaign, extensive media advertisements and visits to key leaders to acquaint them with both sides of the issue. By the end of the year, these efforts had worked, and prices for natural gas were much more reasonable.

In 1982, financial improvements brightened the Company's economic picture as new general rates, authorized by the California PUC, went into effect. The income generated by the new rates increased the Company's revenue for the year, which in turn led to higher earnings and increased cash flow for construction projects. Other rulings by the CPUC included rate increases, a $79 million Energy Cost Adjustment Clause (cost of fuel) increase and various adjustment mechanisms. These various measures, bolstered by improved in-house expense-control procedures, significantly bettered the financial outlook for 1982 and 1983.

The technological advances of the 1970s and 1980s created an increasingly complex business environment for SDG&E and its employees. In order for the Company to keep pace with the ever-expanding customer base, and assist employees in working with the sophisticated new equipment, additional computers enhanced the work environment. The Information Services Division, newly created in 1981, utilized computers very effectively as a management tool. Analysis of business operations, recommendations for improvement, coordination of all corporate activities and automation for high productivity were just some of the aspects of computer activity available to management.

Systems such as maps tracking the Company's underground and overhead distribution facilities, inventory management and word processing proved to be important long-range additions. As with most major companies at this time, conversion to computers was expensive, time consuming and a difficult adjustment for many old-time employees. But the long-range benefits were improved efficiency, greater productivity and better customer service.

CALIFORNIA PUBLIC UTILITIES COMMISSION

The California Public Utilities Commission, formerly the California Railroad Commission, is the regulatory agency that ensures that a utility, which has the exclusive right to serve a specified geographical area, charges fair and reasonable rates for the services it provides its customers. The agency is also charged with seeing that the utility is able to recover the cost of doing business and earns enough profit to attract investment capital.

The connection between the utility and the commission is one filled with confusion and lack of understanding by the general public. Regulatory proceedings conducted by the commission require a complex, lengthy process calling for the services of veritable legions of accountants, attorneys, financial planners and key executive personnel. Batteries of computers are necessary to produce the documents deemed essential to fully document the cases brought before the PUC.

Changes in procedures during the 1970s accompanied the impacts caused by inflation, the Arab oil embargo and third-party involvement in the regulatory process. Special-interest groups became active participants, causing issues to be more complex with slower resolutions.

New laws required agencies, such as the Nuclear Regulatory Commission, to assess long-range effects, thereby slowing the process and spiraling construction costs. Licensing procedures are long and involved, necessitating long-term planning by Company officials. The commission and the utility, while sometimes frustrating each other, both share a common goal—that of protecting the consumer and offering the best energy rates and services that benefit all parties concerned.

Employees' Association 1983 basketball champions, from the team "South Bay," were (from left) Mike Redondo, David Smith, Jonas Jackson, Roger Davis, JuJu Villareal, J.D. Tharpe, Larry Ayers and Dann Ludd.

The advent of computers throughout the Company allowed customers instant access to their records over the phone, or at various satellite offices, such as this one in North Park. Serving customer Bob Fowler are Jamie Stapleton (left) and Susie Conners.

A renewed commitment to customer service by Company executives resulted in new approaches to consumer relations during the 1980s. Rising energy costs and high unemployment rates had created considerable tension among customers. New systems were put in place to train employees to help unhappy consumers understand the issues behind higher rates. Some of the new additions to service during the early 1980s included: increase of telephone-center hours, addition of bilingual customer-service representatives (including employees who spoke eight other languages) to assist Hispanic customers and Saturday service for customers. The introduction of two programs for employees—People Power, for improving communication skills, and Information Exchange, for personnel such as meter readers and linemen—were created to help customer-contact employees answer customers' questions in the field.

In late 1982, the California PUC directed all electric utilities to develop programs that would help to alleviate the burden of potential financial hardship for families already burdened by inflation and unemployment. SDG&E's response characterized its continuing concern for the community when the Company created an annual Winter Assistance Program. A $100,000 shareholder contribution to United Way agencies provided emergency assistance to customers who did not qualify for other government assistance. When Company employees were asked by management to contribute, they did so in a big way. An additional $50,000 for this fund came from the SDG&E employees' Contribution Club.

Home-energy audits by Company conservation representatives continued to be popular with SDG&E customers, and it is estimated that the 29,000

KENNETH ROBERT SHEARER

Tape-drive units are only one part of the Company's computer system. Today, computers operate power plants, oversee distribution of both gas and electricity, and even provide many employees with instant mail communications.

Linemen in training practice their skills with a game of lineman basketball.

home visits generated by this service alone trimmed customers' energy bills more than 21.8 million kilowatt hours and 11.8 million therms.

Remote computers also assisted this program by cycling high-energy appliances in residences, such as air conditioners, off and on during peak demand periods.

Industrial consumers also benefited from innovative cost-reduction programs designed to increase maximum efficiency and conservation of energy. Cogeneration counseling, energy conservation audits and commercial load management were the three most important ways that the Company helped commercial, agricultural and industrial customers to reduce energy usage. Proof that these services were valued by the community at large were seen in such examples as Pacific Southwest Airlines' trimming its electricity bill by one million kilowatt hours a year. The continuing link between SDG&E and the community was substantially strengthened during these years of crisis management through concerted efforts by the Company. Planning to meet future energy needs was seen by SDG&E executives as a joint effort between

Applied Energy, Inc., the Company's subsidiary, supplied chilled water to operate the air-conditioning systems of many downtown buildings. The water was pumped under city streets in special insulated pipes, seen here being installed on B Street in 1982.

the community and the Company. SDG&E Chairman Tom Page stated unequivocally that it would "require a community-of-interest effort to assure adequate energy for the future." Utilities, business leaders, individuals and government representatives would have to work together. This concept inspired new corporate and employee efforts.

The Company instituted an energy-issue advertising campaign, updated the speakers program and developed a series of brochures to help customers gain more understanding of important energy topics. A cohesive advertising campaign was developed to explain to the energy-consuming public the rationale behind high energy costs, the need to purchase power, the value of the Southwest Powerlink, the effects of deregulation and the ways customers could cut their energy consumption through judicious management.

Predictions by national experts of rapid growth in San Diego, both commercial and residential, fueled expansive new plans by SDG&E officials during the decade of the 1980s to meet these changes. Forecasters, such as John Naisbitt in his book *Megatrends,* called San Diego a city of "great opportunity" and stated that San Diego would be the relocation choice of many companies and individuals over the next several decades. A high rate of growth in the area was a phenomenon that SDG&E had experienced many times in its century of existence. Flexibility in service had long been a watchword with the Company as it planned new ventures to improve or expand existing conditions.

Installing ceiling insulation, often blown-in as small particles, was one of the Company's principal programs to help customers save on their energy bills in the 1970s and 1980s. Many other conservation measures were also promoted as SDG&E evolved into an energy management company.

JAMES COIT

Linda Hom checks a roll of drawings against a backdrop of hundreds of roll ends at the Company's Record Center in 1980. During the 1980s, the Company completely computerized its maps, one of the first utilities in the nation to do so.

Many high-tech industries were expected to move into the region, but these businesses had lower, and different, energy requirements. Computers constituted a major component of many of these technologically advanced companies, and quality, as well as quantity, of electric supply was critically important. Fluctuations of electric frequencies could no longer be tolerated as they once were by old-line industrial customers.

New homes under construction featured innovative energy-saving designs to help owners trim costs. While the demand for services from the Company would expand, it would not expand in the same ways that it had in the past. SDG&E had to be prepared to meet a different type of expansion rate and keep cost controls effective. These goals had to be combined with an eye on services that would now satisfy the energy-conscious consumer. The educational programs the Company had undertaken over the previous years had paid off, and customers were now aware of necessary changes and were demanding energy-efficient services.

The traditional course had worked for more than 100 years, but now the strategy had to be untraditional—innovative and designed with flexibility to meet unknown challenges in the years ahead. A multifaceted approach was the answer: supplementation of SDG&E's electric generating capability with increased purchases of energy, cutback on new plant construction, encouragement of other utilities to build the necessary plants and sell energy to the Company, promotion of customer conservation and diversification of the energy resource mix.

Dick Korpan, group vice president–finance, flashed a victory smile after getting a flower-covered "A" when the Company's bond rating was upgraded in July 1983.

A major vote of confidence was received by the Company in 1983 when it achieved a major financial goal—regaining the A bond rating, allowing SDG&E to borrow funds at a lower rate. The bond upgrading was a recognition by the financial community of the Company's successful improvement of financial and operational performance.

Another shift in a favorable direction came in 1983

when natural-gas prices were stabilized. Rates charged to gas utility customers were expected to increase at a pace lower than the level of inflation. Reaching the same stability with the electric rates was anticipated by 1985, achieving the Company's goal of limiting future rate increases to no more than the national inflation rate.

In conjunction with this goal, the computerized Energy Management Center—Mission Control—was put into operation in 1983. This sophisticated center makes available information relative to accessing the cheapest and most practical sources of power throughout the West, Southwest and Northwest. In 1983, average electric rates reached 11.9 cents per kwhr and increased to an all-time high of 12.7 cents in 1985. At this time, fuel costs were responsible for about 60 percent of this peak rate. The aggressive search for low-cost energy for purchase, combined with the switch from fuel oil to natural gas in the Company's generating plants, led to the first decrease in 10 years of the average cost of fuel. In late 1983, after a decade of increases, gas rates finally started to decline, but electric rates did not go down until after 1985.

Another long-awaited project came closer to completion in 1983. Unit 2 at San Onofre was put into service, and Unit 3 was in the final testing stages. The two units were the last of the large generation units planned by the Company, and their completion brought SDG&E one step closer to the planned diversification of the electric energy resource mix. The more diversity, the greater the flexibility in the face of changing environmental and energy concerns.

CHARLES SCHNEIDER

Mission Control is the heart of SDG&E's energy management system. Sophisticated computer equipment helps controllers select the most economical energy to supply customers while maintaining the integrity of the transmission system.

As SDG&E executives faced the future knowing they could build on the successes of the previous few years, it became clear that the utility industry was changing forever. Gone were the old days and old ways of obtaining power; utilities would become energy-management companies. With the uncertain regulatory climate and the desire to move away from a heavy dependence on a single fuel source, such as oil, a more diverse energy mix was needed. Transmission of energy around the nation would become far more important and, ultimately, many of the country's major utility companies would be linked in an integrated nationwide grid. Movement of excess generating capacity and low-priced fuel resources to other regions was expected to become commonplace. Many companies would find it to be less expensive to purchase energy from these sources than invest heavily in more plants with high construction costs and stiff regulatory controls.

SDG&E'S BLACKSMITH

SDG&E was founded in 1881 and employed a blacksmith to shoe the Company's fleet of 20 horses. The "smithy" probably spent most of his time shoeing horses and forging parts for the carriages. One hundred ten years later, SDG&E's current blacksmith, Yanos Vijyada, works in the shops complex. Vijyada, a Hungarian immigrant, is one of the few true blacksmiths left in the county, and he creates unique parts and tools for the Company. He learned the craft as a 14-year-old boy in a small farming village in Hungary.

Vijyada makes and repairs more than 150 different tools, from shackles used to pull cable to probes used to punch holes in the ground near gas lines to search for leaks. One tool he designed was a tong used to pick up telephone and power poles. The tongs used previously were too heavy to handle easily and were weak at the axle. Vijyada designed a 40-pound tong that was certified to lift 4,500-pound poles safely.

The work that Vijyada loves most is still the work he can do by hand, with gripping tools and hammers that he says he envisions as extensions of his body. "I like to work with the anvil the most," he said. "Because you are working with your hands and shaping it to come out into whatever it is you make, you have to have a feel for it."

Besides lifting towers, helicopters were used extensively to ferry work crews, and even heavy concrete, to remote locations during construction of the Southwest Powerlink in July 1983.

CHARLES SCHNEIDER

The efforts to create a turnaround by the Company did not go unnoticed by the local community. The five-part plan was greeted in 1979 with skepticism, but by 1983 it was clear to San Diego leaders that big things were happening at SDG&E. An editorial in *The San Diego Union* in 1983 stated that:

A healthy public utility that is coping effectively with its financial problems can serve its customers with more efficiency and economy than one that is wallowing, decks awash, in a sea of fiscal troubles . . . Tom Page . . . is running a tight ship. He is weathering the storm. The benefits are beginning to show up all down the line, for owners, crew and passengers alike.

In order to keep pace with the expected growth of San Diego as an attractive "destination city" and as part of the general northeast to southwest shift of population in the United States, SDG&E officials planned to spend hundreds of millions of dollars through the final years of the 20th century to meet customers' service expectations. The theme "Energy is everybody's business" underscored the idea that SDG&E and the community had to work together to achieve common goals. During the 1980s, customer growth increased steadily, a major consideration in planning for the future and a strong incentive to Company leaders to work closely with local communities to meet their needs.

Annexation of 3,000 acres in the Otay Mesa area by the City of San Diego in 1984 created a need for major expansion of electric and gas services. The city announced plans to encourage development of this region as part of a proposed international commercial and business center linked to Mexico by a new border crossing. This area ultimately figured in plans for a binational airport.

San Diego's North County was increasing at a rate faster than the rest of the region during the decade of the 1980s. To meet the increased residential and commercial demands for energy, the $2 million Carlsbad substation was constructed. The substation received its energy from the Encina Power Plant, stepping the voltage down to 12,000 volts before distribution to North County customers.

Programs to assist customers already receiving service from SDG&E did not fall behind during these times of expansion. Various efforts were enacted to give low-income San Diegans special help. The low-income weatherization program resulted in 4,590 homes receiving free insulation in 1983 to cut energy costs. Funding of solar systems at low-income housing projects was absorbed by SDG&E. Both of these projects were mandated by the California Public Utilities Commission. Seniors in Trouble Referral was a program to identify older customers with problems who might need special assistance. SDG&E customer contact employees are in neighborhoods on a regular basis and might be the first to notice a problem. More than 400 Company employees participate in a joint effort with the Area Agency on Aging to alert appropriate agencies when a senior citizen needs assistance.

The younger members of the community benefited from SDG&E's involvement in a variety of school activities. Energy education programs focusing on conservation and safety begun in 1975 in the elementary schools continued on a regular basis, and in 1983, these informative efforts were expanded to the high school level. The award-winning energy education programs were designed to introduce young children to basic concepts of energy via SDG&E's Captain Power and the Power Quiz. These programs served as a model for similar educational activities around the country. The Company "adopted" Memorial Junior High School, and 29 Company volunteers tutored and counseled students at the school on a weekly basis.

ARCHAEOLOGY AND THE SOUTHWEST POWERLINK

Archaeology played an important role in the construction of the Southwest Powerlink during the early 1980s. Concern for the environment and cultural resources forms a major part of the preparation that takes place before construction begins on any project. Various types of studies are done to ensure that rare and endangered plants and animals, their habitats and Native American and historical or archaeological sites are protected from impacts by the energy project.

Extensive studies were begun well in advance of construction, with various environmentally oriented surveys conducted along the proposed route and any areas of projected impact. Surveys by biologists and archaeologists determined the location and numbers of rare and endangered species such as bighorn sheep, golden eagles, the Andrews scarab and desert tortoise. Riparian areas called for special attention, as they are the locations of habitats for various species and frequently contain Native American cultural resources such as stone tools, rock art and ceramic remains.

Survey findings identified areas of special impact and avoidance, which were marked with bright yellow flags. Proposed access routes and construction areas were adjusted to avoid disturbing animal habitats and significant prehistoric or historic sites. Helicopters were used for transportation in certain areas to minimize environmental impacts. Continuous monitoring took place at all phases of the project to make sure that SDG&E's environmental-protection standards were enforced.

Employee-education projects included activities like this 1983 "Kids at Work" day at the Beach Cities District. Lineman Mitch Mitchell and daughter Taryn watch lineman Paul Sos install new electric meter.

Another positive note was sounded in 1983 when cost projections for SDG&E's largest construction project, the Southwest Powerlink, were revised downward from $236 million to $215 million, with a completion date of May 1984, two months earlier than was expected. The lowered cost was due to careful planning and close supervision of each stage, economic factors that trimmed costs, and the sale of a portion of the line to the Imperial Irrigation District. The project was 75 percent completed by the end of 1983, despite its unique construction requirements.

Backing the home team was one of San Diego's favorite activities when the Padres baseball team went to the World Series in 1984. Helper Mario Arce displayed a homemade sign while working in downtown San Diego.

Helicopters were used in many areas to airlift equipment and crews into the region when special access roads would have damaged the environment. The varied terrain required equally varied construction techniques, including manually digging holes for tower footings. Special methods had to be devised to ensure that the concrete met rigid standards in the 110-degree desert heat. To conserve the amount of agricultural land taken from production, 99 single-pole structures were used instead of the standard four-legged lattice-steel towers.

Upward progression and accomplishment continued at a steady pace in the "benchmark" year of 1984. The price of the common stock reached a 10-year high of $23.75 while the typical residential bill declined nearly 5 percent. The final goal of the financial recovery program was reached, trimming construction costs to 10 percent of capitalization. In the realm of finance, SDG&E's bond rating went from A- to A+ by Standard and Poor's Corporation, and from A3 to A2 by Moody's Investors Service, the second upgrade in

Terry Winter completes his duties as manager of the Southwest Powerlink transmission-line project as he throws the switch in July 1984. Watching the ceremony are (from left) Charles Embrecht, California Energy Commission, Roger Hedgecock, mayor of San Diego, Tom Page, Leo McCarthy, California lieutenant governor, and Leonard Grimes, CPUC commissioner.

less than a year, and short-term debt dropped to zero in the last half of the year. The Southwest Powerlink was completed ahead of schedule; a second link with Mexico was forged with a 230,000-volt interconnecting system. Peak demand reached 2,342 megawatts on September 5, and more than 30,000 new electric customers were added to the system.

Another element was added to the mix in 1985 with activation of a nonutility subsidiary, Pacific Diversified Capital. The new subsidiary's task was to purchase and develop other companies. In the next two years, four companies were purchased and added to the subsidiary's portfolio.

These accomplishments signaled many positive things for the Company, but most importantly they heralded the new direction undertaken by SDG&E as it created strategies for supplying the energy needs of the area during the 21st century. All over the country, the utility industry had come to realize that different approaches to services and pricing energy were mandatory. Plans were well under way by SDG&E executives to devise ways to control peak demand and take advantage of new opportunities in energy production, coupled with development of brand-new technologies.

Record growth accompanied the change in direction as Company officials mapped out long-range plans. Late in February 1986, the 900,000th customer was added to SDG&E's system. By the end of that year, the total number of electric customers had reached 940,752, marking one of the highest growth rates in the country—5.25 percent. The ratio of gas and electric customers to employees was 319 to one, a figure rating among the highest productivity indicators in the utility industry.

The new strategies were showing positive results and enabled the Company to continue to post record earnings while reducing customers' rates.

Employee Chuck Fimbres helped carry the torch to the 1984 Olympics in Los Angeles after being selected from a number of employees.

Cogeneration projects, like this facility at the North Island Naval Air Station, have become an increasingly important part of the Company's energy resources.

The residential base was growing rapidly, but at the same time the industrial base was diminishing because customers were generating their own electricity. In 1986 alone, more than 40 companies left the system because their own cogeneration systems were in place, with an additional 165 companies expected to follow. This fact of life in the 1980s meant Company officials had to step up the pace and become even more competitive and aggressive in reducing rates.

By 1986, SDG&E's conversion from a traditional utility to an "energy management company" had begun to take hold. In 1986, the concept became a reality, and when oil and natural-gas prices dropped drastically in that same year, SDG&E was well positioned to take advantage of the competitive pricing marketplace. Fuel contract personnel, skilled in negotiating for power-plant fuels, including oil and uranium, moved to apply those skills in the newly emerged natural-gas spot market.

Company buyers moved quickly to snap up these natural-gas bargains. Significant cost savings were achieved by purchases of spot market fuel oil from suppliers in Singapore, Australia, Alaska and California. The CPUC agreed to require SDG&E's sole natural-gas supplier to transport gas that the Company purchased from other suppliers for a fee. Creation of a unique spot market bidding program attracted suppliers from around the country and industry leaders who praised SDG&E for its innovative approach. The fuel-switching flexibility and generating-fuel purchase expertise developed by Company officials led to a drop of 35 percent in natural-gas power-plant fuel costs.

Engineer Wes Goodwin examines a test facility for solar-power cells. The Company experimented with many types of solar, wind and other alternative energy resources.

Power-plant maintenance, like this work on the cooling water condenser at the South Bay Power Plant, helped increase efficiency at Company power plants. Larry Ayers (left) and Ed Bowker use high-pressure water guns to push cleaning scrapers through condenser tubes.

Deregulation of the natural-gas industry would bring about many changes in the years ahead. The Federal Energy Regulatory Commission decided in 1985 to provide for open access to interstate gas-transmission pipelines. In 1986 and the following years, the Company began buying a substantial portion of its natural gas from suppliers in Texas and Oklahoma, with transportation by Southern California Gas Company for a fee.

Two new, coal-fueled energy contracts with flexibility price clauses were signed, which replaced the original contracts with Arizona and New Mexico. A low-cost contract with Mexico for geothermal-fueled energy was also signed. The capacity of the Southwest Powerlink was upgraded from 700 to 1,000 megawatts. In addition, an improved contract with Southern California Edison to provide a backup transmission route to eastern energy sources added another element of diversity to SDG&E's plans for the future.

SDG&E's major partners in wholesale power acquisition began to upgrade their systems during the 1980s. One example was the Pacific Intertie, a joint venture of Pacific Gas & Electric Company, Southern California Edison, and SDG&E to transmit power between the California-Oregon border and Los Angeles. As each company changed its operations, SDG&E revised its contracts to increase flexibility in the face of expanding power needs.

KEN ARNONE

Power poles at the Miramar Storage Yard are prepared for delivery to work locations throughout San Diego County to meet growing energy needs during the booming growth of the 1980s.

Control of fuel costs was only one part of efforts in 1986 to reduce operating expenses. Updating of the business plan included an important long-term SDG&E resource—its 4,815 employees. Introduction of the Performance Improvement Program in July 1986 encouraged individual employees to look long and hard at each aspect of their job to find ways to reduce costs. To increase the incentive to examine cost-cutting measures thoroughly, the Company began offering 10 percent of the first year's savings for accepted ideas. More than 1,000 ideas for "The 10% Solution" were submitted to Company executives, and 44 employees received awards of more than $260,000 in money-saving strategies.

New goals for the second half of the 1980s included: the maintenance of the market share, an increase in earnings, and improvement in generating system use. To implement these plans, Company officials planned to redesign the rate structure to include lower variable rates, increase fixed-fee charges and attract new commercial and industrial customers. Residential customers were increasing rapidly, but to assist the community in drawing more industrial development to the area, SDG&E joined with the San Diego Economic Development Corporation to create strategies to attract industry. Since high energy costs were a deterrent to new business, ways to lower costs while adding increased value were of paramount importance.

By the second half of the decade, deregulation was an accepted reality, and SDG&E executives realized that to compete successfully, strategies had to include marketing wisely, cutting costs while increasing sales. Deregulation was becoming a fact of life for industry leaders, and nonregulated competitors were slowly edging into the energy generation and transmission field.

To be aggressively competitive, SDG&E took a variety of steps to sharply reduce rates to commercial and industrial customers. To back up this plan, increased efforts were made to improve the usage of existing generating plants so as to postpone or avoid building new units. Financial incentives,

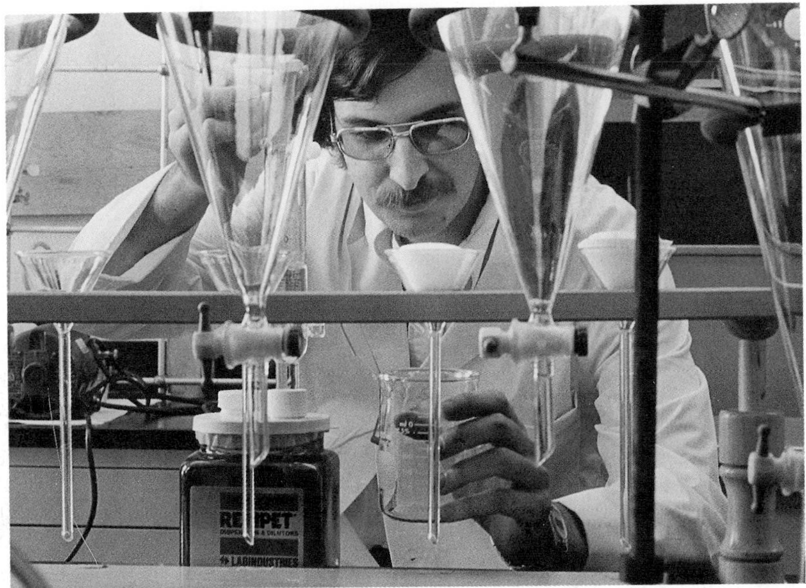

Besides research, SDG&E scientists, like chemist John Bricarello, do extensive materials testing and environmental analysis to ensure good customer service and to protect the environment. The Company has maintained a laboratory testing facility since the 1920s. It is one of the finest industrial labs in the service area.

coupled with marketing strategies to convince customers to shift some of their energy demands to dusk-to-dawn hours, helped to minimize the growth in energy demand. By 1987, more aspects of this program were in effect. Gain Sharing was planned in 1987 and implemented in 1988. The program was an employee profit-sharing system based on achievement of customer satisfaction and budget goals.

Changes in the Company from the late 1970s to the end of the 1980s reflected shifts in the utility industry nationwide. Ten years earlier, SDG&E had more than 40 research programs in operation to help reduce dependence on expensive foreign oil. By the late 1980s, almost all the programs had been discontinued because they were no longer cost effective. California utility companies had been ahead of the nation in research, and by the end of the 1980s, this type of effort was no longer required to give customers the potential for new services once thought necessary by industry leaders.

The utility industry was changing rapidly during these years, and Company officials felt it necessary to switch policies when market indicators suggested that it was prudent. One of the decisions generated by SDG&E's flexible attitude and commitment to its customers was to sell the Heber geothermal plant in 1987. While the plant was a successful research and development project and provided reliable energy, the owners of the geothermal field declined to make additional investments to increase the well capacity that would provide the additional hot-water resource needed by the plant. The costs of operation were too high for the level of operation and, as a result, SDG&E was forced to close the plant and seek recovery of monies for the benefit of the plant owners.

By the beginning of 1988, SDG&E had 4,612 full-time employees and almost one million customers in San Diego County and the southwestern section of Orange County, covering a service area of 4,100 square miles.

The Company's 10 Percent Solution employee suggestion program has produced nearly $12 million in yearly savings since it began in 1986. Employees, like Steve Straub, benefit by being rewarded part of the savings. There have been eight suggestions that have earned the maximum award of $25,000.

TIM STAHL

Thermal energy storage, or TES, represented a lower-cost way to cool many commercial buildings. Ice created in the drums by cheap, off-peak electricity, could be used to cool a building during the day when electric rates were high.

Natural-gas customers totaled more than 625,000 in the county, with service expanding rapidly eastward along the international border. The Company's major assets included the Encina and South Bay power plants; the Southwest Powerlink 500,000-volt transmission line running from San Diego to Phoenix; the natural-gas pipeline system in the gas service area, and a 20 percent interest in three nuclear-generating units at the San Onofre Nuclear Generating Station.

A major issue began in 1988 that would dominate newspaper headlines, disrupt Company activities and rouse the ire of the local community. In June 1988 the company agreed to merge with Tucson Electric Power Company as a strategic move to acquire new generating resources and the potential for future earnings growth. This effort was abandoned after Southern California Edison Company persistently proposed to acquire the Company. In November 1988, SDG&E signed a merger agreement with SCEcorp and its utility subsidiary, Southern California Edison Company, under which the Company would merge with Edison. Favorable votes of both companies' shareholders were received at annual meetings held in April 1989. Directors of SDG&E accepted a $2.5 billion takeover bid by Edison that—if it had been approved by a multitude of government agencies—would have created the nation's largest investor-owned utility.

The vote had not been unanimous, but there was a substantial favorable majority. Company President Tom Page, who was to remain in San Diego to head one of the five Edison divisions, stated that price was the primary consideration. "I had no choice from a financial perspective. It was truly imperative that we accept. This is a different business today, one that is changing. Price was the primary issue, and it substantially increased the value to our shareholders." The merger agreement and its related understandings contained unprecedented protection for the Company's employees and communities.

EVOLUTION OF SDG&E

1881 San Diego Gas Company was founded on April 18 to supply manufactured gas to homes and businesses in the downtown San Diego area.

1884 Jenney Electric Company of Indianapolis began electric generation and service to arc lights.

1887 San Diego Gas & Electric Light Company was organized from San Diego Gas Company and Coronado Gas & Electric Company. The Jenney Company was purchased and incorporated into the new company in the same year.

1892 The generating system of the Electric Rapid Transit Street Car Company was purchased to provide incandescent lighting power.

1905 San Diego Gas & Electric Light Company was sold to H.M. Byllesby & Co. Engineering on April 1. The sale was caused by a lack of capital to expand the system to meet new demand. Extensive improvements were started.

1906-12 Construction of the first transmission lines and distribution systems to La Jolla, La Mesa, El Cajon and National City.

1910 Spreckels' direct-current system was purchased and the Company became the exclusive electric system in San Diego. The first part of Station B was built to supply power for the San Diego Electric Railway Company.

1910 The Escondido Utilities Company began gas and electric service to the city of Escondido.

1914 The Escondido Mutual Water Company established an electric district; began distribution of electricity to 60 customers in the area surrounding the city from two hydro plants, one in Bear Valley and one in Rincon.

1916 The Company bought the Oceanside Electric & Gas Company and operated gas and electric generators until transmission lines arrived.

1917 The Company acquired the Escondido Utilities Company and operated the existing generating plant until transmission lines were put in from Oceanside.

1918 The Company bought the Del Mar Water, Light & Power Company electric distribution system.

1921 The Company bought the San Diego Electric Railway Company's power plant to provide steam, direct current and alternating current.

1928 The Company purchased the Capistrano Substation, the most northern connection in the San Diego electric grid and its interconnection to Southern California Edison.

1930 The Company bought the South Coast Gas Company that served Carlsbad and Oceanside.

1935 The Holding Company Act passed and caused the break-up of utility holding companies. Byllesby owned 34 companies in 22 states, including the Market Street Trolley system in San Francisco, nine light and power companies and 10 utilities providing gas, water, steam, telephone, oil, engineering and management.

1938 The Mountain Empire Electric Co-op was incorporated; SDG&E began power delivery in 1940.

1940-41 The Company became an independent investor-owned corporation, and the name was changed to San Diego Gas & Electric Company.

1948 The Company bought the Rincon substation.

1954 The Company acquired the Escondido Mutual Water Company's electric distribution system.

1968 The Company purchased from the City of San Diego the distribution system that supplied Balboa Park.

1970 The Company bought Mountain Empire Co-op.

1988-91 The Company entered into a merger agreement first with Tucson Electric Power (abandoned) then with Southern California Edison. The latter merger failed to receive PUC approval in May 1991.

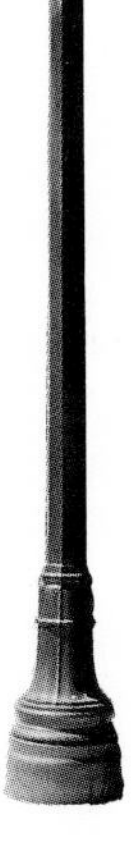

The Orange County District office represents one of several facilities of modern design opened by the Company during the last decade.

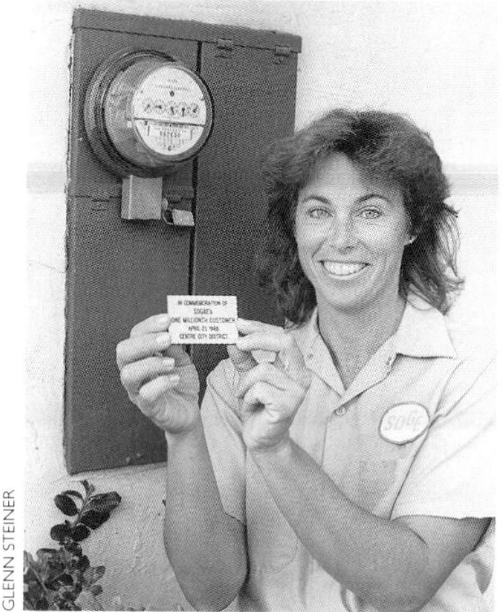

GLENN STEINER

Only a few days after its 107th birthday in April 1988, SDG&E connected its one-millionth electric customer. Meter reader Pam Foland holds one of seven plaques (one plaque for each district) that were attached to the customer's meter to mark the occasion.

Reaction from the community was immediate and vociferous. The San Diego City Council expressed "deep concern" at the potentially adverse economic impact and ordered city officials to challenge the takeover before regulators acted and to explore the feasibility of buying SDG&E and operating it as a city department. Page was faced with not only the fears of the city council, but also concern within the service area about higher rates, loss of a headquarters company and employee uncertainty about jobs and security.

The proposed merger benefited Edison in many ways, including SDG&E's service territory with greater projected growth rates than Edison's, a different customer mix that would provide more stable revenues, and a potential annual operational savings of more than $100 million to keep rates down. For holders of SDG&E stock, the merger provided increased stock value, the use of excess generating capacity on the Edison system to meet SDG&E needs for power, lower and more efficient cost operations and a significant reduction in the need for capital expenditures for new power plants.

From November 1988 until May 1991, the Company rode a roller coaster of criticism from many corners, and employees felt the brunt of customer wrath. Forefront in everyone's mind for those 30 months of hearings and legal decisions was the merger and how it would affect jobs and the community. Ironically, amidst the most tumultuous period in SDG&E's 110-year history, the Company's employees created an amazing track record of accomplishment—low rates, high earnings, record customer-service satisfaction—a record difficult to achieve in serene times. The employees once again rose to the challenge and displayed tremendous physical and mental energy in the face of enormous adversity and created a company more successful than at any other time in its history.

The year 1990 brought record-high levels of achievement in five key

Ken Forsman, K&A Construction, and Marion Stille, SDG&E project manager at the Company's energy-efficient demonstration home, which showed customers how to save money and conserve resources. The 600-square-foot home was constructed inside the San Diego Convention Center for a 1991 home show.

categories: earnings, stock price, customer satisfaction, community participation and employee productivity. During his annual address to stockholders, Tom Page emphasized that "there is no utility in the United States that has the level of productivity San Diego Gas & Electric has. It's due to the combined efforts of our forty-two hundred employees, and I want to tell you that I am very proud of each and every one of them." The policies and programs implemented early in the decade had proven to be wise choices. The Company had dramatically transformed its public image, its financial stability and its customer service despite the wide-ranging pressures from geopolitical problems and environmental issues.

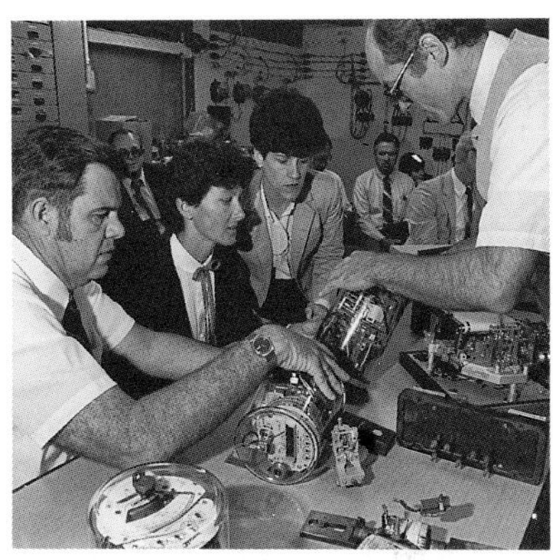

Learning the inside story on electric meters in June 1984 are Hal Larsen (left), Linda Linderman, Lynn Von Gietzen. Richard Smith, electric meter shop, taught the class.

In November 1990, President Bush signed the Clean Air Act Amendments of 1990. This comprehensive revision of existing federal air-quality regulations requires utilities to further reduce the level of several types of air emissions, including toxic air pollutants, and deal with the issue of acid rain. Since the new law was less stringent than existing California laws, it did not result in any new major capital expenditures for the Company. Pacific Diversified Capital (PDC), SDG&E's wholly owned subsidiary, took actions to concentrate its investments in environment-related products and services. As a result, the Company was better prepared to benefit from the worldwide emphasis on improving air quality.

In addition, PDC's subsidiary, Wahlco Environmental Systems, Inc., is the world leader in the manufacture and sale of flue gas conditioning systems, which is a comparatively low-cost option for utilities to help comply with the new federal regulations. WES had designed, engineered and built about 90 percent of the flue gas conditioning systems installed in North America and 75 percent of those installed around the world.

WES planned to continue its marketing efforts in the flue gas condition-

South Bay Power Plant employees Bob Krug (left) and Larry Ayers examine the remains of a huge air preheater bearing for Unit 3. The failed bearing was replaced with a new one (in background) by plant maintenance crews.

ing field and sell systems to utilities and industrial firms as a method for reducing air emissions. At the same time, expansion was planned for the Company's line of engineered products and services through its Bachmann, Metroflex and Wahlco Power companies. New products, joint ventures and acquisitions were pursued to add more diversity to the program. WES continued its business ventures in the United States and overseas, including the United Kingdom, France, Germany, Italy, Hungary, Poland, Australia, Korea, Taiwan and Hong Kong. Expansion to other countries in Eastern Europe and the Soviet Union was under consideration as well.

The CPUC evidentiary hearings ended in August 1990; in February 1991, the administrative law judges presiding at the CPUC hearings, after considering thousands of pages of testimony, issued a proposed decision denying the merger application. The proposed decision was based on a finding that the merger would adversely affect competition. The judges believed that the merger had anticompetitive effects that could not be mitigated. That finding contradicted the recommendation of staff members of the Federal Energy Regulatory Commission that most of the claims of adverse competitive effect were without merit. It also contradicted the determination of the U.S. Department of Justice that, with certain mitigation measures already accepted by Edison, the merger posed no competitive problems. In addition, the judges agreed that the merger would provide more than $1 billion in customer savings by the year 2000 and that all significant environmental concerns related to the merger could be mitigated.

On March 20, 1991, the CPUC heard final arguments from lawyers for 21 participating cities, federal and state agencies and the two local utilities. By April 18, 1991, the 110th anniversary of the Company and possibly its last as an independent company, the mammoth merger hearings had been completed. On May 8, 1991, the decision was announced. Employees stood silent and motionless around office speaker phones that had been specially connected to the CPUC's San Francisco hearing room. The CPUC had denied approval of the merger by a unanimous vote of 5 to 0. The moment of stunned disbelief seemed to last forever, and then everyone started talking, laughing and crying, all at the same time.

The boards of directors of both San Diego Gas & Electric and Southern California Edison voted on May 16, 1991, to end their efforts to merge the two utilities. "We are disappointed in the CPUC's decision to deny the merger of SDG&E and SCE. We continue to believe the merger is in the best interests of SDG&E's customers and shareholders. After reviewing the CPUC's decision that denied our request to merge, we have concluded that we will not appeal the Commission's decision," said Tom Page. As part of the agreement to end the merger process, Edison paid SDG&E $15 million, which covered the majority of expenses the Company incurred during the merger process.

The rejection of the merger was a financial loss to the Company, but SDG&E management had planned an alternative to the merger. Page stated that the Company would remain a strong, viable company, well positioned to meet the future. "We have said all along that the merger is the superior option, but we have been on a parallel planning tack to move forward as a stand-alone company if we needed to."

When it became definite that SDG&E would stay intact and continue to provide services to the residents of San Diego, a fresh spirit took hold of the Company. Throughout the organization, from top to bottom, everyone felt that SDG&E was poised on the edge of momentous events. A belief that the next decade and the next century would be one of the most exciting and challenging in the Company's history prevailed at all levels, and employees looked forward with anticipation to the coming years.

The skilled and dedicated Company employees had created some of the most dramatic changes in the Company's history during the 1980s. They had carefully crafted the strategy that would keep SDG&E in the forefront of the industry and well able to cope with the increasingly complex energy industry in the 21st century. Within days, CEO Tom Page, the board of directors and key management leaders had drafted extensive plans to channel the same energy displayed by employees consistently during the years of uncertainty into a new formula for success in the future.

ROY ROBINSON

Brian Sibold, in uniform, receives a $500 send-off from Donald Felsinger, vice president–marketing & resource development, when Sibold was called to serve in the 1990–91 Persian Gulf War. A check to each employee called to duty has been a Company tradition since World War II. Those who also served were Ray Enama, Patrick Gorgas and Michael Nesbit.

SDG&E in ice was the centerpiece for the Company's employee post-merger party in June 1991.

> An oil painting titled *San Diego Gas Works* c. 1930 by Anna Marie Valentien, a San Diego artist who illustrated the new industrial age of the 1920s and 1930s. In the foreground she has recorded the appearance of the original small structure built in the 1880s. The belching smokestacks add a note of drama to the composition. (Photo courtesy of the San Diego Historical Society.)

Inset—The San Diego skyline of 1991 showing SDG&E's headquarters at left and new skyscrapers at the harbor's edge.

STEPHEN SIMPSON.

A view looking west down Broadway about1910 showing street lights and the newly completed U.S. Grant Hotel. (Hand-tinted photo courtesy of the San Diego Historical Society.)

The California Tower and dome of the Museum of Man built in 1915 in Balboa Park reflect San Diego's Spanish heritage.

An evening view of San Diego's cityscape taken in 1963 reveals the new skyscrapers built during the late 1950s and early 1960s.

Connecting electric service to the famous Mt. Palomar Observatory in the early 1950s. The remote installation had used its own generators for several years.

Station B Power Plant turbine room in the early 1980s. Except for some new control systems, the equipment has remained unchanged since the plant was finished in 1938.

A nighttime view of the lighting system at the San Diego County Administration building on Harbor Drive, a WPA project dedicated by President Franklin D. Roosevelt on July 16, 1938.

CHARLES SCHNEIDER

The Silver Gate Power Plant turbine room, showing generators on a flagstone deck. The plant featured the first single-unit boiler-generator design when it began operating during World War II.

Reddy Kilowatt was a popular parade figure in the late 1950s as the Company worked to boost the sales of electricity in many of San Diego's new homes.

Important legislative bills are considered at California's capitol building in Sacramento. Company Vice President Ronald Fuller and Sacramento office staff member Jeanette Bunch discuss a pending issue.

STEPHEN SIMPSON

From the Coronado side of San Diego Bay, a construction crew in the late 1940s begins laying a 12,000-volt submarine cable to provide more power to Coronado and the U.S. Navy.

Construction of gas and electric distribution systems has been a constant undertaking for a growing San Diego.

At sunup, Kelly Ward and Dan Lancaster load polyethylene gas pipe on their truck at the Beach Cities Service Center. About 1,400 employees begin work at or before 7 a.m. to meet the needs of customers.

Dan Dietrich, underground electrician, adjusts equipment for 12 kilovolt distribution cables in an underground vault near the Company's Station B Power Plant.

The Heber Geothermal Demonstration Power Plant was built in the1980s as one of several alternative-energy research projects undertaken by the Company.

Several solar-energy projects, such as this one near Warner Hot Springs in San Diego's North County, explored clean alternatives to meet growing energy demand.

Kirk Fink, SDG&E agricultural representative, measures light level in a greenhouse as part of the Company's energy conservation efforts in the late 1970s.

Tankers delivering oil were a familiar sight offshore from the Encina Power Plant during the late 1970s and early 1980s.

Fuel loading of San Onofre Nuclear Generating Station Units 2 and 3 took place in 1982. Both units became operational in the mid-1980s and helped replace thousands of barrels of imported oil.

Large-capacity insulators in the Encina Power Plant switchyard in 1957.

> The South Bay Power Plant, during construction of Unit 1 in 1960.

The Southwest Powerlink in the early 1980s required extensive use of modern construction systems to surmount the rough desert terrain between San Diego and the Phoenix, Arizona, area. Worker at bottom marked the route with high-tech survey equipment. Construction workers (below) assembled the huge towers in sections, many of which were then lifted into place through mountain terrain by a giant flying crane (right).

Gale-force winds and lightning make line repair hazardous for SDG&E crews who work around-the-clock to restore service to customers affected by power outages during storms.

Keeping SDG&E power lines in service involves maintenance and repair in all areas.

STEPHEN SIMPSON

San Diego's modern convention center features a sail-like roof to blend in with the city's waterfront. SDG&E helped design the facility's air conditioning system, which uses natural gas instead of electricity.

Chapter 12

1991–2000
The Past as Prologue

"We will build alliances with all of our constituencies on issues of mutual interest. We will provide proactive leadership dealing with these issues, while being responsive to the needs and desires of others."

1991
Population*
2,498,016
Electric
Customers
1,111,240
Sales in kwhr
14,171 million
Average cost / kwhr
9.27 cents
Gas
Customers
680,593
Sales in therms
663 million
Average cost / therm
48.04 cents

PALA
SAN DIEGO COUNTY
BORREGO SPRINGS
OCEANSIDE
ESCONDIDO
JULIAN
DEL MAR
LAKESIDE
PINE VALLEY
TECATE
MEXICO

SDG&E Service Territory

*County population based on census 10-year estimates

Six weeks after the announcement that the state PUC had denied permission for the merger, the above goal was created by Company management at a meeting on June 25, 1991. SDG&E planned to develop energy alliances with not only existing constituencies but with "adversaries who historically have been in opposition to the Company." This plan, along with the goal to remain the lowest-cost energy supplier in California, would provide the cornerstone for future growth and development in the decade of the 1990s and into the 21st century.

SDG&E President Tom Page revealed more of his ideas about future directions at this meeting. "If you subscribe to the belief that the future will be based on building partnerships, building coalitions and building allies — then it's time for us to be an energy alliance company. This will complement and not replace 'the energy management company' or the 'energy utility company' which we've operated as in the past." Page gave his definition of the alliance to the gathered listeners: "The world today is no longer made up of loners, it is made up of coalitions and allies working toward a common cause to be successful. The definition of the word 'alliance' is 'to be in close association for a common objective.' In my mind there is not a term that will be more descriptive of how SDG&E will be successful in the 90s." Summing up SDG&E's position on the brink of a new era, Page predicted:

We can shape our own future, control our own destiny and channel the same energy that created the most successful company in its history into an

The Company symbol for the 1990s advances conservation efforts promoting clean energy and environmental restoration.

< Fisheye view of San Diego from high above the bay. (Photo by Rocky Thies.)

DON BARTLETTI

President and CEO Richard Stegemeier of Unocal (left) and Tom Page fuel an automobile with natural gas at one of the Company's NGV fueling stations. Partnerships with oil companies to expand the availability of natural gas for vehicle use will be a key activity in the 1990s.

independent entity even more vibrant and alive than before. Everybody wants a second chance. We now have it. All 4,200 of us have a second chance at establishing our own goals, not somebody else's—and doing our darndest to meet them. We can make SDG&E whatever we want it to be. This is a positive time for us, a good time for us. And with a track record like our employees blazed the last three years, who's going to doubt their ability to carry it out?

Page also predicted that the Company would "be allies with all of the constituencies with which we do business—employees, customers, regulators and the general public." This "new" company would be laden with fundamentals—some new and some old—but nearly all familiar to SDG&E employees. The base for the future would be built on key aspects of 1990 and 1991 as all-time record years: high productivity, customer satisfaction, rates among the lowest of investor-owned companies in the state and an exceptionally sound financial picture.

Building on this sound base developed in the decade of the 1980s, and having learned from their mistakes, as well as successes, Company executives devised strategies to deal with future energy needs. In the not-so-distant past, it was common for utilities to begin planning 10 years ahead for a large-scale power plant. In 1991, forward-looking energy providers rely on a combination of smaller power-producing efforts requiring shorter lead times

Future energy projects may have multiple roles. At the South Bay Power Plant, SDG&E Vice President Ron Fuller (right) talks with San Diego County Water Authority's General Manager Lester Snow (left), SDG&E's Bruce Williams and CWA's Gordon Hess about adding a water desalting facility and a new generator to the plant.

to meet their future energy needs. It was also easier in the past to estimate the future availability and costs of various energy resources. In prior times, SDG&E tended to depend on a single energy resource to meet energy needs, such as oil. Now there would be an emphasis on fuel diversification, developing a mix of different energy sources.

In today's and tomorrow's energy marketplaces, the most successful companies will be those that implement short-term strategies to achieve long-term goals. They will always be ready to respond quickly to new challenges and opportunities. This would be one of the key goals as the Company heads into the future.

In contrast to previous decades, one of the major issues facing the San Diego region in the 21st century could be the possible relocation of industry to other sections of the country or world where production costs may be less expensive. Lower gas and electric rates, cheaper labor, lower taxes and fewer government controls in other areas encourage companies to relocate. The recession of the 1990s, costs of construction, prolonged development time and ever-mounting environmental requirements, combined with a serious drought beginning in 1986, will seriously affect decision makers in their relocation choices. All these different issues could potentially combine to push rates higher and make anticipation of customers' needs more challenging to determine.

The wave of the future for SDG&E is to buy power in a bidding process to complement its selective program of building plants. Independent power producers will build plants and sell the electricity to power companies. Leasing of transmission lines could make companies such as SDG&E common-carrier transporters carrying energy for others. More independent power producers emerging in the 1990s will produce a different cost structure. SDG&E faces a difficult situation because it is the only utility in the state that needs new power plants or other energy resources in the next 10 years. Construction of new transmission lines or the costs of new generation to meet the needs of continuing community growth will possibly add more costs to customer rates. Environmental impacts could add to the upward pressures.

To meet the challenges of the coming years, Company executives developed a nine-point strategy of fundamental goals and objectives to keep SDG&E in the position of a low-cost utility company. The goals included an increase in shareholder value; improvement of electric product reliability and gas system flexibility; enhancement of Company relationships with regulators, government agencies, customers, shareholders and suppliers; evaluation of all environmental, safety and health factors when weighing decisions; adoption of resource planning to implement environmental concerns—all while improving service and maintaining SDG&E's position as one of the lowest-cost energy suppliers in California.

THOMAS A. PAGE

Thomas A. Page joined SDG&E in 1978 as executive vice president and chief operating officer, having left a position as executive vice president at Gulf State Utilities in Beaumont, Texas. He had joined that company in 1973 and was a member of its board of directors, as well as president of its nonutility business operations. Prior to 1973, Page served as treasurer and controller of Wisconsin Power & Light Company in Madison, Wisconsin.

A native of Niagara Falls, New York, Page earned a bachelor of science degree in civil engineering and a master's degree in industrial administration from Purdue University. In addition, he is a certified public accountant and a licensed professional engineer with membership in many professional organizations.

Page has served as director and chairman of the Pacific Coast Gas Association and the San Diego Economic Development Corporation. Currently, he serves as a director of the American Gas Association and of the California Economic Development Corporation. He is a member of the Policy Committee on Energy Resources of Edison Electric Institute and a member of the board of overseers of the University of California at San Diego. Page also serves as trustee emeritus of Scripps Clinic and Research Foundation and as a trustee of La Jolla Cancer Research Foundation. He is a member of the California Business Roundtable and continues active relationships with the Krannert and Engineering Schools at Purdue.

In 1981, Page was elected SDG&E's president and chief executive officer. The board of directors elected him to the position of chairman in 1983.

JACK E. THOMAS

Jack E. Thomas, a graduate of Oregon State University, serves as chief operating officer of San Diego Gas & Electric. He became president of the Company as of January 1, 1992. Thomas joined SDG&E in 1957 as a junior engineer and, over the next several years, held positions in engineering, construction, operations and planning. This diverse experience led to the position of manager and then vice president of the electric division.

In 1974, Thomas was named vice president of power-plant engineering and construction. He assumed responsibility as group vice president of customer service in 1980 and was elected executive vice president–utility operations in 1985. He became chief operating officer in 1986.

Thomas is a registered engineer in the state of California and a member of the American Society of Mechanical Engineers. He is vice chairman of the board of directors for the Sharp Healthcare System and president of the Pacific Coast Electrical Association. He serves on the executive committee of the San Diego Council, Boy Scouts of America, and is past president of the council. He is a member of the Pacific Coast Gas Association and the Rotary Club of San Diego.

The nine-part strategy was part of the plan to guide SDG&E if the merger failed. Company officials developed these ideas as a backup plan to be the official approach for the coming years. Staying flexible, weighing a wide range of new options, utilizing emerging technology, and building on the strong base of SDG&E employees will be the guideposts of the future. A redefinition of utility companies and the way business is handled will take place as the industry meets the challenges imposed by the 21st century.

One of the first attempts to address customer needs in the new century, while adhering to the new goals and policies outlined by Company executives, took place with the submission of SDG&E's Biennial Resource Plan Update (BRPU). This report is filed every two years with the state Public Utilities Commission by California's three large investor-owned electric utilities. SDG&E is most likely to be more affected than the other utilities because it has the greatest need for new electric resources.

In late August 1991, SDG&E submitted several energy-resource plans that complied with new PUC rules requiring utilities to consider the cost to society of air-pollution emissions caused by generating facilities while projecting customers' future energy demands. The plan the Company preferred encompassed more than $1 billion worth of possibilities, including repowering generating units at the South Bay and Encina power plants and possibly building a combined-cycle generation plant at an SDG&E site in Blythe, California, in the year 2001.

SDG&E's plan is designed to balance air-quality costs, rates to customers, and local community impacts and concerns. The Company's preferred plan calls for minimal rate increases and significant reductions of air emissions from current levels, since repowering a unit with state-of-the-art technology decreases the air emissions from the unit by up to 90 percent. The new program strikes a sound balance among SDG&E's long-range strategic goals. The plan will enable the Company to provide reliable energy while continuing to be the lowest-cost energy supplier in California and achieving an increase in earnings.

ROY ROBINSON

Company President Tom Page accepts an award presented by Gil Contreras from the Mexican American Business and Professional Association and the Chicano Federation of San Diego County for SDG&E's contributions to the Hispanic community. Pictured (from left) are Tony Delfino, Contreras, Anita Valencia, Margot Kyd, Page and Lex Smuts.

In the future the industry will face an ever more competitive environment calling for greater creativity and efficiency in operations. Former product cycles were 30 years long, and construction schedules routinely encompassed 10 years. Today, business opportunities might have a life of 12 months, requiring Company executives to act quickly and move projects to completion in record time. The need to identifiy and capitalize on new methods of increasing earnings will be critical in the highly competitive markets of the future. Flexibility and an open mind to all potential opportunities will be vital to operations. Such innovative ideas as selling corporate services to other companies, new power-purchase opportunities, and acquisition of additional non-utility companies to complement Wahlco Envi-

John Dawsey, environmental health administrator, measures electric and magnetic fields (EMF) below a power line. Evaluating environmental concerns like EMF will be an important part of the Company's future business operations.

The Company's gas-making plant in the mid-1920s. This photo was taken from Ninth Street looking east.

BOARD OF DIRECTORS

SDG&E's chief executive officer, Tom Page, chairs the seven-person board of directors and its executive committee. Members of the board chair various committees that provide guidance and policy decisions for Company goals. Former United States Congressman Clair Burgener, long active in San Diego real estate and local politics, joined the board in 1983 and chairs the nominating committee. Malin Burnham, chairman of John Burnham & Co. and Burnham Pacific Properties, Inc., became a director in 1967 and currently heads the audit committee. Dr. Ralph Ocampo, a San Diego physician and surgeon, and a board member since 1983, leads the finance committee.

Daniel W. Derbes, president of Signal Ventures and an expert in advanced technologies, joined the board in 1983. Other directors on the board are Fred S. Stalder and Catherine Fitzgerald Wiggs. Stalder, a private investor, joined the board in 1969 and witnessed the difficult times during the 1970s. Wiggs, a vice president in the human resources development department at Security Life of Denver, became a director in 1979. A management consultant in organizational effectiveness, she chairs the executive compensation committee.

ROCKY THIES

(From left): Fred C. Stalder, Malin Burnham, Ralph R. Ocampo, Thomas A. Page, Daniel W. Derbes, Catherine Fitzgerald Wiggs and Clair W. Burgener.

ronmental Systems will be under consideration by management. Creativity, combined with commitment, will be the signposts of the 21st century.

SDG&E started out in 1881 as a fledgling enterprise located within a city with poor odds for survival. Situated on the edge of the continent, at the end of the railroad lines and with no real resources to build a city, San Diego managed to survive and ultimately prospered. If the original founders of SDG&E had weighed their alternatives, they would have realized that the attempt to start a utility company in an "energy desert"—a location with absolutely no energy resources—was risky at best. No hydroelectric power, no coal reserves, no oil or natural gas were present in the area to assist those optimistic souls on their quest to bring power to the city. So what led these men to strike out on this desolate path through the energy desert?

Faith, an excellent climate, and an innocence of the obstacles to overcome, all combined with a belief in the future of the region, allowed these early San Diegans to make plans. Certainly these men of exuberant optimism could never have envisioned the extensive development of Southern California or the crucial role that energy would play in its growth over the next century. At each phase of San Diego's development, San Diego Gas & Electric Company was present, preparing a path through the "desert" with both gas and electric services. SDG&E was always in the vanguard of development as the city moved outward or expanded its inner resources.

Nearly every activity in the county has been augmented or assisted in some fashion by the presence of SDG&E. The growth of the region and the Company has been entwined for 110 years, a process that will continue long into the future. SDG&E employees have the legacy of past traditions and those pioneering optimists as an example for the future. This positive outlook, which has served so well in the past, will continue to be the beacon of the future, lighting the way into the 21st century.

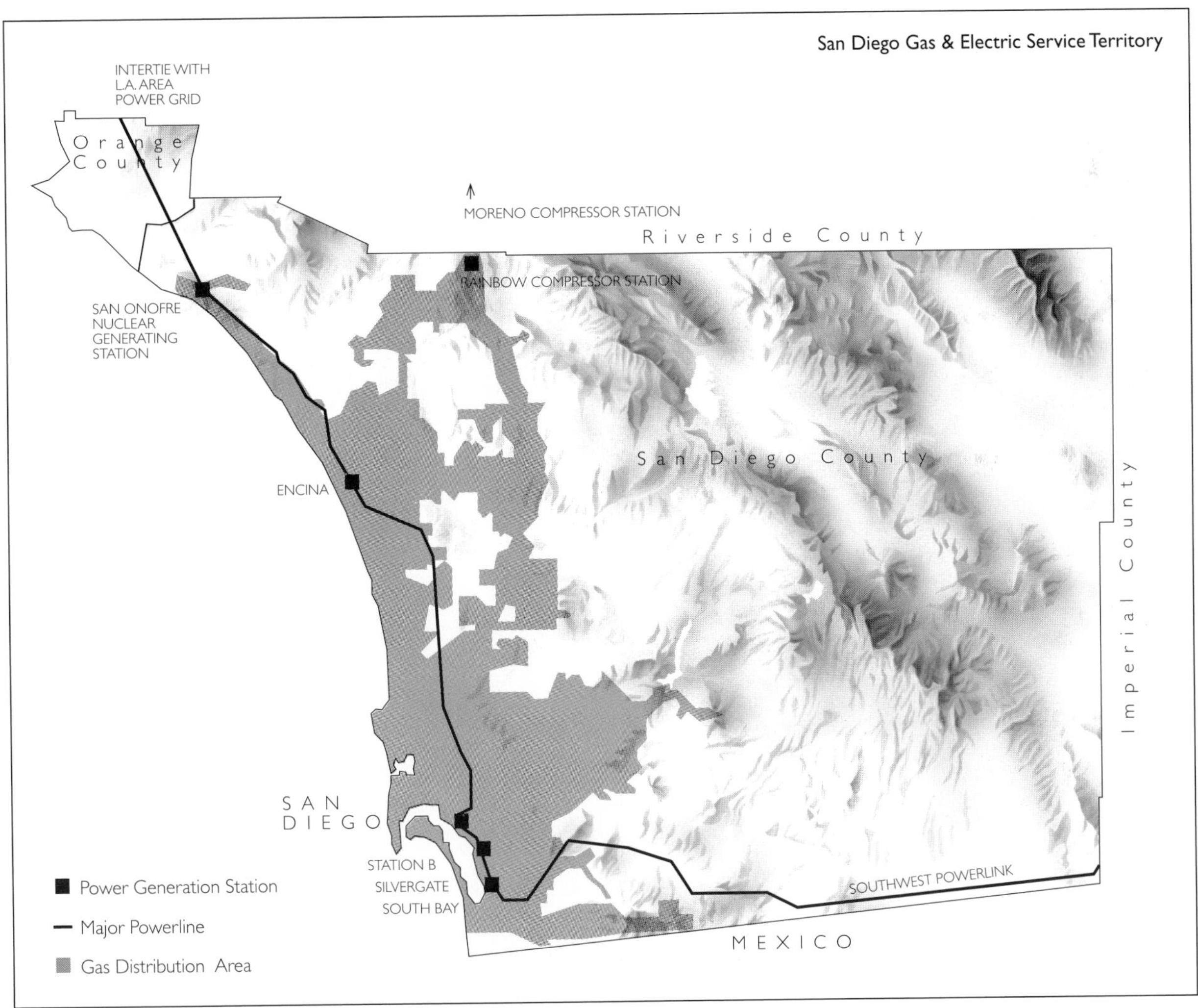

The faces behind SDG&E's success

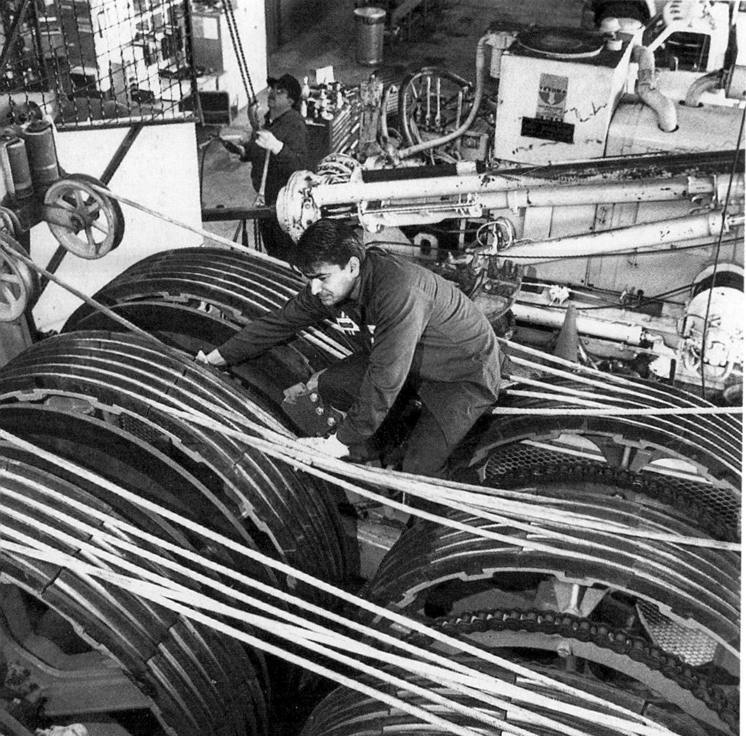

SEATTLE
WASHINGTON

SECURITY
SDGE

SDGE

COMPANY OFFICERS

The management structure of SDG&E has constantly evolved since the Company's founding. Looking back 110 years to the first organization meeting on April 18, 1881, Oliver S. Witherby was elected chairman, Bryant Howard treasurer and Ephraim W. Morse secretary. As the size of the service district and the kinds of operations grew, so did the number of persons in leadership roles. On the Company's birthday on April 18, 1991, the following persons, with the date of their first employment, were the officers of the Company:

THOMAS A. PAGE
Chairman, President and Chief Executive Officer (1978)

JACK E. THOMAS
Executive Vice President and Chief Operating Officer (1957)

Senior Vice Presidents

STEPHEN BAUM
General Counsel (1985)

GARY D. COTTON
Engineering and Operations (1968)

ALTON T. DAVIS
Customer Services (1968)

R. LEE HANEY
Finance and Chief Financial Officer (1972)

Vice Presidents

DONALD E. FELSINGER
Marketing and Resource Development (1972)

RONALD K. FULLER
Governmental and Regulatory Services (1974)

EDWIN A. GUILES
Corporate Planning (1972)

MARGOT KYD
Administrative Services (1980)

RICHARD L. MANNING
Public Relations (1981)

GEORGE A.F. WEIDA
Human Resources (1983)

FRANK AULT
Controller (1969)

MALYN K. MALQUIST
Treasurer (1978)

DELROY M. RICHARDSON
Corporate Secretary (1971)

SDG&E PRESIDENTS

Oliver S. Witherby
April 18, 1881—April 15, 1886

William J. Hunsaker
April 15, 1886—April 15, 1887

O.S. Hubbell
April 15, 1887—May 31, 1887

David C. Reed
May 31, 1887—January 17, 1889

Dr. Robert M. Powers
January 17, 1889—June 27, 1905

Col. Henry M. Byllesby
June 27, 1905—January 9, 1907

Fred W. Jackson
January 9, 1907—April 9, 1907

C.E. Groesbeck
April 9, 1907—March 11, 1912

Adelbert H. Sweet
March 11, 1912—March 12, 1912

C.E. Groesbeck
March 12, 1912—November 18, 1912

Henry Harrison Jones
November 18, 1912—May 24, 1924

Maj. Gen. George H. Harries
May 24, 1924—September 24, 1924

Robert J. Graf
September 24, 1924—July 24, 1931

William F. Raber
July 24, 1931—August 25, 1941

Hance H. Cleland
August 25, 1941—December 9, 1946

Laurence M. Klauber
December 9, 1946—April 26, 1949

Asher E. Holloway
April 26, 1949 —October 22, 1951

Emery D. Sherwin
October 22, 1951—April 25, 1961

Hiram G. Dillin
April 25, 1961—September 1, 1963

Joseph F. Sinnott
September 1, 1963—January 1, 1971

Walter A. Zitlau
January 1, 1971—November 17, 1975

Robert E. Morris
November 17, 1975—April 29, 1981

Thomas A. Page
April 29, 1981—January 1, 1992

Jack E. Thomas
January 1, 1992—Present

Restored glass-plate photo of Company office interior between 1895 and 1898. (See page 25.)

A

B

C

D

H

I

J

Station A during the late 1890s

K

L

M

N

Engineers (from left) W. C. Drummond, Carl Wenz, George F. Phythian, Walter Zitlau and Ralph Wise were involved in the construction of the Silver Gate Power Plant in March 1943.

Q

R

S

Company band at the 1922 employees picnic at Pacific Beach

V

W

Y

Z

Company Employees' Picnic in 1923, held at the Barn in Grossmont.

ACKNOWLEDGMENTS

The authors wish to express their sincere appreciation to the numerous persons who so willingly helped in the preparation of this book. In a study such as this, it is often difficult to record contemporary events with the same broad perspective and dispassionate outlook used in surveying institutions far removed in time and place. Fortunately, we were asked by management to write as complete and honest a story as possible. Chairman Tom Page asked that all Company records be made available and that we be given the full cooperation of all employees. These instructions were carried out graciously, even when normal schedules were interrupted. The only limitations we experienced were those imposed by time and our ability to condense in a few months 110 years of history.

SDG&E could not have chosen a more talented, patient and helpful design team than Tom Gould, Stephanie Swiggett Gould and John Odam. They produced the excellent graphic illustrations, maps and tables. John Odam was responsible for the overall design. Stephanie has our special gratitude for making many last-minute changes without a moment's hesitation. Tom Gould, with his eye for composition, selected the final color shots. We are indebted to the City of San Diego for allowing us to use Charles Reiffel's 1937 painting *Harbor Night*.

At SDG&E we were fortunate to have the assistance of Pauline McKnight, manuscript editor, with her encyclopedic knowledge of people and events, as well as her familiarity with all of the Company publications. She never rested in her pursuit of an elusive detail. We would also like to thank Fred Vaughn, photographic editor, for his many extra hours of work in searching through the Company's more than 50,000 photographs to select just the right ones for the narrative. His picture captions have lent depth and color to the work. His efforts in locating early records were most helpful. We would also like to express our appreciation to Corporate Secretary Del Richardson and his staff for making all corporate records easily accessible.

For reading and commenting on various stages of the manuscript, we would like to acknowledge the expertise and suggestions of Chairman Tom Page, Executive Vice President Jack Thomas, Vice President Dick Manning, Treasurer Malyn Malquist and Director Clair Burgener as well as staff members Tom Murnane, Dave Smith, Elizabeth Pecsi and John Britton in Corporate Communications, and Val Crane in Corporate Relations and Research. Technical reviewers included Bob Lacy, Dave Hopkins, Carl May, Bill Velte, Greg Barnes, Al George, Sid Gilligan, Jim DeVore, Larry Hall, Walt Wendland and Gary Akin. We also appreciate the time granted by Tom Page, Jack Thomas, Alton Davis, Phil Klauber, Margot Kyd, Del Richardson, Stuart Crump, Edith Thomas and Terry Sinnott for interviews about various aspects of Company operations. We are grateful to Rafael Allende, Matthew Herndon, Graham Blair and Jim Frank for their efforts to fill statistical gaps.

NOTE ON SOURCES

This history is based primarily upon documents in the archives of the San Diego Gas & Electric Company, the San Diego Historical Society, early newspaper accounts from *The San Diego Union* and *San Diego Sun*, personal interviews and photographic sources. Extensive use has been made of Company minute books, correspondence, employee publications and annual reports. For general background information regarding the utility industry, the authors consulted Charles M. Coleman, *PG&E of California: The Centennial Story of Pacific Gas and Electric Company 1852-1952* (New York, 1952); Nicholas B. Wainwright, *History of the Philadelphia Electric Company, 1881-1961* (Philadelphia, 1961); and William A. Myers, *Iron Men and Copper Wires: A Centennial History of the Southern California Edison Company* (Glendale, 1983 and 1986).

We would especially like to thank Richard Amero, an employee of the Company since 1952, who, during the past several years, had gathered together almost all local newspaper accounts about the Company's beginnings during the 1880s and continuing well into recent times. He had also collected pertinent data on many of the early events and shared all of his material with us. We are also indebted to the staff of the San Diego Historical Society, especially Executive Director James Vaughan, for providing continuous assistance with research and document reproduction. Tom Adema, in the photographic department, gave his complete cooperation and shared his extensive knowledge in locating and pinpointing illustrative material. Larry and Jane Booth also lent their expertise in identifying photographs.

We are grateful to copy editor Shaun Doole for her perceptive editing and careful proofreading at every stage. For additional proofreading we appreciate the efforts of Cindy van Stralen. For other varieties of encouragement and assistance over the course of preparing this book, we wish to thank Rodrigo Tapia of the University of San Diego and Judy MacInnes, Cheryl Moreno and Rita Nuño of SDG&E. We also thank James W. Freeman of Precision Lab for expert photographic print processing and Summer Todd for historic photo restoration.

In addition to patience and understanding, daughters Kristin Engstrand and Kristina Lincoln contributed in photographic preparation, manuscript copying, and in a host of ways that made the work flow more easily.

Finally, we would like to acknowledge the cooperation and support of Project Manager Betty L. Timko, Community Relations, who saw this book through from its inception to completion. She coordinated all aspects of this production with ability, grace and a necessary sense of humor.

As historians, we have tried to provide accuracy and balance to the story of a complex organization. Because of a goal to produce this history in 1991, we know that the collection and presentation of information is, in many aspects, incomplete. Nevertheless, in these reflections about SDG&E, we have done our best to revive memories, enrich the knowledge of the reader, and give broad perspective and understanding about the Company's evolvement through the years. All those who took part made this book a better product; we, however, take responsibility for errors or omissions. We hope that further in-depth studies will be inspired by and grow out of this basic overview of SDG&E's historical development.

Iris Engstrand
Kathleen Crawford

COMPANY PHOTOGRAPHERS

The first identified photographer of Company activities was Carl Wiggins. Some of his photos date from 1895, shortly after he joined the Company. Well-known San Diego photographer Herbert Fitch took many photos between the turn of the century and the late 1920s. Other Company photographers, starting in the 1910s, included Les Kobler, Forrest (Frosty) Raymond, Al LeGrand, Jack Stevens, Eric Lund-Jensen, Tom Larimore, Art Brackley and Andy Suarez. Additionally, many other employees over the past century have contributed pictures of people, places and events in SDG&E's corporate life.

Today, SDG&E's photo collection includes an estimated 50,000 negatives and prints. The earliest known photo of a Company facility is probably from 1884, only three years after the Company's gas works went into operation. Many of the early photos (several of which are used in this book) were taken with cameras using 8- by 10-inch glass plates.

SDG&E's photo collection may well be one of the most valuable historical reference sources in San Diego County.

Al LeGrand poses with his camera.

Iris H.W. Engstrand, professor of history at the University of San Diego, received her Ph.D. from the University of Southern California, where she specialized in California, Latin America and the American West. Dr. Engstrand, who chairs the board of editorial consultants for the *Journal of San Diego History,* joined the faculty at USD in 1968 and received the Davies Award for Faculty Achievement in 1984. She was awarded a Haynes Foundation Fellowship from the Huntington Library in 1988. Her published works include *San Diego: California's Cornerstone*; *Spanish Scientists in the New World: The Eighteenth Century Expeditions*; and *The First Forty Years: A History of the University of San Diego 1949-1989*.

Kathleen Crawford teaches history at the University of San Diego, United States International University and Grossmont College. She is the author of several corporate histories, ranging from transportation to banking, and articles on San Diego history, including "God's Garden: the Grossmont Art Colony." Former assistant curator of collections at the San Diego Historical Society and assistant education coordinator at the San Diego Museum of Man, Ms. Crawford is active in the field of historic preservation, conducting architectural and historical surveys of San Diego County for various agencies. She holds a bachelor of arts degree in both anthropology and history and received a master of arts degree in history in 1987 from the University of San Diego.